Benjamin Cohen
855 Queen Anne Rd.
Teaneck, NJ 07666

Raising Roses
Among the Thorns

Raising Roses Among the Thorns

Bringing Up Spiritually Healthy Children in Today's Society

Rabbi Noach Orlowek

FELDHEIM PUBLISHERS
JERUSALEM　NEW YORK

First published 2002

Copyright © 2002 by Rabbi Noach Orlowek

ISBN 1-58330-519-x

All rights reserved. No part of this publication may be translated, reproduced, stored in a retrieval system or transmitted, in any form or by any means, electronic, mechanical, photocopying, recording, or otherwise, without permission in writing from the publishers.

FELDHEIM PUBLISHERS
POB 35002 / Jerusalem, Israel

202 Airport Executive Park
Nanuet, NY 10954

www.feldheim.com

Printed in Israel

In
לעילוי
Memoriam
נשמת

לזכר נשמת   ומורי ורבי ורעיתו זצ"ל
הורי היקרים זצ"ל
זעליג בן ר' נח יהודה   אלעזר שמחה
אסתר בת ר' יהושע אפרים   בן מורינו הרב אלחנן בונם
       פייגע רחל בת רב מאיר

ת.נ.צ.ב.ה.

Rabbi CHAIM P. SCHEINBERG	הרב חיים פינחס שיינברג
Rosh Hayeshiva "TORAH ORE"	ראש ישיבת "תורה אור"
and Morah Hora'ah of Kiryat Mattersdorf	ומורה הוראה דקרית מטרסדורף

פעיה״ק ירושלים, תובב״א, י״ג תשרי תש״ס

ידוע לכל העוסק במלאכת החינוך היום כמה קשה ומסוכן הוא השפעת הרחוב. בכל צעד ושעל הילדים שלנו חשופים להשפעות העלולות חלילה להחריבם מבחינה רוחנית. ללא ספק היום, יותר מתמיד, זקוקים אנו לבתים ספוגים ביראת ואהבת תורה, ויחס החם בין ההורים לילדים כדי שההורים יצליחו להחדיר מסורה זו לילדיהם.

לכן שמחה גדולה היא לי לראות שתלמידי היקר כבר למעלה משלושים שנה, הרב נח אורלוויק שליט״א, עומד להוציא לאור ספר הדרכה להורים איך לבנות, בצורה מעשית, קשר חם ויעיל עם ילדיהם. ר' נח, מתלמידי המובהקים של ישיבתנו הקדושה, וכעת משגיח בישיבתנו, נודע כבר עשרות שנים כאדם המחונן עם סייעתא דשמיא בהדרכתו למחנכים ולהורים - ולילדים עצמם. ולכן אני מברך אותו שחיבור זה יתקבל בציבור היראים והשלמים ושיצליח בעבודתו הפוריה להרבות כבוד שמים, ולהמשיך לעזור לאלו ששואפים לגדל ילדיהם לתורה ולתעודה, עד ביאת גואל צדקינו, בב״א.

בברכת התורה והמצוה
חיים פינחס שיינברג

Rabbi CHAIM P. SCHEINBERG
Rosh Hayeshiva "TORAH ORE"
and Morah Hora'ah of Kiryat Mattersdorf

הרב חיים פינחס שיינברג
ראש ישיבת "תורה אור"
ומורה הוראה דקרית מטרסדורף

Yerushalayim, 13 Tishrei 5760

It is well known that we live in times when the influence of the street and the media preach a life of materialism and selfish pleasure-seeking, devoid of spiritual meaning. Our children can easily fall victim to these influences. There is no doubt, however, that the Ribono Shel Olom has provided us with the means with which to protect our children from these incitements. A warm home, where parents build the relationship with their children that enables them to transmit the timeless truths of Torah to their children, is one of our major defenses against the exposure to the street and the media.

It is most gratifying to see that Rav Noach Orlowek, shlita, my talmid of more than thirty years, and today a mashgiach in our Yeshiva, has gathered, in book form, practical and pertinent advice on how to build a relationship with children and imbue the home with an atmosphere which will cause our children, with Hashem's help, to choose the timeless truths of Torah as their beacon in life, and not, *cholila*, fall prey to the destructiveness of the street.

Rav Noach, for several decades, has been internationally known as an expert on teacher training, childrearing and other domestic issues. May Hashem bless him with continued siyata dishmaya in helping parents and teachers prove that we can successfully raise our children to live a life full of Torah and yiras shomayim.

רחוב פנים מאירות 2, ירושלים, ת.ד. 6979, טל. 1513-537 (02), ישראל
2 Panim Meirot St., Jerusalem, P.O.B. 6979, Tel. (02) 537-1513, Israel

ישיבת גבעת שאול
ירושלים תובב"א

ב"ה ג' ג' תשנ"ג

הרה"ג ר' נח אורלוויק שליט"א הוציא ס' נפלא
על המוסף והמחנכים

"לגדל שושנים בין חוחים".

ספר זה הוא מדריך (נפלא) להורים בארצות הברית, כיצד
לחנך את צאצאיהם ברוח טהורה של תורה ומצוות, שלא
יהיו מושפעים מההפקרות המוסרית השוללת ברחוב.

ספר זה יהי' ה' עזר גדול לכל הורי שומרי תורה ומצוות
שיזכו לגדל צאצאיהם ליראי שמים ואוהבי תורה בסייעתא
דשמיא. זכות גדולה היא להרב הגאון המחבר שליט"א עבור ס' זה
ויהי רצון שהספר יימצא בבית של שומרי תורה ומצוות
דוברי אנגלית!

שלמה וולבה

ב' תמוז תשנ"ג

ידידי הגדול הרב הגאון מגדולי בעלי המוסר והמחנכים
ר' נח אורלוויק שליט"א הוציא ספר בשם
"לגדל שושנים בין חוחים"

ספר זה הוא מדריך נפלא להורים בארצות הברית, כיצד לחנך את צאצאיהם
ברוח טהורה של תורה ומצוות, שלא יהיו מושפעים מההפקרות המוסרית
השוטטת ברחוב.

ספר זה יהיה עזר גדול לכל הורי שומרי תורה ומצוות, שיזכו לגדל צאצאיהם
ליראי שמים ואוהבי תורה בסייעתא דשמיא. זכות גדולה היא להרב הגאון
המחבר שליט"א עבור ספר זה, ויהי רצון שהספר יימצא בכל בית של שומרי
תורה ומצוות דוברי אנגלית!

ב' תמוז תשנ"ס

בירקא דאורייתא,
שלמה וולבה

שמואל קמנצקי
Rabbi S. Kamenetsky

Study: 215-473-1212
Home: 215-473-2798

2018 Upland Way
Philadelphia, Pa 19131

בס"ד ב' לחג האורים תשס"ב

למע"כ הרב הגאון מרביץ תורה ומשפיע לעדרים וכו' מוהר"נ ארלאוויק שליט"א

אחדשה"ט בכל הכבוד ובברכת שלום כמשפט.

עברתי על ספרו הכי חשוב איך לגדל שושנים בין החוחים. בימים אלו שכל העולם במצב כל כך מושפל וקשה מאוד לעמוד על המשמר ולכוון החינוך הנכון שמוכשר בזמן הזה.

מאד נהניתי מהצעותיו והדרכותיו ומקוה אני שלוקחי דבריו ישמעו ויצליחו, כי אור ספרו יציל מן הקוצים ומן הברקנים ומכל מיני פורעניות.

יזכה כבודו להמנות ממצדיקי הרבים שצדקתם עומדת לעד.

מנאי המכבדו כערכו הרם

שמואל קמינצקי

Rabbi Nachman Bulman
Yeshivat Ohr Somayach
Ohr Lagolah

הרב נחמן בולמן
ישיבת אור שמח
אור לגולה

בס"ד

מוצש"ק קדשים תש"ס פה ירושלם ת"ו

To whom it may concern,

Rabbi Noach Orlowek, *shlita*, has become a widely treasured resource for thousands who seek guidance in facing the spiritual and psychological travail and anguish of our times. He speaks to thousands orally and has won an exceptionally wide readership for his first two major works — *My Disciple, My Child* and *My Child, My Disciple*. We are privileged now to benefit from a third work — no less distinguished than his earlier ones — *Raising Roses among the Thorns*, on raising a healthy generation in a hedonistic society.

Paradoxically, the present crises are a side effect of the triumphal revival of Torah in our times.

Rabbi Orlowek does not pretend to "solve" all of our problems, but he does shed vital light, often unconventional, but always richly rooted in Torah sources. Behind his "official" thematic, a subtle and richly nuanced perspective seeks for balance between authority and discipline, between self-esteem and submission to Torah. Many will be inspired and genuinely helped to find anchorage on our stormy seas. Can there be anything more precious than wise counsel for those buffeted about by upheavals beyond compare in this hoped-for generation of the impending final *geulah* — redemption?

הכותב למען כבוד אלה אשר משליכים את נפשם מנגד לרפא לבבות
נדכאים ושבורים — אשר הם קרובי תשובה. יהי"ר שבזכות ספרים כאלה
נזכה לראות בקרוב בבנין אריאל ובהשכנת שמחה בלבן של ישראל.

נחמן בולמן
ישיבת אור שמח פה עיה"ק

137/21 Ma'alot Daphna, Jerusalem 97762 Israel • Tel: 02-824321 : טל • 97762 ירושלים 137\21 מעלות דפנה

יוסף הלוי עליאש
RABBI JOSEPH ELIAS
7 LEON DRIVE
MONSEY, N Y 10952

It gives me the greatest pleasure to put on record my admiration for *Raising Roses among the Thorns* by the outstanding Torah educator and my good friend, Rabbi Noach Orlowek, *shlita*. I had the opportunity to read the manuscript at an early stage and immediately realized the great contribution it could make to our community.

Parenting is a topic of prime concern to contemporary society. Changing social and moral approaches and the breakdown of traditional family values and moral standards leave parents frustrated and at a loss how to raise their children. Unfortunately, the Torah community is in many ways even more challenged in this respect than society at large: we have a firm commitment to an educational ideal which we must defend in the face of the constant change in general society. This task is made even harder by the fact that many of our parents do not have a clear, detailed picture of the principles and procedures that Torah educators demand; yet they are crucial to our efforts to mold our children in the right spirit.

Rabbi Orlowek, as in his earlier books, has the ability to focus on the key issues that should concern his readers, and to present them in a most readable manner. In this volume he analyzes concrete steps parents must take to guide their children in their daily life. In the process, they will hopefully develop in their children a pride in their Jewishness that will form a solid foundation for a life of Torah and *avodas Hashem*.

Rabbi Joseph Elias

The reason that a little bit of light drives away a lot of darkness* is because the light is real and the darkness isn't

---

* Duties of the Heart *(Chovos HaLevovos)*, Gate Five (Wholehearted Devotion), chapter 5.

NOTE:

Wherever the words
"Mori VeRabi"
("My Teacher and Mentor")
appear they refer to *Mori VeRabi HaGaon*
Rav Simcha Wasserman, zt"l.

Acknowledgments

I am indebted to Hashem for all the wonderful people He has granted me the privilege of knowing, both in life in general and during the many years which went into preparing this book. It is truly a fearsome task to write acknowledgments, lest I omit someone's name.

Mrs. Sarah Shapiro, editor of this as well as my previous books, took on the task with her usual skill and dedication to the principle of effective parenting. She worked long and hard, and I am grateful to her. Mrs. Miriam Stark Zakon reviewed the entire book twice and gave it her valued professional approval.

Rav Shea Fishman, *shlita*, executive vice-president of Torah Umesorah, saw, early on, the importance of the subject matter covered in the book, and gave it his unstinting moral and financial support. Rav Shea brought in Rav Shlomo Goldberg, *shlita*, of Los Angeles, whom I consider one of America's premier *chinuch* experts, to help shape the book's contents into what will eventually be practical, interactive parenting workshops.

Words cannot express the gratitude I feel for those overwhelmingly busy, expert *mechanchim* (educators) who took time to review the manuscript during its various stages. Rav Nachman Bulman, *shlita*, who for many years has been an inspiration for me, reviewed the entire manuscript. Rabbi Joseph Elias, *shlita*, and Mr. Avi Shulman, *shlita*, gave early versions of the manuscript their wise attention, combining over a century of *yiras Shamayim*, learning from the Torah giants of the previous generations, and their own enormous *chinuch* capabilities.

My oft-time host and friend in Philadelphia, Rav Sholom Kamenetsky, *shlita*, also reviewed with his keen mind the entire manuscript. Rabbi Irwin Katsof, *shlita*, looked at the manuscript and offered his unique, practical suggestions.

Mr. Dovid Grossman, *shlita*, with his uncommon common sense and computer skills, had a direct hand in helping with the technical challenges that were encountered while writing this book. Mrs. Eden Chachamtzedek and Mrs. Leah Goldstein helped greatly with their capable and reliable inputting of the text onto disk. Mrs. Sarah Lipman put her heart and considerable graphic abilities into producing the beautiful design with which this book is blessed.

Reb Yaakov Feldheim, *shlita*, has, as always, been a valuable friend and advisor. For this book it has been my pleasure to have made the acquaintance of his son Mendy. I would like to express my gratitude to the members of the editorial and production staff of Feldheim Publishers in Jerusalem for their professional work, especially Mrs. Deena Nataf, Mrs. Bracha Steinberg, and Mrs. Joyce Bennett.

Mr. Ben Gasner has lent his magnificent talents to producing the cover of this book and I am grateful to him.

I would be remiss if I did not publicly thank the person who put so much heart and soul into organizing this book. He, to my regret, requests anonymity, but I feel compelled to thank him publicly.

Last, and certainly not least, I must continue to express my gratitude to Hashem for giving me my life partner, Rena, to whom I can never say "Thank you" enough.

Noach Orlowek
Jerusalem
Nisan 5762 / April 2002

A Vital Word to the Reader

We cannot start anything, much less a book about raising children in difficult environments, without the humble recognition at the outset that we are absolutely incapable of accomplishing anything on our own. Our success as parents is totally dependent upon Hashem.

Parenting is a difficult job under any circumstances. Today, however, we are confronted with an almost overwhelming challenge. Instant global communication by way of the media and the internet, along with the drastic lowering of moral standards worldwide, have created a situation in which parents can feel helpless before the incredible power of environmental influences.

Many important ideas will be stated, *b'ezras Hashem*, in this book. I hope and pray that they are of practical help to the reader. It is vital that we understand that we are never in total control of how our children turn out, and can never judge anyone for their apparent lack of success. There is a famous saying that "the apple doesn't fall far from the tree." Why, then, do we find that even children from illustrious Torah homes are straying from the path of their parents? One answer has been beautifully stated: the apple doesn't fall far from the tree when the winds are mild, but when there are gale-force winds the apple will fall far from the tree. *Today we are living in times where unbelievably powerful winds are blowing.* Even the Gemara[1] states that we can never fully understand why the greatest of people (such as King Chizkiyahu) can have an evil child (King Menashe).

Ultimately, no matter how perceptive we are, and how expert the advice we receive, we are *completely* dependent upon Hashem's help. As the Yiddish saying goes, *"Meer tuen, Gott tut off,"* "We act, Hashem accomplishes." Surely we must do our best, but our efforts will bear fruit only if Hashem wills it. This knowledge, above all, will enable us to derive benefit from this book. May we all merit His mercy.

---

1. *Berachos* 10a.

USING THIS BOOK

The Tug of War

There is an underlying tug of war going on throughout this book, both on the printed page and in the author's heart and mind. On one hand there is the intense desire to reach out and give specific, practical, hands-on advice. On the other hand, however, it is not possible, nor desirable, to give specific advice regarding so individualistic an endeavor as child-rearing. *This book is a storehouse of advice, not a toolbox of solutions. The parent must invest his or her heart and soul into understanding the individual child, who is unique in all of Creation.* Parents must understand the dynamics that lie behind the correct handling of the manifold challenges that each one of them faces today. Too much detailed advice may cause the reader to feel incompetent and can straightjacket him into a rigid, and often mistaken stance. *This book is a detailed guide, but batteries have not been included. The batteries, the insight and inspiration and dedication of the parent, must come to the fore if the advice given is to be properly used.*

Please, do not blindly follow the advice you see here. It is only intended as a directional aid, with the true compass in the hands of parents who are objective, God-fearing, and willing to consult competent advisors in their community.

This book is best used if it is read in its entirety. There are several major themes that keep appearing; this is not meant solely to repeat or reinforce an idea, but, more importantly, to show that if an idea is true, it will appear in many of the facets of parenting. A complete reading helps the reader grasp "where the writer is coming from" in a general sense, and then the details of each chapter can be better understood.

Except for one footnote, psychological sources are neither quoted, nor, indeed, consulted. Our Torah is a powerful guide to all areas of life, and certainly to the all-important area of parenting. In order to balance the desire to make the book easier to read, but still give the reader an opportunity to explore the Torah sources quoted, much information has been relegated to footnotes, with only the Torah concepts vital to understanding the central idea appearing in the text itself.

It is truly a fearsome task to commit to writing advice and insights on parenting, for one can never know when such advice will be misunderstood or taken out of context. I am deeply indebted to my editor, Mrs. Sarah Shapiro, for the many hours of reading, rereading, and tireless efforts to make sure that the ideas presented here are clear and as concise as possible. I pray that both parents and children benefit from this book and that it be the catalyst for improving that bearer of the Divine Presence, the Jewish family.[1]

---

1. See *Alei Shur*, vol. 1, p. 255; and *Kiddushin* 70b.

TABLE OF CONTENTS

Approbations

Acknowledgments

A Vital Word to the Reader

Using this Book

PART ONE
Understanding Children:
Where We're Coming from — The Basis of this Book

CHAPTER 1: Children: Who Are They? 3
CHAPTER 2: Children Are Different from Adults. 9
CHAPTER 3: The Right and the Left Hands 19
CHAPTER 4: Fearfulness in Children 25
CHAPTER 5: Teenagers 35

PART TWO
Indispensable Tools You'll Need to Reach Your Children

CHAPTER 6: Listening. 55
CHAPTER 7: Empathy 73
CHAPTER 8: Talking to Each Other. 79
CHAPTER 9: Talking to Children. 87

PART THREE
Tackling Life's Challenges

CHAPTER 10: Quiet Time and Renewal: Principles for Life . 99
CHAPTER 11: Taking Responsibility for Our Attitudes . . 115
CHAPTER 12: Change: How Much, How Fast. 125
CHAPTER 13: Tackling Overwhelming Problems:
　　　　　　　Principles of Problem-Solving 131
CHAPTER 14: Practical Problem-Solving 155

Part Four
Building a Warm Home in a Cold Environment

Chapter 15: The Two Dynamics of Love 181
Chapter 16: The "Triple A" —
 Attention, Appreciation and Affection. . . . 195
Chapter 17: Three Expressions of Love 203
Chapter 18: The Greatest Gift You Can Give Your Child. 209
Chapter 19: Building Self-Esteem in Children 217
Chapter 20: Sensitivity and Oversensitivity. 233

Part Five
Enemies of a Happy Home

Chapter 21: Sibling Rivalry. 243
Chapter 22: Criticalness 251
Chapter 23: Successful, and Unsuccessful, Criticism. . . 263
Chapter 24: Confrontations: Where There Are No Winners. 275
Chapter 25: Children and Domestic Strife 293

Part Six
Coping with a Hostile Environment

Chapter 26: Compete Where You're Strongest. 301
Chapter 27: The Big Question 311
Chapter 28: TV, Videos, and Who Knows What Else:
 Not Only a Torah Issue. 321

Part Seven
Using the Lessons of History to Build a Better Future

Chapter 29: Bridging the Generation Gap 331
Chapter 30: The Ba'al Teshuvah Family in a Torah Society 345
Chapter 31: Being a Parent: The Example of Yaakov . . 357
Chapter 32: A Rose among the Thorns. 361

Epilogue: Exile as an Opportunity

Glossary

Raising Roses
Among the Thorns

PART ONE

UNDERSTANDING CHILDREN

WHERE WE'RE COMING FROM — THE BASIS OF THIS BOOK

CHAPTER ONE

Children: Who Are They?

CHILDREN AND FLOWERS

Mori VeRabi, zt"l, was once leaving his apartment building in the Mattersdorf neighborhood of Jerusalem. He turned to the person accompanying him and said, "Aren't the flowers beautiful?" The person was bewildered for there were no flowers anywhere. Mori VeRabi then explained, "The children. Don't you see the children?"

Flowers. The Jewish People are likened to flowers many times, as Hashem's beautiful expression of love for His people.[1] Flowers give us joy in their beauty, but they are soft and need gentle tending. If that care is insufficient, they wilt. So too, Heaven forbid, can our children.

We can take the flower analogy further. In many fruits, the flower is the harbinger of the fruit soon to come, at which point the careful tending is to be accompanied by diligent watching — to protect the fruit from the natural elements, and from its natural

---

1. *Shir HaShirim* 2:2.

enemies. This is true, also, of the developing and maturing child: Children need diligent watching, firmness and discipline, but this firmness must be administered against a backdrop of love, attention, and protection from the "elements," those harmful aspects of the society in which we live.

Sometimes the only way we can protect our children from these dangers is to teach them how to successfully interact with them. Achieving that balance between shielding them from the dangers and teaching them how to weather such exposure is one of the most urgently important jobs that modern parents must come to grips with.

How We Are Affected by the Environment

Rav Yeruchem Levovitz, *zt"l*,[2] notes that we are affected by our environment because it is human nature to adapt to the norms of one's dominant culture. Children are even more susceptible to this nature, for they learn good and bad from what happens around them. As *Mori VeRabi, zt"l*, said, children are like new immigrants. Just as new immigrants seek to acclimate themselves to their new environment, so, too, do children. They come to a new country (this world) and begin behaving like everyone else. Children pick up everything that goes on around them and are quick to imitate, and eventually internalize, whatever they see. They are the likeliest candidates to want their environment to accept them.

What this means is that we must do two things:

1. **Instill Self-Respect.** *People who respect themselves have less need to find favor in the eyes of others.* We must, at every opportunity, build up our children's sense of self-esteem. One facet of this is

---

2. Rav Yeruchem Levovitz (1875–1937), the illustrious *mashgiach* of the Mirrer Yeshiva in Europe, is widely considered one of the greatest Torah educators of the twentieth century. This concept appears in *Da'as Torah, Vayikra*, p. 148.

the knowledge that they are always beloved to Hashem, and are His children.

Children need devoted care, love and respect. These are conveyed primarily by nonverbal means. This is especially true with younger children, although it is vital to verbalize with them as well. When we respect them deeply and consistently they will respect themselves. We are the most important people in our children's lives, and what we say and do counts more than anything else they'll hear or see — provided that we are maintaining the relationship as it should be maintained.

2. Instill a Sense of Belonging. Family, though, is not enough. Today, because of the pervasive lure of the world outside the home, a child needs a smaller society of his own. He must get a sense of belonging. For a child, this need is filled most often by the school, and this sub-society is a bulwark against the feeling of not being a part of the greater culture, and of missing out on its seductive attractions.

Sometimes youth groups, in addition to the school, are an important asset.

THE SCHOOL TODAY

In our generation the role of Torah schools has changed. In earlier times, the school could concentrate mostly on imparting Torah information, and not concern itself so intently with preserving the child's loyalty to a Torah way of life. A strong family, in conjunction with a society which was not that "sick," meant that when it came to spiritual matters, there wasn't such a terrible threat out there. Today, however, for several reasons, the school must assume the role of being *mekarev* — that is, it has to draw its students close to a wholehearted, emotional loyalty to Torah ideals, and cannot concentrate only on curriculum. Some of these reasons are as follows:

1. **In the United States and the world at large, the family is a beleaguered institution.** As we all know, divorce rates have escalated alarmingly, and it is becoming less and less likely that a child will have a secure and nurturing family to come home to at the end of the school day. There is also a rise in the number of families undergoing marital problems that fall short of formal divorce. Sometimes, unresolved situations such as these are even harder for the child to cope with than an actual breakup of the family.[3]

In addition, more and more families are dependent upon the mother's financial contribution to balancing the family budget. This leaves the home with less of the maternal nurturing that is essential to the soul of a child. This diminished amount of nurturing can put the child more at risk, especially if the street seems to be offering other forms of attention and happiness.[4]

2. **The prevailing culture is riddled with materialism,** and it is all packaged so alluringly that the magnetic pull on the child's most basic urges can be overwhelming. *In order to fight these natural inclinations, the child must be in a happy frame of mind.* A person does not have the psychic energy to make difficult decisions, or to resist the understandable lure of the dominant society, unless he feels happy.

This means that the school must consciously make its goal the inculcation of happiness in learning. It must bring about in its students an identification of school with pleasure; school has to be a

---

3. Rav Shneur Kotler, *zt"l* (1908–1982), once wrote that sometimes the mitzvah of *redifas shalom*, pursuing peace, is fulfilled when there is a divorce. Such a decision, however, must be reached only after much effort and with the agreement of a competent *rav*.
4. This is not to say that a mother should not work. This is a complicated question, for the fiscal pressures that can result from her not working can be even more harmful to domestic tranquility than her not being home. In addition, it is common today for a woman to need to be outside the home, and to be engaged in other activities, in order to feel she can completely give of herself when she is home. Each situation must be judged individually, and with a good deal of *yiras Shamayim*.

place they like to be. This includes the redefining of a "good teacher" as one who not only teaches well, but reaches well.

This is not to say that learning has to be primarily "fun," or that teachers must feel that they have to worry, like politicians, about their ratings in the student polls. But teachers today, more than ever, are engaged in a life-and-death struggle for the souls of their students. They must realize how deep is their students' need for their teachers' appreciation and respect.

❧ Points to Remember

We are the most important people in the lives of our children, and what we say and do counts more than anything else they'll hear or see.

Children pick up everything that goes on around them, and are quick to imitate, and eventually internalize, whatever they see.

Achieving the balance between shielding our children from danger and teaching them how to weather such exposure is one of the most urgently important jobs that modern parents must come to grips with.

A child must have a sense of belonging.

People who respect themselves have less need to find favor in the eyes of others.

A person does not have the psychic energy to make difficult decisions, or to resist the allures of the dominant society, unless he is in a happy frame of mind.

CHAPTER TWO

Children Are Different from Adults

MATURITY

In order to understand our child, we need to understand his language, the language of emotion.

Maturity is expressed by the ability to balance one's emotions with one's intellect.[1] Until the intellectual growth is such that this balance is achieved, a person will be dominated by his emotions.

Thus in any relationship with a child, the emotional mode of communication is going to be the primary one.

According to the evil Achashveirosh's edict, each household was forced to speak the language of the father, *umedabber kilshon amo.* In reality, the opposite is what is called for. It is the responsibility of the father to understand and communicate in the language of his "subjects," and his ability to do so is what makes him a true leader. *We need to know how emotion differs from the intellect.* If we lack this understanding, we can't hope to reach our children, nor to inspire trust in them, nor, even, to educate them.

---

1. *Shem MiShemuel, Vayikra,* p. 378.

Some of the points mentioned in this chapter will be reiterated several times in this book, for many of the solutions we shall be offering are predicated upon this assumption, that children have a powerful, dominant emotional quotient, and that it's up to us to communicate in that language. For some of us, this means having to relearn, or become sensitive to, the language that as children we ourselves once knew.

One way of putting this is as follows:

> *Generally speaking, adults first **hear** what you have to say, then decide what they think of you. Children, on the other hand, first decide what they **feel** about you, then whether or not to bother listening.*

This is so because words are the language of intellect, and adults have a strong intellectual component.[2] The first difference between the emotion and the intellect is that the intellect responds to words, while emotion responds to the nonverbal.

Verbal Versus Nonverbal Communication

The verbal parts of speech, that is, the words themselves, address the intellect. The nonverbal parts of communication are, among other things, the expression on your face, your tone of voice, and the sincerity with which you speak. These address the heart.

There are also other nonverbal messages such as a gentle touch, or time spent together privately, or your remembering and alluding to something your child has said on an earlier occasion. Messages such as these convey nonverbally that he or she is important to you.

---

2. Even in adults, the emotional component of our perceptions, opinions, and decisions remains powerful.

These points will be raised later on in this book. In fact, this entire book revolves around the ideas in this chapter, and how to integrate them into our parenting.

AN IMPORTANT DIFFERENCE BETWEEN VERBAL AND NONVERBAL COMMUNICATION

When a person uses words, he seeks to impress upon your mind the justness and correctness of his words. That is, he wants to transfer what's in his mind into yours. Once they have already made up their minds about something, however, people are often resistant to having their opinions changed or influenced.

This is where the power of nonverbal communication comes in. In nonverbal communication, the message is addressed to the emotional part of the listener, who then comes to his own conclusions about you and what you stand for. People respect, and defend, their own conclusions far more than they do anything they've been "taught."[3]

EMOTION IS TOTAL

If you've ever spent time observing a very young child, you may have noticed that his emotional self is the totality of his being. Either he's entirely joyous or totally depressed. This is because emotion itself is total. When you're depressed, you're depressed from the top of your head to the tips of your toes.

The intellect, on the other hand, says, "But…". Its strength lies in its ability to discern pluses and minuses in a situation, to perceive

---

3. As *Mori VeRabi, zt"l,* stated, this is a way of understanding the verse (*Tehillim* 1:2), "And with *his* Torah [i.e., his own conclusion] will he occupy himself day and night."

details, to not be completely swayed by the depth of one's feeling on any given matter. Whether a person is sad or glad, the intellect isn't all wrapped up in just one aspect of a situation. It gives consideration to the feeling, but does not necessarily act upon it.

EMOTION IS ANCHORED IN THE PRESENT

Emotions, in order to excite us, must be part of our present, and not just a memory which we have recalled. For instance, when a person is angry with someone for what he did twenty years ago, it's not merely that the person is *recalling* what happened back then. He's pulling that memory into the present.

Emotion knows only the present. We all remember times when we thought our present emotion would stay with us forever, but noticed later on that somehow the emotion had passed. For example, when a person is angry, he can imagine that the feeling will last forever — though, of course, it does not.

Sometimes, on the other hand, we experience positive emotions, such as love and inspiration, which we wish could last eternally. This will be possible only if we learn how to draw that emotion into our present. The intellect has the capacity to remember, but if we don't have the ability to draw that emotion into our present, we will not regain the emotion.[4]

---

4. If you wish to recapture an emotion — to feel again, for example, the exhilaration you got one day years ago upon successfully finishing an important task, or the sense of inspiration that was once yours upon seeing a majestic scene in nature, or the love that you once felt for someone — then remember as many details as possible of your surroundings at the time of your initial experience. Was it light or dark, cold or hot, noisy or quiet? Was there music playing, and if so, which music? Who was there? What were you wearing? What activity were you engaged in? The intellect, which has the power of recall, has the power to draw forth the memory, and with it the associated emotion. I often give this advice to newlyweds, to treasure the happiness of those initial times together.

Children, who view the world primarily with their emotional component, live in the present. It looms large before them. The younger the child, the less that the future — even the near future — seems to figure in his computations. Tell a hungry toddler, one who understands your words, that if he stops crying for ten minutes, you'll make him the richest person in the world ten years from now — and your words will have no impact.

This point is brought into focus by the following:

> *A wise Jew in Israel, Rav Tzvi Greenhaus, shlita, once said that we often see very young children fighting sleep. They rub their eyes, cry, etc. We think, if you are tired, why not just go to sleep? Tomorrow's another day. The answer is that for a baby, tomorrow is not another day! Going to sleep is tantamount to dying, and all of God's creatures fight off death with whatever means they have at their disposal.*

THE TRULY WISE MAN

In both the Oral and Written Laws, wisdom is associated with the sense of sight.[5] This refers both to looking back into the past and to looking ahead into the future.

Responsible action is a blend of intellect and emotion. It is the intellect that sees the "big picture," charts one's course, and makes decisions. It is emotion, though blind, that supplies the energy necessary for carrying out the will of the intellect.[6] The wise man sees a picture in his mind's eye — either by recalling images from the past or by projecting into the future — and then incorporates it into his present, where the emotion can act upon it. Indeed, Judaism

---

5. *Koheles* 2:14; *Tamid* 32a.
6. See *Chochmah U'Mussar*, vol. 2, *ma'amar* 13, and *Alei Shur*, vol. 1, p. 143.

understands wisdom as maturely bringing together the energy of the emotion with the foresight of the intellect.[7]

How Children Are Similar to Adults

As important as it is to note that children are different from adults in many significant ways, there are several areas of similarity. I want to mention just a few, and, again, this is so vital to our subject that these points will be reiterated several times throughout this book.

1. People Appreciate Being Heard. People appreciate being heard. Knowing that what they tell you is going to be taken seriously can make a big difference. *When your children anticipate that their words are going to be meaningful to you, they won't close down communication.*

Opportunities for problem-solving and bonding will thus always be within reach.

2. People Appreciate the Effort We Go Through to Understand Them. The emotional value of something is innately related to the effort expended to achieve it. I feel loved when someone does something for me that was difficult for him. I also value things that have been brought about with effort.

The effort we make to understand our children is not lost on them. Even if they don't seem to appreciate it, we will see the fruits as time goes by.

3. People Respond to Those Who Appreciate Their Strengths. A person's future is to a great extent contingent upon his ability to

---

7. For example, if someone is causing us grief in the present, we can utilize the intellect to influence our emotion by looking into the past and imagining him as he was years ago as an innocent baby, unscathed by life's sometimes negative experiences. See *Tomer Devorah* (*The Palm Tree of Devorah*), by Rabbi Moshe Cordovero (1522-1570).

access and utilize his strengths. We know this instinctively, for we tend to gravitate to those activities in which we excel.

Even when a negative trait, or any kind of weakness, is present, often the best way to rectify it is to channel the person's strengths into that area. The weakness will be compensated for, or will simply atrophy by itself, spontaneously.

Parents must recognize and show respect for the strengths of their children. When battling those facets of life that endanger their children's healthy development, utilize those strengths as you would any highly valued ally.

THE MOST POWERFUL TEACHING — BY EXAMPLE

Since children are deeply affected by what they see, it cannot be overemphasized that the true leader teaches by example. This is the case in regard to all aspects of living, but especially so when it comes to Torah observance.

> *There was once a man who was known for his prodigious diligence in learning. He spent many, many hours absorbed in his Torah books. None of his children, however, followed in his scholarly footsteps. When the family was observing the week-long mourning period for him, a visitor asked to see the departed person's study. The books were all well-used, and the margins were filled with the man's notations. When the visitor inquired as to why none of the children had become scholars in their own right, the children replied that when their father had gone into his study to learn, he had always locked himself in, and none of them had been allowed entry.*[8]

---

8. Rabbi Paysach Krohn, *Along the Maggid's Journey* (New York: Mesorah Publications, 1995), pp. 69–70.

Outside the home, our children may not have many opportunities to see the happiness of a Torah life. They must see it in us. If we wish to impart to them a love for Torah, or trust in Hashem and love for Him, then we must exemplify these things ourselves. If we want our children to love *bentsching* (saying Grace after Meals), we must love it ourselves.

Never should we give the impression that "it's hard to be a Jew," the phrase which, according to Rav Moshe Feinstein, *zt"l*, ruined an entire generation. People aren't interested in doing difficult things. So remember, feel the love and joy of a Torah life and there's a good chance your children will, too. Certainly there is a street out there, but the street can't compete with the joys of a truly spiritual life.

❧ Points to Remember

IN ANY relationship with a child, the emotional mode of communication is going to be the primary one.

EMOTION supplies the energy necessary for carrying out the will of the intellect.

PEOPLE respect and defend their own conclusions far more than they do anything they've been "taught."

PARENTS must recognize and show respect for the strengths of their children.

WHEN your children anticipate that their words are going to be meaningful to you, they won't close down communication.

THE STREET can't compete with the joys of a truly spiritual life.

CHAPTER THREE

The Right and the Left Hands

Our Sages[1] have said that children need to be pushed away with the left hand and brought closer with the right. This means that children need to feel love, trust and closeness with their parents, at the same time that they feel the respect and awe that come with a certain degree of distance.

The left hand must be the weaker of the two, just as it usually is in a physical sense. In other words, the parent–child relationship should be predominantly a close and caring one, with an element of distance and respect. The *halachah* provides us with ways to manifest this respectful distance, such as not contradicting a parent or sitting in his or her place. These *halachos* serve a particularly significant purpose today, when children have so much pulling at them that can take them away from the ideals of the parents.

A child wants distance between himself and his parents when it is accompanied by love, because distance fulfills the child's natural need and desire to look up to his parents. Respect for parents, which is expressed, in part, through the distance that separates him from

---

1. *Sanhedrin* 107b.

them, helps a child sense the difference between his home and the society beyond it.

A Child's Love and Respect Are Natural

Under normal circumstances, children naturally develop this love and respect for their parents more and more as they mature. Thanks to that deeply felt, instinctive need to trust their parents and view them positively, these emotions need only be nurtured and encouraged, not instilled in them from scratch by anyone.

It's vital that parents bear this in mind. The fact that love and respect for parents are inborn means that even if these feelings seem to have been eroded away by negative experiences, the chances for regeneration are excellent.

This optimistic mindset is going to be a necessity when the parent–child relationship runs into hard times, or when parents feel as if they've failed irrevocably, or if they initially get little reciprocation from their child when trying to reopen the channels of communication in a marred or even shattered relationship.

Which Comes First

Although the right hand is the stronger one, the Sages spoke of the left before the right. This refers to a child who is mature enough to be educated in the proper way of relating to parents. The love and closeness he feels for his parents will thus be enhanced by his innate respect and awe.[2] This idea of the left push-

---

2. It must be noted, however, that in the natural process of growing up, Hashem has set right before left — closeness and love before distance and respect. For example, the younger the child, the less capable he is of feeling gratitude toward his parents — and the more Hashem instills unconditional love into the parents' hearts.

ing away before the right can engender proper closeness is an example of how sometimes we must, in order to achieve our goals, go first in the opposite direction.

Awe and Respect for Parents

The awe and respect that children feel for parents should derive from two factors:

1. Mutual Respect — Innate Dignity. If children are to respect us as parents, we must respect each other — and ourselves. This respect must be deeply rooted in the innate dignity which Hashem has bestowed on all of us. Anything that lacks deep roots is an unstable, impermanent thing — unless, of course, it's held in place with a lot of policing and enforcement.

Many civil laws are not enforced, or even enforceable, in our days, because they do not reflect the realities of the population they seek to regulate. For example, a prohibition on vodka would probably not be enforceable in Moscow, but would in all likelihood work in Salt Lake City. If one tries to enforce respectful behavior from one's child yet does not show others in the family that respect, then one will be fighting a losing battle. Moreover, if respect for parents needs to be enforced or demanded, this in itself brings about a lowering of parental dignity.

If one spouse is disrespectful to the other, the children will follow suit. Eventually they, too, will stop respecting that parent — or more likely, both parents.

The following is a true story related to me by Rav Avraham Alter, *shlita*, of Chicago:

> Rav Alter once entered a store and after a few moments became aware that a young man was speaking disrespectfully to the woman standing behind the counter. When he realized that the woman was this young man's mother, he was about

to chide the son for his lack of respect, but before he could do so, another man appeared. The woman, noticing his entrance, remarked, "Oh, someone called but I forget who it was."

"Haven't I told you a hundred times to write down messages? You're always forgetting! You never learn!"

Rav Alter had nothing to say. He realized that the son was doing as he had been taught so well by his father.

2. Halachah. *Halachah* requires strict adherence to laws governing respect for parents. This respect is inviolate, and has its source in our relationship with Hashem; it is one of His Commandments.

Even though there is so much obvious logic behind the obligation to respect parents, *Mori VeRabi, zt"l*, said that it is also a *chok*, a law that we follow even without our perceiving any logical underpinnings for it.

It is of paramount importance that we follow the halachic specifications as to what constitutes respect and distance in relation to parents. This will ensure that it continues to apply even when parent and child are at odds. On account of the emotional component in every parent–child relationship, there will always be times that a child will not want to be respectful. When that happens, if the *halachah* has been internalized as a given, this will prevent at least the worst violations of parental honor.

❦ Points to Remember

A CHILD wants distance between himself and his parents when it is accompanied by love, because distance fulfills the child's natural need and desire to look up to his parents.

BECAUSE love and respect for parents are inborn, even if these feelings seem to have been eroded away by negative experiences, the chances for regeneration are excellent.

IF CHILDREN are to respect us as parents, we must respect each other — and ourselves. This respect must be deeply rooted in the innate dignity which Hashem has bestowed on all of us.

CHAPTER FOUR

Fearfulness in Children

A Frightening World

Today's world, even the very street that a child lives on, can be a frightening place. In addition, the media graphically portrays every tragedy and brings it to our doorsteps. Young minds that are exposed to television are at particular risk. They view thousands of scenes of fearsome violence and deceit, and to a young child a picture is a reality, whether the story is true or not.

Parents, even those who don't expose their children to television, need to grapple with this problem on several levels. They must take care:

1. To teach their children about the real dangers that are out there, without turning them into fearful persons.

2. To protect their children from the influences of a society in which violence has become a normal way of responding to situations.

3. To teach genuine trust in Hashem.

Dealing with Fear in Children

Before discussing how to help our children deal with their fears, we need to know certain things about how to deal with emotions in general, and our negative emotions in particular. Then we can apply this to dealing with fear.

How Can We Be Commanded Regarding an Emotion?

The Ibn Ezra asks how is it that the Torah can command us not to covet.[1] Certainly one can be commanded concerning one's actions, but how can a person be commanded to have or not have a particular emotion? The same can be asked about any of the positive emotions which the Torah commands us to have.

One answer to this question is that the Torah is commanding us to *do* something that will help us *experience* the desired emotion. The Rambam, in the second chapter of *Hilchos Yesodei HaTorah*, seems to use this approach. When he discusses fear and love of Hashem, he asks, "What is the path toward achieving love and fear of Him?" and then goes on to describe actions that lead to these emotions.

Mori VeRabi, zt"l, suggests that the reason the Torah commands us to eat meat and drink wine on a festival is in order to foster the emotion of joy, which is a Torah commandment. This is why women and children are supposed to be given other means of experiencing joy, such as new clothing or jewelry, and it is the responsibility of the husband/father to provide these.[2] We are enjoined to *do* something which will foster the required emotion.

---

1. *Shemos* 20:14. The Ibn Ezra (1092–1164) was one of the Jewish People's all-time great poets and thinkers.
2. See *Shulchan Aruch, Orach Chayim*, section 592:2.

What this means is that when we wish to feel a positive emotion (such as love and fear of Hashem, or joy during a festival), or wish to not feel an emotion (such as a paralyzing fear), we can find a way to achieve this. Sometimes this won't be something we do physically; rather, it will be a thought or an attitude that we intentionally place in our minds, one which will help to ward off negative emotions.

THE FIRST THOUGHT IS BEYOND OUR RESPONSIBILITY

Several years ago, Rav Mattisyahu Solomon, *shlita*,[3] made a point which I believe to be nothing less than one of the fundamental underpinnings of mental health. He said that we are not held responsible for an improper thought that *enters* our mind; we are only held culpable for *holding on to it*.[4] If we don't retain the thought, then we're not responsible for it having entered our mind, for over that we had no control.[5]

In other words, *we are not responsible for the thoughts that enter our minds, we are responsible for what we do with them once they're there.*

It follows that when we have thoughts or emotions that we would rather not dwell upon, we should not bemoan the fact that

---

3. *Mashgiach* of Beis Medrash Govoha, Lakewood, N.J.
4. Rav Mattisyahu points out that an improper or worthless thought cannot enter a person's mind during Torah study, for a person cannot hold two thoughts in his mind at one and the same time. It is during a break in Torah thought that the foreign thought can enter. The remedy, then, is to return to learning, and the unwanted thought will be pushed out of one's mind as a matter of course. The implication here, says Rav Mattisyahu, is that the improper thought is really Hashem's way of calling us back to our study.
5. I think that Rav Mattisyahu's principle finds support in Rav Tzadok's *Tzidkas HaTzaddik*, section 235, in which he says that a person who unwittingly daydreams during learning, but puts his mind back into Torah when he realizes his mind was wandering, is not guilty of wasting time from Torah study, for one is not held responsible for thoughts that unwillingly entered his mind.

they have appeared, but rather, find means of effectively eliminating them. In other words, it is our responsibility to determine what thoughts or emotions we dwell on. How is this done?

Taking Control of Our Minds

As Rav Michel Twersky, *shlita*, of Milwaukee once said, a person can allow improper thoughts to occupy his mind by constantly thinking about them, even while trying to ignore them. Rav Michel compared this to someone is knocking at my door whom I don't want to let in. If I focus on his knocking, he still has control over my consciousness. Even if I don't let him in, his knocking preoccupies me. Trying to ignore a thought by pushing it out of my mind by force is another way of actually holding onto it, albeit indirectly.

If you don't want to let the one knocking into your home, be busy with guests whom you *do* wish to entertain. The best way to stop thinking about green is to think about blue, rather than constantly thinking about not thinking about green.

> *Dr. Yitzchok Twersky, a psychologist whom Rav Shlomo Wolbe, shlita, and others, hold in high regard, once counseled one of my students who was plagued by inappropriate thoughts. He suggested that the boy compile a list of pleasant, happy thoughts, each of approximately two-minute duration. When beset by a negative thought, he was to replace it with one of these, and was to repeat this process several times. The boy, a person beset by various problems, was much helped.*

This is another example of the principle that the best way to avoid something negative is to be involved in something positive. Be involved in positive thoughts and the negative ones will pass.

FEAR AS A SIGN OF INTELLIGENCE

When in Los Angeles not long after a terrifying series of earthquakes and aftershocks, I was asked to address a group of parents whose children were afraid of experiencing another one. The first thing I told them was that their children were behaving normally. Anyone who has been in an earthquake will testify that it is indeed a trauma. The thing we most depend on is the ground we stand on, and when that proves to be unreliable, it is frightening.

Fear, like pain, is a sign of awareness, and it's a healthy reaction. Just as our lives would be lacking a vital human dimension if we felt no pain (or guilt, or worry), so, too, with fear. Fear, like the other emotions mentioned, is an aspect of human intelligence and an indication that we're facing reality. As we are taught, *Yosif da'as yosif ma'achov*, more intelligence can breed more pain (through increased awareness).[6]

Whether or not a given emotion is healthy can be determined by examining it through two prisms:

1. Am I in control of the emotion, or is the emotion in control of me? To what extent is it related to an intellectual awareness, and experienced under the "aegis" of the intellect?

2. What effect is this emotion having on me? Is it productive and energy-producing, or depressing and debilitating? Sometimes we understand in advance, from experience, what effect a given emotion will have. Sometimes we don't know until it hits us.[7]

---

6. *Koheles* 1:18.
7. See the Introduction to *Divrei Yehoshua*, Rav Yehoshua Heller, *zt"l* (1814–1879), in which he explains that some people know how to deal with the Evil Inclination because of their greatness of understanding, while others can give advice because they have gone through the trials of the Inclination themselves. See *Vayikra* 19:32, in which we are enjoined to honor the young person who is possessed of wisdom, and the elderly person who has life experience. These two forms of wisdom seem to parallel the two ways we know things, by tradition and by self-discovery.

Recognition that fear can be a sign of good mental health relates to an important aspect of dealing with that emotion.

How We React — Emotionally

Much will depend on how we as parents react, on an emotional level, to what goes on around us. If we ourselves are gripped with terror, then there's precious little we can do to spare our children the same agony. If, however, we admit our fears but are emotionally calm, our children will internalize that attitude. (Regardless of whether or not most of the people around children are in a state of panic — and we hope they won't be — parental emotions have the greatest effect.) We do what we can to prevent misfortune, and then we stay calm, placing our trust in Hashem. The Brisker Rav[8] did all he could to protect himself from harm. Then he'd become calm, as the following beautiful story indicates.

> *During the 1948 War of Independence, the Brisker Rav always took care to find and enter bomb shelters during the Jordanian shellings of Jerusalem. Once, during a fierce torrent of shells, he was seen leaning against a wall, studying Torah as calmly as if it were a beautiful sunny day. When asked how he could be so calm — even though he was fearful enough, apparently, to usually seek shelter — he replied that it was not the shells he feared, but the Torah's injunction to guard one's life.[9] Once he had done all he could to find shelter — whether or not he succeeded in doing so — he felt that he had fulfilled the mitzvah to the best of his ability. Then he could be calm and return to his studies.[10]*

---

8. Rav Yitzchok Ze'ev Soloveitchik (1889–1959), one of the twentieth century's greatest Torah giants and educators, who was also noted for his great fear of Heaven.
9. See *Sefer HaChinuch*, mitzvah 546.
10. This idea — that one should do all he can and then calm down — is expressed in the Torah. Miriam did all she could to save her baby brother, Moshe, by putting him into the river in a waterproof basket. She then stopped, and waited, ready to spring into action should any additional opportunity to save her brother present itself. See Rav S. R. Hirsch on *Shemos* 2:4.

While we may not be capable of that level of fearlessness, we would do well to emulate the Brisker Rav's example of doing our best and putting our trust in Hashem.

How can we be calm? It's a lifelong project. We must internalize the powerful realization that Hashem loves us and that in the final analysis, what happens is for our good. This includes death. One of the reasons the Written Law doesn't elaborate on what the next world is all about is that we're expected to realize that if Hashem loves us, then we needn't ask where He's taking us.[11] Much as a child doesn't interrogate a father about where he's taking him but follows along joyfully, confident in his father's love, so can we go along joyfully wherever Hashem takes us.

FEAR AND TRANQUILITY ARE NOT A CONTRADICTION IN TERMS

Children mirror our emotions. Even if we recognize that a situation is a fearsome one, our children are more likely to keep their cool if we parents do.

Some time ago I heard this story:

> *In a plane which seemed about to crash, a mother, in her mid-thirties, was staring full in the face of her daughter, who appeared to be around four years old. She was about to place herself over the child, in an attempt to absorb the shock of the crash with her body, and perhaps save her child's life. The mother began speaking and the child listened closely, sensing the importance of her mother's words.*

---

11. *Sefer HaYoshor*, Fifth Gate, p. 52 (Eshkol ed.). Although the authorship of *Sefer HaYoshor* is unclear, it is commonly attributed to the famous Rabbeinu Tam, a twelfth-century Tosafist and grandson of Rashi.

The mother spoke in a soft, sure tone. She said, "I love you very much. Do you know for sure that I love you more than anything?"

"Yes, Mommy," the child responded.

"I am now going to place my body over yours. If anything happens to me, it is not your fault." The child sat there calmly and listened.

Stay calm, and so will your children.

Never Say, "It's Nothing"

Never, never say, "It's nothing" to a child. To him the fear is real and palpable. It's a part of his emotional reality. To say that it's nothing is to invalidate his feeling, which does *not* nurture the potential for a close relationship. In addition, it will make him feel that you really don't understand him, or worse, that you don't care.

What you can do is tell him that you, too, are afraid of things sometimes, and that this is a natural human emotion. This will validate his feelings, and give him renewed confidence that just as other people's fears can pass, so can his.

Trust in Hashem

Trust is a greater sign of a deep, permanent relationship than intellectual understanding. If my obedience to Hashem is based on my understanding, then when I cease to understand, I cease to obey.

Prayer is one of our most powerful means of connecting to Hashem. Nonetheless, *trust* in Hashem is an even deeper manifestation of a close relationship with Him. Internalizing this trust can be even more effective than prayer, insofar as it is trust that makes the human being more open — more available, so to speak — for receiving all the goodness that Hashem wishes to bestow upon him.

Trust in Hashem is an enormous bulwark against fear, whether it be fear of hardship, misfortune, tragedy, or of the dominant society's rejection.

❧ Points to Remember

WE ARE NOT responsible for the thoughts that enter our minds, but we are responsible for what we do with them once they're there.

FEAR, like pain, is a sign of awareness, and it's a healthy reaction.

NEVER, never say, "It's nothing" to a child.

CHILDREN mirror our emotions.

WE MUST internalize the powerful realization that Hashem loves us and that in the final analysis, what happens is for our good.

TRUST in Hashem is an enormous bulwark against fear, whether it be fear of hardship, misfortune, tragedy, or of the dominant society's rejection.

CHAPTER FIVE

Teenagers

The Torah gives us the timetable by which people reach maturity and are therefore punishable for their transgressions. In a human court, it's age twelve for a girl and thirteen for a boy. In the Heavenly Court, it's twenty for both of them.[1] It is interesting to note that what falls between these two points is *teenager*.

A teenager is in "transit" from childhood to adulthood, and there's a general rule that all transitions are difficult. When a person is in transit, it means he really isn't anywhere, or that he's in more than one place at a time. In any case, none of these places can be called home.

---

1. It seems that the difference between a human court and the Heavenly Court lies in how the judgment is made. The human court judges the act itself: even if it's clear that the guilty person is repentant, and would do many good things were he permitted to go on living, the court has no license to forgive. In truth, Rav Hutner, *zt"l*, says (*Pachad Yitzchok*, Shavuos 44:8) no man has the right to judge another. The court therefore can only rule in areas where God has given them jurisdiction. He gave them the jurisdiction, and hence the obligation, to decide if a crime has been committed, and if so, to punish. This they must do, and no more. The court is not going to decide if the person is a good human being, for they cannot see into the recesses of someone's soul. The Heavenly Court, on the other hand, judges the person. Whether or not he has truly repented, and what he can become in the future, are indeed taken into consideration.

A teenager is part child, part adult. Not half-and-half, but rather, sometimes all-child, sometimes all-adult. Treat him always as a child and you'll have a revolution on your hands; treat him always as an adult — relying on his conscience, offering him great responsibilities and great leeway — and both of you might end up wishing he were a little kid again.

Wanting to Feel Strong

A teenager is someone who wants to feel strong, but feels weak. This is one of the reasons that good youth organizations are so vital. They offer teenagers the chance to be part of something large and important, without having to do it alone. The positive social interactions in a well-oriented and well-run youth group are also of incalculable value in preventing negative relationships from forming.

People who feel weak are often preoccupied with feeling strong, because in general, people who feel they're lacking in some area are often keenly conscious of it. This leads us to our next point.

Many areas of Torah become clear by way of this principle, but they are outside the scope of this work. What is clear, however, is that the Heavenly Court takes into consideration the big picture, while the human court only sees the specific act. This, indeed, is a good measure of maturity — the more mature the person, the bigger the picture he is expected to see. At twelve or thirteen, the person is expected to understand the act, and to be held responsible for it. At twenty he is already obligated to see how his future is affected by his deeds. This seems to be what the *Sefas Emes* means when he says (*Beha'alosecha*, p. 78, section beginning "*B'inyan*") that at age thirteen a boy becomes a bar mitzvah and at twenty he becomes a *ben Torah*. As *Mori VeRabi, zt"l*, said, the difference between Torah and mitzvos is that a mitzvah is likened to a candle (see *Mishlei* 6:23), which only illuminates a small area, while Torah is compared to light, which lights up an entire vista. So too, the mature *ben Torah* is expected to see the entire vista, while a bar mitzvah is only expected to understand the importance of a particular action.

POWER AND RESPECT

There is a general rule: those who are most obsessed by power, money, or glory, are those who feel they don't have it.

Teenagers often feel that they don't have enough power and autonomy over their lives, that their parents don't trust them, that their parents consider them incapable of making decisions about their own lives. And the teenagers are often right in these assessments. This isn't to say that the parents are completely off the mark, but it is possible to alleviate what is often an emotionally charged situation.

Like teenagers, we see that little children like to break or drop things, especially from highchairs. Perhaps this is because they like to affect their environment. I think this instinct is related to many other areas of learning. For example, the way children learn to speak is by repeating the sounds that bring results, even when the need for those results has passed. (An example of this is a child's saying, "waller" and getting water, then continuing to say it even when he's no longer thirsty.)

TWO-YEAR OLDS AND TEENAGERS

The favorite word of both teenagers and two-year olds is "no,"[2] and often there's a good reason for it: both teenagers and two-year olds are in search of their identities. The two-year old is becoming aware of his basic identity as a person apart from his mother. The

---

2. Throughout the exile, the Jew was also busy saying "no" to the dominant culture. This is the secret of our survival. See the commentary of the Vilna Gaon on *Mishlei* 10:20, regarding Moshe's defense of the Jewish People before God. Moshe said they were indeed stiff-necked, as Hashem had charged, but this trait would make them the most loyal nation in the world to Him. The difference between that "no" and the "no" of a two-year old or teenager, is that the historical "no" was prompted by inner conviction, while the child's is prompted by the desire to establish an as-yet-unclear inner identity, and to "win" a confrontation.

teenager is engaged in the same process on many more fronts, and for him it's happening vis-à-vis his entire family. "No" is his way of saying, "I'm also here."

This is important, for our "emotional temperature" shoots up when we think our child is being unreasonably obstinate, or that we're being spited. We worry about "how he's going to turn out," bristle at being related to disrespectfully, wonder where we've gone wrong, and if we've failed. Then we get defensive, which often translates into going on the offensive.

Much of the time, none of these emotional assumptions about what's motivating him, or about what his behavior portends for the future, reflect reality. At such moments, it's our responsibility to calm down and seek to understand what really lies behind his "no."

Why Discipline Is a Problem

Every society needs limits in order to function. One of the problems in today's world is that in many situations people feel they shouldn't have to accept any restrictions on their "freedom."

> *A number of years ago I was on a flight to New York. Those were the days when I prepared my talks on the flight instead of sleeping, and I was soon at work during takeoff, notebook open on my lap. The flight attendant, having nothing to do while the plane was climbing, asked what I was doing. I said I was preparing classes on discipline in the home and school. I pointed to the emergency exit door which was right near us, and asked if he would kindly allow me, at this point, to get up, pull the lever down, and push the door out. He very solemnly shook his head no. I went on to explain to him that every society — and the people traveling on a Boeing 747 are also a society — needs rules, guidelines, and yes, limits, or else we cannot exist.*

While it's true that problems sometimes appear when parents present limitations, this is often more an issue of the *manner* in which rules are presented, and the quality of the authority figure's past relationship with the children, than the limitations themselves.

Often, schools have problems with teenagers for the same reasons that parents do; that is, not enough thought is put into how the rules should be formulated and presented. In addition, in school, as at home, personal tensions between students and authority figures may still be lingering from past conflicts.

Teenagers Are Judgmental

Teenagers chafe if they feel they're being treated like children, even though they often invite this approach, since in part they still *are* children. Therefore, they prefer to think that adults are "out of it."

In the same vein, teenagers are likely to sit in judgment upon their parents or teachers, and often find enthusiastic support for this from their peers. They also tend to be highly opinionated, and, because of their child-component, often see things in terms of black and white, with the parents and all they stand for definitely on the dark side of things. For parents — who not so long ago had a child who was trying his best to imitate Mommy and Daddy, and for whom they were the epitome of all that was right and good in the world — this can be frustrating, baffling, and at times, infuriating.

Some Guidelines and Attitudes

In light of all the above, it is worthwhile to set down some guidelines for good relationships with teenagers, at home and at school.

First let's examine some of the mind-sets that are necessary for dealing coolly, calmly, and *lovingly* with a teenager.

1. It Will End. Someone once described a high school as being like a bath. People get out cleaner than when they started, but leave behind a lot of dirty water. Parents need to look past these sometimes nerve-wracking times with the knowledge that their children are basically good and will come out of it.

They can look for proof of this simply by observing their older children who are no longer teenagers. These older children can be astute observers of what is really going on in their teenage siblings' minds. Or, in the absence of older children, parents can see what is going on in other families.

Things generally right themselves if parents learn to lean with the prevailing winds (and hurricanes) of adolescence.

2. It's Unnatural to Be a Teenager. Up until quite recently, historically speaking, children went directly from childhood to the responsibilities of adulthood.

Once we realize there was no such thing as "adolescence" until modern times, we can better appreciate the real difficulties that adolescents experience. Society has created an artificial, and hence troublesome, stage. In the non-Jewish world, down through the centuries, people in this age-bracket left school at a relatively young age. Then, if they survived a variety of plagues and childhood illnesses, they married and went off to work (or off to war). Even in religious Jewish Eastern Europe, most young men didn't continue on to "higher education," not in yeshiva and certainly not in university. They married and learned a trade, embarking upon "the hard work of life" at a young age. For better or worse, the world wasn't technologically enough advanced, and there simply wasn't enough wealth spread around, for people to stay in school beyond their early teens.

3. Wanting to Be Independent — A Sign of Health. Bear in mind that the desire to be independent is a sign of health. The

Maharal[3] teaches that the word *chayim*, "life," denotes the ability to maintain oneself, which is why well or spring water, which can replenish itself, is called *mayim chayim*, "living waters." Maintaining oneself involves independence; choice, *bechirah*, manifests this independence, and is what life is all about.[4] When a person dies, he loses that gift of free will, which is the essence of what it means to be human. That is one of the reasons we mourn a person's passing.

Just as they instinctively resist physical death, so, too, do human beings fiercely resist the "death" of being dominated. Children can sometimes be so dominated or browbeaten that they lose any sense of confidence or initiative. This is pathology, and not the way people are meant to be.

There are many times in life that in order to get where you want to go, first you have to go in the opposite direction.[5] Before becoming independent a person must first learn the art of being dependent, but it can be difficult for a teenager to hear this. By this time in a child's life, sadly enough, we may have already lost his or her respect. He may know in his heart that there's a lot he has yet to learn and understand, but the last people on earth he'd admit this to are the very ones whom he sees as being so completely "out of it."

4. Successful Chinuch — Especially With Teens. Remember this principle: *Successful chinuch is actually an ongoing transfer to the*

---

3. Rabbi Yehudah Lowe (d. 1609). See *Nesivos Olam, Nesiv HaTorah*, chapter 4, paragraph beginning "*U'vaperek Eilu Treifos.*"
4. This, on a deeper level, is at the root of the first man's desire to eat from the Tree of Knowledge. He wants to choose to do the right thing, and not be programmed to do it. See *Michtav Me'Eliyahu*, vol. 2, pp. 137–145. This explains why we see two-year olds pulling the spoon out of their mother's hand. They want to feed themselves.
5. Such as time spent in silent reflection before meaningful speech; or overall flexibility that gives one the room to be inflexible, on occasion, without ruining the relationship; or digging deeply before building a skyscraper.

child of responsibility for his decisions and his fate. This process starts at an early age and accelerates as the person approaches the teenage years.

Even in the earliest days in school, the teacher must create an atmosphere in which the children *want* to follow along, even though it's quite easy to coerce people of kindergarten age. We don't necessarily design the classroom explicitly for the purpose of having fun, but we do want them to develop the attitude that learning is something they desire.

When a child shows a pull toward independence, this is not a sure sign that something is wrong, and that what's called for now is to counter that impulse with some "discipline." Such a pull toward independence only becomes pathology:

If the recurrent theme is, "Whatever you want, I want the opposite." I'm not speaking here of what often emerges in the course of a particular confrontation, in which the negativity is a reaction to a specific conflict. I'm referring to an oppositional attitude that has become a child's general state of mind. It is not a healthy sign if children don't want anything their parents treasure, and do want whatever their parents disdain.

If arguments and disagreements are a frequent, high-profile occurrence. This would indicate that there's more here than meets the eye. There is probably a backlog of emotion fueling the tension and confrontations, and hence their frequency and high volume.

5. A Swiftly Changing World. *Today in the United States, and in many other parts of the world, "teenage" can begin somewhere around age nine.* There are many reasons for this, not the least of which is that the world is changing so swiftly that indeed, parents can easily be perceived by their children as being ignorant of many of the "basics." Among these, of course, is computer technology.

Rav Dovid Abramov, of the Bnos Chava Seminary in Jerusalem, once said to me that today a generation consists of about two or three years — not twenty, as it always has been traditionally. What this means is that parents need to keep pace with what's happening.

Though the pace of today's word is ultra-swift, our best equipment is eternal and unchanging. Equipped with knowledge of the age-old truths that work with all human beings, and the natural, inborn love and respect that all children have for their parents, they can weather any storm. The Torah is called the Torah of Life, for it has within it all the "active ingredients" to deal with all sorts of problems.

> *I will never forget visiting, with Mori VeRabi, zt"l, a school for turned-off teenagers. In the morning classes, they were barely attentive to a young Israeli teacher from the very same background as their own. There was little communication.*
>
> *In the afternoon, Mori VeRabi taught the same group and had them eating out of his hand. There were no obvious connections between him and the students. Mori VeRabi was a European who had spent forty years in the United States, teaching people who bore no resemblance to those before whom he was now standing.*
>
> *What happened was that Mori VeRabi was the personification of those timeless truths that enable one to reach anyone, anywhere.*

6. We Need to See What's Right. As with all areas of problem-solving, parents need to see what's right about a situation and the people who are involved. When we can see what's right, we get strength to deal with the real problems at hand.

> *A woman I know well was having difficulty with her husband, who had no idea "where she was" emotionally, and who regarded "feeling down" as a weakness of character. She told me that she had good days and bad days. On the good days, she could ignore her problem and feel good. I replied that this was the wrong approach. On good days she needed*

to see the whole picture, the whole perspective. She had to face the fact that she had a problem, but that there was a lot of good in her life as well. If she ignored the "bad" on the good days, then on the "bad" days everything that was making her unhappy would jump out at her like a coiled spring and overwhelm her.

We, too, need to keep our perspective. When we see the good with the bad, the intellect can take the helm. In problem-solving, this is always the best approach.

Once we're able to see the problems we're having with our teenagers from a less emotional perspective, with some degree of understanding as to where they are developmentally, we can try to draw them closer, using some of the truths that are taught in our Torah.

Show Them that You're "With It"

When I say "with it," I don't necessarily mean that parents need to be involved in the same things as their children; rather, we can help them if we understand what's important to them. One of the great educators of our time, Rav Mendel Kaplan, *zt"l*, showed how Torah is indeed a Torah of Life, and can be applied in all situations by those who truly understand it.

*Rav Kaplan, after a disastrous first day of teaching in a Chicago yeshiva, showed up the next day with a Chicago Tribune under his arm. He couldn't read or speak English very well, but when he asked the students to read aloud the news of the day, they could see how well he **understood** everything that was going on out there in the world.*[6]

---

6. Rav Yisroel Greenwald, *Reb Mendel* (New York: Mesorah Publications, 1994), p. 44.

Rav Mendel's students saw how a truly great Torah personality can take his learning and apply it to all situations, even in a foreign country where he had just arrived and where he had little firsthand knowledge of the culture. In this case, the Torah taught Rav Mendel to *understand* the *Chicago Tribune*.

Although I cannot, even in a small way, compare myself to Rav Mendel, I, too, during my travels, have found the issue of relevance to everyday life to carry weight with teenagers:

> *I remember speaking one Friday night to a group of modern American teenagers in the South. I had no idea how to reach them. Hashem gave me the idea to suggest teaching them how to capture an emotional memory, to be able to "freeze" it and draw it out when necessary. They liked the idea because it related to their lives.*
>
> *On another occasion, in the Midwest, I had a similar group one Shabbos afternoon. I asked them what they wanted most from their parents, because maybe I had their parents' ears and could be of help to them. There was no dearth of participation, and some amazing revelations came to light.*

While I have said that being "with it" doesn't necessarily mean being excited by the same things children are, it would be a very good idea to ask them about their lives, their concerns, their observations. If you're sincere, if you truly seek to understand the pull that certain things exert on children, they'll open up and share their world with you. "If it's important to you, it's important to me." If it seems to them that what's important to them is important to you, there's a chance they will try to understand your world, and perhaps not find it as archaic as they had thought.

It is a deep expression of respect to attempt to understand someone else's world. As we have said, teenagers perceive a lack of respect from the adult world, yet when respect is sincerely offered, it can have a powerful impact.

Tzniyus Issues

With regard to the highly sensitive subject of *tzniyus* (modesty) in clothing, the same issue of being "with it" holds true. When girls see that a woman can understand and relate to their desire to dress a certain way, they're more open to listening to her about these issues. That modesty is not only a matter of clothing is a vital point. The desire to wear clothes that are currently in style but that may attract the wrong people must be discussed, openly and honestly, with someone whom she respects and who understands her needs. When a girl understands that *tzniyus* is not only a halachic issue, but pertains to the very essence of who she is, then the matter appears in a different light. A teacher has to be able to honestly empathize with the struggle that some students face when shopping, when they come upon a less-than-modest outfit that they'd love to have.

Truth be told, *tzniyus* is not strictly a girls' issue. Those who deal with boys also need to know how to approach this subject as well.

Avoid High-Profile Conflict

When disciplining teenagers, be extra sensitive to the fact that they're acutely conscious of how they look to others, especially to their peers. Experienced teachers know that having a public confrontation with a teenager is a no-win situation; if the student loses, he becomes a martyr, and if he wins, he wins big. At such a time the wise teacher turns away from the student, continues coolly with his teaching, and waits for a quiet moment to privately administer the consequences.

A teenager can recover from a punishment for misbehavior. If, however, he feels you have slighted him publicly, this won't be easily forgiven, and probably never forgotten. What's true for teachers is equally true for parents at home, especially in front of their children's friends.

VALUE THEIR INPUT

It's good for a teenager to feel his input carries weight with you — in as many areas of his life as possible. As stated, power is important to those who feel they don't have any.

Your desire for his input must be genuine. Teenagers value "upfrontness." You should seek his opinions not just in order to get his cooperation, but because you value him as a person. I'm not saying your teenage child always should have his way, but that as often as possible you should seriously consider his side of things and try to accommodate him.

Consider the following extreme example of how much a teenager values your consideration:

My *mechutan*, Reb Meir Saslow, aside from being a top teacher in *yeshivos*, also taught in an inner-city New York public school. He was known for the class decorum he kept, even though he had nothing in common culturally with his students. I once asked him for some of his secrets. He told me the following anecdotes.

> *A teenager missed an important test because he had been wounded in a shootout with the police, and it was up to Reb Meir to decide whether to allow him to make it up. There was no lecturing, no value judgments. The boy was allowed his makeup test.*
>
> *Once, the mother of a student came to school, and Reb Meir said to her, "It's a pleasure to have Pedro in my class." The son gave Mr. Saslow a look of disbelief. No one had ever said that about him, much less a teacher to his mother. For the rest of the year, whenever Pedro would start to get out of hand, Reb Meir would say to him, "Pedro, you owe me one," and Pedro would settle back into being a model student.*

It is entirely possible that Pedro was a terror right before and right after Reb Meir's class, but during Reb Meir's social studies class he was a model student. There's a golden rule here: Children will often behave according to how they're treated.

Without a doubt, this also applies to *our* teenagers. Thank God, they don't get wounded in shootouts, but their need for our completely serious attention is every bit as urgent.

Another Teenager

People in the field know that often the best influence on a teenager is another teenager. That's whom he'll trust, for better or worse. If you want to dissuade a teenager from taking a path that can lead to self-destruction, introduce him to someone who has gone that way and has come to regret it. Since the emotional facet of the teenager is still strong, the present is what affects him. The *yetzer ha-ra*, which is so powerful at this stage of life, also has regard only for the present. To teach him a lesson show him someone, in his here and now, who can be a model of how dangerous it is to take that path.[7]

This World and the Next

Rav Mordechai Amram Yaakovson, a student of the Chazon Ish, *zt"l*,[8] has for the past fifty years been one of Bnei Brak's premier educators of teens. When I was a *mashgiach* in a school for gifted teenagers, he once told me that teenagers are interested in this

---

7. See Rashi, *Vayikra* 16:1. The *Divrei Yehoshua*, in his introduction, points out that we know things either from personal experience or from wisdom. Another teenager, someone your child can relate to, often possesses a combination of the two, which enables your child to imagine the result of embarking upon a given path.
8. Rav Avrohom Yeshaya Karelitz (1878–1953), one of the twentieth century's greatest Torah leaders.

world, not the next.⁹ For instance, they are more likely to be concerned about their reputation among their peers than any projected punishment in the Next World. When seeking to influence a teenager as to the merit or disadvantage of a certain path, make sure he can see it in terms of the benefit or the loss in this world — not reward or punishment in the next.

Make sure that your words are relevant to the teenager in his present situation, without relying too much on future repercussions to influence his decision-making. After all, a teenager is still part child, and the present weighs heavier on him than any possible future outcome.

Stay in Touch

The fact that a teenager isn't acting out cannot be taken as a sure sign that he's not at risk. Teenagers are prone to internal struggles that you may not be aware are going on. Keep your fingers on your teenager's pulse by having positive, frequent contact with him. Keep in touch with his world. It's likely to be changing faster than you imagine. He will appreciate your sincere interest in where he is and what's important to him.

If you have lost touch with him, it is crucially important to find someone else who can be there for him until you can rebuild your own relationship.

Modern Democracy and Teens

We must bear in mind how much at risk our children are. When I asked my *mashgiach*, Rav Tzvi Feldman, *zt"l*, of the Mirrer

---

9. See *Chochmah U'Mussar*, vol. 1, p. 66, where he explains why we are affected less by the consequences for a misdeed in the next world. This is because we have no picture of the next world, and it is a picture which affects us most.

Yeshiva in Brooklyn, what the best form of government (aside from *Mashiach*) is from a Torah viewpoint, he swiftly replied, "Democracy. Don't think that in a dictatorship there's only one dictator. Every policeman on every corner is a dictator, because there's no one to turn to for justice." From the look in his eye it was obvious that the truth of his words arose from his own life experience under the Russian heel and in Siberian exile. There can be no question that Jews owe a deep debt of gratitude to the United States and other democracies that have allowed them to pursue, unhindered, the ideology that they espouse.

At the same time there is a profound danger lurking in modern democracy. In a world in which pleasure is a top priority, it's natural for each generation to say to the one before, "Whatever excited you isn't enough for me. I deserve something more." That "something more" can be drugs, unbridled promiscuity, or worse.[10] In a democracy, the people rule. When everyone else seems to want, and get, a particular thing, individuals usually find it hard to refrain from going after it.[11]

Combine the atmosphere of a permissive democracy with teenagers whose natural human drives are at their peak, and we can understand the pressures that young people are under. This should make us more patient and respectful of them, and more appreciative when they seek to maintain the standards their school and home have set for them.

---

10. See Ramban, *Devarim* 29:18, in which he talks about where an unbridled, pleasure-seeking personality is headed, may Hashem protect us.
11. Early in the twentieth century there was an attempt to prohibit the production and sale of alcohol. It has been said that the money earned by organized crime during that era spawned today's powerful crime syndicates.

❦ Points to Remember

A TEENAGER is "in transit" from childhood to adulthood; as a general rule all transitions are difficult.

A TEENAGER is someone who wants to feel strong, but feels weak.

PARENTS need to look past these sometimes nerve-wracking times with the knowledge that their children are basically good and will come out of it all right.

PEOPLE who feel weak are often preoccupied with feeling strong. Those who are most obsessed by power, money, or glory, are those who feel they don't have it.

THE DESIRE to be independent is a sign of health.

PUBLIC confrontation with a teenager is a no-win situation.

SUCCESSFUL *chinuch* is actually an ongoing transfer to the child of responsibility for his decisions and his fate.

WHEN we can see what's right, we get the strength to deal with the real problems at hand.

LOVE means, "If it's important to you, it's important to me."

PART TWO

INDISPENSABLE TOOLS YOU'LL NEED TO REACH YOUR CHILDREN

CHAPTER SIX

Listening

Of all the parenting skills that are important in establishing a relationship with our children, knowing how to listen heads the list. Good listening is an absolutely indispensable part of drawing our children close to us, helping them to fend off the effects of the surrounding culture and to identify with the ideals of the home.

THE ELEMENTS OF PROPER LISTENING

The Hebrew word *lishemoa*, "to hear," has three basic meanings in the Written Law, each of which is crucial to parents. According to the Vilna Gaon,[1] "to hear" means three things:

1. Hearing in its simplest sense
2. Understanding
3. Accepting

---

1. 1720–1798, one of the Jewish People's all-time great scholars and teachers. See his commentary on *Mishlei* 4:1.

If we examine each of these three facets of hearing, we will, *b'ezras Hashem*, discover the path to better communication with our children, with all the blessings that it brings.

1. Hearing

"Hearing" means to actually, physically, "catch the words" of another person. While this may seem patently obvious, nevertheless, important lessons emerge from this idea when we examine it more closely.

We hear better when it's quiet. Even if we catch someone's words in a noisy or busy environment, there's a palpable difference in the quality of our conversation when there are no distractions. The words of a child, sometimes spoken softly or in half-sentences, certainly don't need any competition, and it goes without saying that the child himself can be even more easily distracted by his environment than we can. This can seriously affect his ability to speak, much to the chagrin of his parent.

There is still another point to consider. The fact that we take the trouble to find a distraction-free area is in itself a nonverbal message to the child: *I really want to hear what you are about to tell me.*

The environment can have a profound effect upon how we behave or feel. Taking a child out of the home, where there may have been tension and conflict, can help him or her to open up. He'll be better able to speak, and you'll be better able to hear him.

2. Understanding

Once the physical environment is conducive to good physical hearing without interruption, we come to the second stage of effective listening: understanding. There are two aspects to effective understanding: understanding what's said, and — especially with children — understanding what's not said. This kind of understanding — of what lies behind the words — involves intuiting what the child is really worried or disturbed about. Sometimes he or she can't express it because of fear or confusion. Often the child is himself unaware of what else is on his mind. However, when the environment is quiet *and the parent is at ease,* then he or she can often pick up what the child himself does not. It can't be overemphasized how important it is for the parent to be at ease, because the child's ability to speak, or even to think, is deeply affected by his parent's degree of calm.

Children are bound to feel misunderstood sometimes by their parents, and this in itself isn't abnormal or serious. But it can become very serious indeed if this situation becomes extreme; in other words, if it's an ongoing element in how the child views his parents. The Alter of Kelm[2] mentions that one of the main reasons a child may be lacking in love for his parents is that he thinks they don't truly understand his needs.

There are a number of ways to convey to our children that we do understand. To name a few:

Facial Expression. We cannot underestimate the importance of facial expression during conversation, especially with children. When it comes to listening, we show interest, attention, and understanding with our facial expression.

Many years ago, Rav Avigdor Miller, *zt"l,* told me that the statement of the Sage Shammai, which tells us to receive every person

---

2. Rav Simchah Zissel Ziv (1824–1898), one of the major exponents of the *Mussar* Movement, who wrote *Chochmah U'Mussar,* a 3-volume anthology of insightful *mussar* (Torah ethics) thoughts. This idea appears in *Chochmah U'Mussar,* vol. 2, p. 207 (*ma'amar* 225).

with a shining countenance,[3] should be examined word by word. First, Shammai tells us that we must *seiver*: our faces must display an expression. Second, we need to face the person who is talking to us, *panim*. Third, the facial expression should be *yafos*, a pleasant one. Shammai also notes that we must do this with *"kol adam,"* everyone.

When "receiving" our children, this is doubly true.

The following two stories reveal the importance that the great teachers of Israel placed on facial expression:

> *Rav Isser Zalman Meltzer, zt"l,[4] who received many people for private audiences, would take a few moments between each person to remind himself to greet the next person with a shining, happy face and make the person feel he was glad to see him.[5]*

> *Rav Yisroel Salanter, zt"l,[6] during the period immediately preceding the Yamim Noraim,[7] the Days of Awe, was once walking with some people, when a pious, God-fearing person passed them going in the other direction. Rav Yisroel greeted him, but the person, whose solemn expression mirrored the awe he felt regarding the upcoming holy days, neglected to return the greeting. Rav Yisroel did not regard this very highly. He mentioned to those who were with him, who had witnessed this interaction: "Just because he has yiras Shamayim (fear of Heaven) doesn't mean I should have to suffer."[8]*

Appropriate Interjections. We can show that we're still listening by interjecting a short phrase that shows we're still there intel-

---

3. *Pirkei Avos* 1:15.
4. 1870–1953, Rosh Yeshiva of Slutsk, Russia, and Yeshivas Eitz Chayim, Jerusalem.
5. See *The Maggid Speaks*, by Rabbi Paysach Krohn (New York: Mesorah Publications, 1987), pp. 154–6.
6. 1810–1883, founder of the *Mussar* Movement.
7. The commonly used term referring to Rosh Hashanah, the New Year, and Yom Kippur, the Day of Atonement.
8. *Nesivos Ohr*, paragraph beginning *"V'Seepair lanu Admor."*

lectually and emotionally. Statements such as, "What you seem to be saying is...." show that you understand what has been said. Comments that reflect back the other person's emotions, such as, "That must have made you feel terrible," or "That must have felt really good," will encourage him or her to continue. It can be of great value just to express your empathy for the person, to show him that he is not alone.[9]

We can also show we're listening by asking for clarification. We needn't be ashamed to say we don't understand. Not only is this no cause for embarrassment, on the contrary, it's an indication of our sincere interest. This, of course, is only so if the request for clarification is done in a non-confrontational manner, in a tone that bespeaks simply the desire to understand.

If a parent can recall something the child has said in the past that supports or helps him or her to understand what the child is presently saying, it's usually a good idea to mention it. This could be something like, "I remember that you made this point several weeks ago, I should have known you felt this way," or, "The point you mentioned several days ago fits in well with what you're saying now."

This type of interjection sends a powerful message to the child: "What you say is important to me. I remember, or try to remember, what you have to say."

Expressing appreciation afterwards for the child's having shared his thoughts or feelings with you is also an appropriate expression of your eagerness to continue this dialogue.

---

9. See *Tehillim* 90:15, and the Malbim ad loc. One of the primary functions of visiting the sick or the mourner is to give him the feeling that there are others who feel his pain. It is only when the mourner or sick person seeks counsel that we give it; until then we are simply to be there, affirming to the person that he is not alone in his grief. Others may not be able to feel what he's feeling, but he is not alone. This subject deserves a wider treatment, but is beyond the scope of this work.

Summing Up. When the child seems to have finished speaking, it's usually a good idea to sum up what he's said. Upon hearing his words repeated, he may well make a correction, or realize that though those are the words he used, it was not what he really meant. This summing up completes what should have been an ongoing demonstration on your part that your child's words are important to you.[10]

Sometimes it is advisable to wait a bit after the child has finished talking. After a brief silence, and sensing your desire to hear as much as possible, there is a good chance that he will resume speaking.

After hearing and understanding, the third step, often a difficult and painful one, looms before us.

3. Accepting

According to the Vilna Gaon, the final aspect of listening is acceptance. Building on this idea, we can say:

Agreeing with All or Part of the Child's Side of Things. After hearing the child's side of the story, the parent may well agree with the child's viewpoint, and on the basis of this new understanding,

---

10. The necessity of being able to hear the other side affects our ability to rely on our conclusions. Have we considered all sides of the matter? Were we able to hear a differing, even diametrically opposed opinion? If the answer is yes, then we can be more confident that our conclusions are reasonable and dependable. As the Chazon Ish wrote in his Letters (#33), "The main (element in) growing in Torah is (the ability) to *always* (emphasis mine) hear the opposing opinion." This is why it is traditional to study Torah in pairs. Rav Shlomo Wolbe, *shlita*, explains that when the Talmud (*Eruvin* 13b) states that we rule according to the opinion of Beis Hillel, it is because they would state the opinion of Beis Shammai (their traditional opponents) before stating their own. This is not a matter of etiquette. It refers to the ability to state the other party's opinions, to demonstrate total comprehension of the dissenting argument, and then to still differ. This is the hallmark of truth, and we therefore rule according to Beis Hillel.

can sometimes offer to make some changes. The beauty of this type of change is that it's not a capitulation, such as what can happen in a confrontation, but instead is the natural outcome of a new perspective, and the dignity of both child and parent is thus preserved. Furthermore, such change is proof to the child that the parent truly understands his position. The change can consist of abolishing or modifying an irksome house rule, or an improvement — from the child's point of view — in the way the parent communicates. Sometimes the parent will agree only in part to what the child has to say. That's also fine. What's important is that the interchange be open.

There is yet another way to interpret accepting. It can be a truly painful step, but carries with it the potential for rich returns in terms of a deeper relationship. It is as follows:

Accepting that this is the Child's Reality. Sometimes it is vital that the parent accept a certain reality before attempting to change it. If your child feels unloved, misunderstood, etc., accept this reality. Even if it's clear to you that the child's perception is wrong, do not seek, as yet, to change it. The first step toward his allowing himself to be influenced is the dignity you afford him by valuing and accepting where he is now holding. This is especially true if the child feels, as is often the case, that the parents have never really heard, much less valued, his side of things.

It's a sad truth that when I ask parents what their child is thinking or feeling, the most they can often come up with is, "I think…" Sometimes one of the most difficult tasks for them is to go back and find out what their child really perceives as the reality of what's happening, and his views about a given situation. I'm talking even about a four- or five-year old, and certainly an older child.

Words such as, "I hear where you're coming from and it's understandable you feel this way," can go a long way toward helping the child let down his defenses and hear the parents' side of things. Another good way of putting it would be something along the lines of, "It certainly makes sense, after hearing you out, that you feel (or act) this way."

There's no question that when the parent has taken these three steps, to hear, understand and accept, it will then be a lot easier for the child to do the same. I believe that as mature adults, the parents need to take the first step. This will allow the child to behave likewise, both on account of having seen the behavior modeled, and because the parental initiative helped the child save face. Now he doesn't have to feel like a "loser."

This process of hearing, understanding, and accepting, sets the stage for the next step.

The Right to Disagree — And the Ability to Negotiate

Disagreement is a natural occurrence in mature human dialogue, and negotiation to resolve differences can be done in such a way that it causes no rupture of the relationship.

Most often, the truth of what lies behind any misunderstanding or damaged relationship is somewhere in between each party's opinion. When both sides have shown each other the mutual respect that comes with listening, understanding and accepting, then the relationship can weather the strain. This is the golden rule, mentioned elsewhere in this book: if there has been a sufficient investment in building a basically healthy relationship, then negotiation and compromise become possible. *Healthy relationships can take a strain.* Often the seemingly most unsolvable problems can be untangled, if good will and a desire for mutual accommodation create an atmosphere in which love can flourish.

This atmosphere of love and understanding is the very air that happy children breathe.

THE MOTIVATION FOR LISTENING

Good listening can be difficult, especially if there are any old habits working against a new dynamic. It would therefore clearly be in order to consider here why it's so important to do this hard work. Some of the reasons that listening skills are so vital are:

1. To Serve as a Role Model. When we listen to our children, we are role-modeling. It's well-known that all people, but especially children, are influenced by what they see in others, especially in their parents. Like many other skills, we learn best how to listen by seeing how it's done. In the child's world-view, the one who does the talking can be perceived as the "smart" one. He's the one who has what to say. When parents listen to children, listening loses its connotation of being characteristic of the weaker, "less smart" one. If parents — adults with greater experience and power — listen, then it's okay for the children to listen as well, without losing status.

2. Kamayim HaPanim LaPanim. There is one tried and true rule in human relationships, which bears repeating an infinite number of times. We'd do well to contemplate it anew every single day: *Kamayim HaPanim LaPanim,*[11] *people reflect each other's emotions.* We respond to others according to the way we perceive they're responding to us. When we show an interest in what someone has to say, there's a good chance he'll show an interest in what we have to say.

3. To Clear Up Misunderstandings. Even the most intelligent and mature people sometimes misread a situation. This can happen on account of misinformation, or a mistaken presumption, or because of a character fault such as hastiness. When we take the time to listen, we often discover we're mistaken. Had we opened our mouths first without taking the time to hear our child out, it could have set the stage for a very great misjudgment indeed.

---

11. *Mishlei* 27:19.

4. Your Child Will More Likely Feel Understood — And Therefore Ready to Listen. When we hear someone out, the speaker feels understood. Then he'll be more likely to consider seriously the listener's opinion because it's coming from someone who understands the situation and the feelings it has invoked.[12]

5. Emotions Cool. Our Sages teach us,[13] *Da'agah b'lev ish yasicheno.*[14] when we're carrying an inner emotional burden, we should speak to someone. This will soothe the emotion, even if no constructive advice is forthcoming. Rav Dessler, *zt"l*,[15] explains this in light of the relationship of heart to mind: The heart, nerve center of emotion, inspires the person, while the mind perceives things from a more dispassionate vantage point. I think that what Rav Dessler means can be expressed by the following allegory: The intellect — "colder" and more impassive than emotion — is the place where words are formed. The heart, repository of the emotion, is, so to speak, "hot" and nonverbal. When you translate an emotion, which is by nature "hot," into words, you are in effect passing the emotion through the brain and giving it a "cold shower." The result is a feeling of relief.

It follows that when you listen, the child is encouraged to speak. This brings about a lowering of his emotional level. His message will become more coherent and he'll feel much better. When you finally do get your chance to speak, you'll have a calmer, more attentive audience.

6. You Know "What's Doing" in Your Child's Heart and Mind. Perhaps the most important result of learning to listen to your chil-

---

12. Perhaps the Hebrew word *eitzah*, "advice," stems from the word *eitz*, "wood," which is the toughest material in the plant world. Many words denoting power seem to have this word as their root (such as *atzum*, "powerful," *atzmai*, "independent," and many others). What this means is that *to give advice is to give someone internal resolve*. This can only come about if the person seeking advice feels understood, and therefore has faith in the words of the advisor.
13. *Sanhedrin* 100b.
14. Based on *Mishlei* 12:25.
15. Rav Eliyahu Eliezer Dessler, *zt"l* (1891-1953), a great scholar, thinker, and educator, served as *mashgiach* of the famed Ponevezher Yeshiva until his passing.

dren is that they'll be more likely to tell you what's going on in their heads, and in their hearts. We need to be supremely careful not to close them off, either by not listening properly, by discounting their reactions, or worse, by denigrating their feelings. This begins, as many things do, even with young children. The following true episodes put this into focus. The first:

> *A five-year old, grieving over the death of a beloved grandfather, tells his mother that he wants to die and be with Grandpa.*

How to Respond

The response to this child must consist of the following elements:

- An expression of empathy.
- Happiness that the child shared his feelings with you. In addition, it would be good to express the hope that feelings would be shared in the future as well.
- Validation, or understanding of the child's feelings.
- A reorienting, after the first three steps have been taken, of the child's view of the situation. This is a gentle form of disagreeing.

The parent's response would be something as follows:

> **(After listening carefully in a quiet place:)** *"I'm really glad that you shared this with me. Grandpa's passing really hurts. It hurts me a lot, too. The pain is a sign that you really loved Grandpa and we would all want him back with us. However, Hashem has decided otherwise, and both He and Grandpa want you to stay here with us. We love you very much and your place is here with us in this world. Please let me know, as often as it happens, when you're feeling again that you want to be with Grandpa, and we can talk about it."*

Notice that the steps taken follow the three types of hearing that the Vilna Gaon had pointed out:

1. Hearing
2. Understanding
3. Accepting

Then, and only then, has the parent earned the right to gently reorient the child to a different way of seeing things.

Another example:

> *A young girl came home one day, demanding that from now on she should be paid for babysitting her younger sister. The mother was advised that she should tell her daughter that just as she, the mother, wasn't paid for babysitting, so, too, should her daughter not ask for payment.*

I think that the advice this mother received was poor, for the following reasons:

With regard to our young girl, what probably happened was that she discovered that some other child in her class was being paid to babysit a sibling. Shouldn't she be paid, too? The child feels it's not fair. She feels exploited, taken advantage of. *It makes no difference whether she's right or wrong. Feelings of being exploited, if allowed to fester, will develop into a very dangerous emotion.*

What this mother was told to say would, in my opinion, cause the child to feel that she had no right to feel the way she felt. In addition, it would seem unfair to the child that there were so many areas of life in which she didn't have her mother's level of freedom, yet was asked to do something because her mother did it.

Moreover, such a response from the mother indicates a lack of appreciation for, or an inadequate effort to understand, what's going on in the child's heart. A child who feels exploited is at high risk for eventual alienation from her parents. Such a child can easily become closed.

The mother needs to take the time to understand what the child is thinking, and *why* her daughter made the request for money right now. This effort to understand the child includes *asking* her directly why she wants payment. Let us not forget that in a healthy relationship, the best way to know what the other person is feeling is to ask. In a healthy relationship, a sincerely stated question will receive a sincerely stated answer.

Many diseases are curable, provided they're caught early enough. *A closed child, if not yet suffering from what could be called an outright disease, is suffering from an abnormality that can be forestalled by early action.* (If a child is closed, he wasn't born that way. I've never seen a closed two-year old!)

A different kind of approach might be:

> *First, the parent can listen carefully, in a quiet place, while the child is expressing her thoughts and feelings. Then come expressions of empathy, that it must be hard for her to be feeling she really deserves to be paid and isn't receiving any money at all. The parent can say how much nachas she has that her daughter babysits for her younger sister, and how sure she is that the younger child loves her big sister for it and appreciates it, or will appreciate it when she gets a bit older. Babysitting is a great act of love.*

It is my firm belief that children should not be paid for doing chores, or for taking responsibility for the family's normal functioning. Children can be rewarded, but not with money; they are *not* hired help. In a case such as this, the parent can then (depending on the age of the child and the younger sibling) continue with something along the lines of:

> *"You'll have to decide whether you want to continue babysitting, but as a parent, I'm not willing to pay for it. It*

doesn't matter what happens in other homes. Sisters in our family babysit for free, or not at all. I understand how hard it is sometimes to babysit for your sister. I want you to tell me when that's the way you feel. Maybe we can make it easier for you, or you can do it less often. I'm sure that Suri loves it when you babysit her; she loves having you near her. Perhaps there are other things you can do, as part of the family, to help the family run better. I love having you around and really appreciate your help."

If the home is generally a happy one, and people feel good about being part of the family, then the above conversation should be helpful. If that's not the case, then there are other problems that need addressing — above and beyond whether to pay for a sister's babysitting.

It is clear how crucial it is to develop the ability to listen to our children. Like all skills, it may be difficult for us at the beginning, but with time and practice we can hone our skills and form lifelong bonds with our children.

7. Listening Increases Your Child's Self-Respect. Children look to us as their earliest barometers as to whether they're worthy people, whether their ideas are worthy of expression, whether their words are worth listening to, and whether their feelings are important.

If we wish our children to be able to say "no" to the seductions of a dominant culture, they must have a healthy regard for their own opinions and feelings. Without this self-confidence, they can be convinced very easily that the outside world has something important to offer, for within themselves they're quite unsure of who they are.

May all of us fully recognize how much depends upon listening to our children.

❧ EXERCISES

1. With your spouse, practice…

    …Tone of voice that denotes sympathy, sincerity and caring.

    …Facial expressions that denote, interest, disinterest, empathy.

    …Interjections that show interest, empathy, understanding.

    …Soft, caring, eye contact.

    This practice should be done with a tape recorder going. The spouse doing the speaking can then listen to how she or he sounded.

2. One of the parents should speak, and the other turn his head away. Alternatively, the parent doing the listening can put on a deadpan face or a bored expression, or can be busy doing something else while the other one is talking. See how it feels!

3. A. Choose a quiet place, conducive to talking and listening. Make sure that the surroundings are comfortable and carry no unpleasant memories or associations. Many children close up because they think that what they have to say won't make a difference anyway. If there's reason to believe that the child won't want to speak about anything too "meaningful," then light conversation should be the rule. The parents should express a desire to hear their child — about anything.

    Often "anything" won't evoke a response, and then the parent should ask the child's opinion about something specific, something non-threatening. (For instance: "We're having a problem with Joey doing his homework. Do you have any suggestions?" Or, "We'd like to take the children out for a treat. We're not sure if we should go to... or to.... What do you say?")

    B.   If none of the above works, sometimes a parent can talk about how his or her day went, and this may prompt a response. Sometimes he or she can talk about how they felt when they were growing up. Children are almost always interested in this.

4. Parents need to learn how to state, lovingly, when and if they disagree with something the child wants. This has to be done in such a way that it won't drive parent and child apart. If the child is to be educated, the parents cannot just "go along" with whatever the child wants, nor can they automatically rubber-stamp all of his or her ideas.

    These "disagreements," however, must come with some partial agreement or concession, or, at the very least, acceptance that this is where the child is emotionally. When the parent has successfully been able to hear the child (and the child believes that he/she has been heard), try, with your spouse, to find some way of changing something in the home that would make things more to the child's liking, while at the same time keeping intact what the parent considers to be fundamentally important in the home.

    Ways of phrasing disagreement can be as follows:

    "It's clear to me now how frustrated you feel about…
        (for teenagers:) …how we've ignored your needs as far as curfew goes…."
        (for, say, a ten-year old:) …your younger brother's bothering you…."

    "…I hear you and want to try to change things as much as possible. Please understand that I cannot turn things around the way you'd like. Maybe such and such would be a good compromise. Perhaps, for starters, we can…."

∼

"I hear how frustrated you are. But I can't think of a good, totally acceptable solution right now. Maybe in the meantime we can try the following partial solution."

∼

"I know that there are things we disagree on. I'd like to make a list, together with you, of things we do agree on."

5. Discuss, with your spouse, why it is sometimes so difficult to listen to your children. Some of the questions you could discuss might be: What are our prejudices that are blocking our ability to hear where they are emotionally? What is making it so hard for us to hear their complaints?

❧Points to Remember

FINDING a distraction-free area to listen to your child sends the nonverbal message: "I really want to hear what you are about to tell me."

WHEN you listen, the child is encouraged to speak.

IF YOUR child feels unloved, misunderstood, etc., accept this reality.

IF THERE has been a sufficient investment in building a basically healthy relationship, then negotiation and compromise become possible.

WE RESPOND to others according to the way we perceive they are responding to us.

EVEN the most intelligent and mature people sometimes misread a situation.

IF WE WISH our children to be able to say "no" to the seductions of a dominant culture, they must have a healthy regard for their own opinions and feelings.

CHAPTER SEVEN

Empathy

When we speak about proper listening, one of its components merits special attention: the quality of empathy. Parents must be able to convey to the child that they empathize with whatever he is feeling, be it joy, pain, the satisfaction of victory or the frustration of failure. Empathy is one of the most powerful tools we have for drawing people closer.

EMPATHY: A CONDITION FOR LEADERSHIP

Empathy is an indispensable tool for the parent who truly wishes to guide his child. Moshe Rabbeinu was not chosen for leadership until he demonstrated that he had this quality, first as a shepherd who felt the pain of a young sheep,[1] and then as the person who could leave the king's palace and feel the suffering of his people.[2] Rabbi Yehoshua rebuked Rabban Gamliel for insufficient

---

1. *Shemos Rabbah* 2:3.
2. *Shemos* 2:11. See *Chochmah U'Mussar*, vol. 1, for a beautiful description of the progression of the levels of empathy that Moshe felt for others. First he intervened when he saw a Jew being beaten by an Egyptian, then he intervened when two Jews were quarreling, and then, even as a refugee fleeing for his life, he stopped to rescue the daughters of Yisro from injustice at the hands of the other shepherds.

empathy for his people, and expressed it in these words: "Woe to the generation that has you as their leader, for you do not feel their suffering."[3]

EMPTYING YOURSELF OUT AND FEELING THE OTHER PERSON'S FEELINGS

Empathy develops when a person begins dismantling the main barrier to feeling the feelings of others: his own ego. The Alter of Kelm in his monumental work, *Chochmah U'Mussar*, says:

> *We have learned: The first and last (i.e., the most all-encompassing) condition for (successful) community service is to distance oneself to the greatest degree possible from self-love.*
>
> *We have learned: To the degree that one distances himself from self-love will he be able to draw himself closer to the truth.*[4]

It should be made clear that the Alter does not mean that a person should feel self-denigration. *If a person denigrates himself, he can neither appreciate, nor love, anyone.* I believe that this is so because a person cannot bear to live in a world in which he feels: *I am the only one who is no good.* Inevitably he'll begin tearing everyone else down too. The Torah tells us that in order to love our fellowman as ourselves, we first have to love ourselves.[5]

My brother Dovid once told me that when he listens to someone, he empties himself out in order to let the other person in. This is a more down-to-earth expression of what the Alter has just taught us.

---

3. *Berachos* 28a.
4. Vol. 1, p. 23.
5. *Vayikra* 19:18.

THE ROOT OF CHESSED

Chessed, lovingkindness, is, I believe, rooted in the Hebrew word *chass*, to have mercy on that which is yours.[6] What this means is that true lovingkindness consists of extending the mercy you feel toward yourself to others.

Rav Avrohom Grodzinsky, *zt"l*,[7] writes:

> *Before a person develops a... sense of self-love... he loves others. Every child[8] loves (other children), by dint of his innocent soul, the love that every creature has for its own kind. As the person matures, he becomes more aware of differences, and chooses to be near those who are like him, whether in height, dress, or financial status.*[9]

Rav Avrohom then goes on to give an amazing piece of advice, which can help a person acquire that sense of love for others that he once possessed as a child, and later learned to ignore. He enjoins us to:

> *Choose a good friend, even one, and... love him as yourself.... With this [you] will break the iron wall of self-love....*

TO CONTAIN EVERYONE, AND HAVE HUMILITY

In order to understand — and feel — the inner world of someone else, you have to already have some of him within yourself.

---

6. See *Siddur HaGra* on the *Shema koleinu* prayer, where it is taught that the word *chus* (חוס) refers to the mercy that we feel toward something that we relate to as our own.
7. 1884–1941. He was the last *mashgiach* of the Yeshiva of Slobodka in Europe, may Hashem avenge his blood.
8. I think the author means when the child is about four or five years of age.
9. *Toras Avrohom*, pp. 465–6.

This will explain why Moshe was the ideal leader, since he contained within himself all the roots of the souls of the Jewish People.[10]

We spoke before of the ability to "empty yourself out." This ability comes from humility, which is the power to take yourself out of the picture. Even if a person isn't going to contain within himself all the souls of the people whom he is to lead — that's a bit much to expect — at least let him have the trait of humility.[11]

We can now build on the above idea and see that the Torah's injunction to love others as yourself ends with the words, "I am God." These three words are the root of our love for ourselves, and then, by extension, our love for others. Such a love is permanent, just as Hashem Himself and His commandments are.

The more a person empties himself of pride, that is, of the feeling that he has special self-worth not possessed by others, the more "room" he has for Hashem to become part of his daily reality.[12]

Your Child Is Not Yours

Mori VeRabi, zt"l, said many times that the key to successful parenting is the realization that the child is not yours, but rather, a

---

10. See the *Be'er Moshe, Shemos*, p. 42 and the *Ohr HaChayim, Shemos* 3:8. This seems to be what Moshe was asking for when he requested that a leader be able to understand each person separately (see Rashi, *Bemidbar* 27:16).
11. This, I think, is exemplified by the verse (*Shemos* 33:11) "ומשרתו יהושע... נער". The word נער seems to have the connotation of emptying, for the word לנער means to shake out. A youth is called a נער since he is young and empty. It was Yehoshua's ability to be a נער, to empty himself out, that was his greatest credential for succeeding Moshe as the leader of the Jewish People. The Midrash says (see *Michtav Me'Eliyahu*, vol. 2, pp. 227–8, which mentions the *Tanchuma Yoshon*), that the word נער refers to a prophet — as this term is used for both Yehoshua and Shemuel. I think this is because a prophet must "empty himself out" in order to receive the Word of God, so he can become an accurate transmitter of God's words to others.
12. *Sotah* 5a: "I [Hashem] am with the downtrodden [i.e., the humble]."

creation given on trust from Hashem. When you as a parent realize this, it becomes easier to empty yourself out, to truly understand and feel where your child is, both in his mind and in his heart.

Develop this ability to empathize and it will be a powerful deterrent against losing your child to the values and lifestyles that you find detestable. It is almost certain that your child will not find such empathy in the street.

❧ Exercises

1. Look at your child's face, and try to feel what he or she is feeling.

   Look at your spouse's face, and try to feel what he or she is feeling.

   If you cannot do the above, ask your child and your spouse how they are, and truly try to feel that feeling.

2. Find the face of a stranger, and, without staring, try to see where he or she is emotionally.

3. When an ambulance passes, take a moment to reflect that someone's loved one is in danger, and say a short prayer for his welfare (heard from Rav Avigdor Miller, *zt"l*). Likewise, when you hear or read about a tragedy, take a moment to feel the pain of those directly involved.

❧ Points to Remember

PARENTS must convey to their child that they empathize with whatever he is feeling.

TRUE lovingkindness consists of extending the mercy you feel toward yourself to others.

IF A PERSON denigrates himself, he can neither appreciate, nor love, anyone.

THE MORE a person empties himself of pride, the more "room" he has for Hashem to become part of his daily reality.

THE KEY to successful parenting is the realization that the child is not yours, but rather, a creation given on trust from Hashem.

CHAPTER EIGHT

Talking to Each Other

We human beings bond with, and understand, each other through speech. Rav Shlomo Wolbe, *shlita*, writes that the prime function of speech is to enable us to better understand and appreciate each other.[1] This is why the Gemara states, "The reward of a wedding is the words."[2] The words of genuine praise that the bride and groom hear about each other make them appreciate and love each other more.[3]

Mori VeRabi, zt"l, said that there is a direct connection between happiness and one's understanding of one's purpose and function, as well as the purpose and function of all things. The more we know what something is for (and especially when we know our own function!), the happier we are.[4] *Mori VeRabi, zt"l,* also quoted the

---

1. *Felach HaShetikah VeHahodayah*, chapter 1. This is why the four groups of people who will not merit the Divine Presence in the Next World (mockers, flatterers, liars and tale-bearers) have as their common denominator that they have used speech, whose function is to bring people together, to instead drive them apart. See *Sotah* 42a. [Rav Shlomo Wolbe, *shlita*, is one of our great contemporary Torah thinkers, author of the acclaimed *Alei Shur* and other important works.]
2. *Berachos* 7b.
3. *Felach HaShetikah VeHahodayah*, ibid.
4. See the *Sefas Emes, Bemidbar*, p. 16, the section beginning *"B'midrash Havieini,"* in which he says that the principal desire of a person in this world is to know why he was created.

Rambam as saying that *wisdom can be measured by the ability to identify function.* There is therefore a direct connection between happiness and wisdom. This seems to be the implication of the verse, "The wisdom of a person will light up his face."[5]

Aside from comprehending the function of speech, we need to understand how best to use the power of speech; in other words, how to talk to each other. For the purposes of this book, we will be focusing on talking to children.

It is important to bear in mind that in fact, speech has two components: speech and silence. Although they may seem like opposites, they really work best, Rav Wolbe writes,[6] when used together. We will explain.

SILENCE

Silence is, or should be, the time when we're speaking to ourselves — when we understand, and polish, our inner world. Thus silence is always a prelude to speech, for proper speech accurately reflects what we feel in our hearts. While we needn't always speak what is in our hearts when we or our listeners are not yet ready, when we do talk it should, generally speaking, make the other person a party to what's going on inside our hearts. Children, especially, are letting you into their hearts when they speak. Tread with caution before you violate that tender and fragile part of their psyche,

---

5. *Koheles* 8:1. I think that part of wisdom is the realization that this world is a good world, and the wise man's connection to reality makes him happy. It is told that the Chofetz Chaim once recommended that a certain person be accepted for the position of *mashgiach* in a yeshiva in Eastern Europe. Shortly afterward, the person came to the Chofetz Chaim, unaware that the Chofetz Chaim had made such a recommendation. He complained to the Chofetz Chaim about how unhappy his life situation was. After the session, the Chofetz Chaim telegrammed the yeshiva, withdrawing his recommendation. Life can be difficult, but for someone truly plugged into the reality of Hashem's goodness, it is not cause for ongoing unhappiness.
6. *Felach HaShetikah VeHahodayah, Hilchos Dibbur U'Shetikah.*

either by discounting out of hand what they say or by betraying a confidence.

Speech and Silence

It is possible to understand a concept from its opposite.[7] For instance, white can be understood by comparing it with black. Freedom can be understood by truly understanding slavery. True opposites, after all, are similar insofar as they mirror each other exactly.

At other times, opposites can be good partners, as complements to each other. Speech and silence are opposites, yet when used in tandem, they're far more effective than when used independently of each other. Our Sages teach us: "The words of the wise are (better) heard when they are spoken softly,"[8] and that one should teach in as brief a style as possible.[9] Both of these teachings reflect the idea that when speech is used together with silence, either through softness of tone or by way of a terse teaching style, the speech itself is enhanced.[10] Sometimes, silence and speech work best when the person is silent before he speaks, that is, if he carefully considers his words beforehand.[11]

---

7. Maharal, *Netzach Yisroel*, chapter 1. Rav Yitzchok Hutner, *zt"l*, uses the verse in *Tehillim* (119:98) which states, "From my enemies will I grow wise," to teach us that we can learn how to serve Hashem by studying the wiles of the Evil Inclination and incorporating those same strategies into our service of Hashem.
8. *Koheles* 9:17. See also *Shabbos* 34a and *Gittin* 7a, in which it states that the man of the house should speak gently, in order that his words be (better) heard.
9. *Pesachim* 3b.
10. The softness of tone denotes self-control, which is the hallmark of a leader. A terse teaching style encourages students to listen, for neither will the talk be overly tedious, nor can the student daydream and count on keeping up with the talk's theme, since a missed word or sentence can cause the student to lose track.
11. Before we recite the *Shemoneh Esreh* we say, "Hashem, open my lips," for we should be so seized with awe that we are unable to utter a sound (Rav Sholom Shwadron, *zt"l*).

Silent "Speech"

Sometimes we "speak" with our silence. This is essentially the nonverbal aspect of speech, and it's far more powerful than the spoken word. When we listen, we are giving to the speaker our minds. That's the most precious thing we possess and it's an enormous nonverbal compliment. Listening not only has a technical function, to help us know what the other person is thinking or feeling, but serves an even more important function — *listening conveys respect.* And when a person feels respected, there's a far greater chance that he or she will reciprocate.

Rabbi Yaakov Horowitz, *shlita*, of Monsey, New York, is successful in making contact with that most difficult of species, the turned-off teenager. He once shared with me one of his secrets: When a teenage "client" enters his study and takes his or her seat, Rabbi Horowitz makes a point of either pulling the telephone jack out of the wall or taking the receiver off the hook. The effect is often magical, for Rabbi Horowitz has already sent this message to his visitor: "Talking to you is more important to me than talking to anyone else who might call right now."

Children — A Top Life Priority

While it's a good idea to plan time for speaking and listening to each child separately to ensure that at least you'll be "touching base," often the impromptu, unplanned conversations are the ones that yield the greatest harvest of love and understanding. This is because emotions and ideas don't naturally lend themselves to scheduling. Just as every speaker or author knows, inspiration can come at the oddest times, and so, too, will a child sometimes feel a yen to talk to you when you're busy with something else. While I'm not saying you should always drop everything in order to talk to a child, remember this: If you don't respond to your child's desire to talk, it will lessen the chance of his approaching you again. It is therefore necessary, when you absolutely cannot reschedule your day to talk with your child at the very moment he requests it, to at least take a few moments at that time to schedule a time to speak, as soon as possible. *Children need to know that they are an important, perhaps the most important, priority in your life.*[12]

> *Mordechai's mother died when he was eleven. He was my student at age fourteen, and his father, remarried, lived outside of Jerusalem. The father, a busy and wonderful man, would come to Jerusalem to visit his elderly father. Before returning home, would drop in at the school to visit his son.*
>
> *I told him that I wanted him, at least once, to travel to Jerusalem, come directly from the Central Bus Station to the school, spend time with his son, and make a point of letting the child know that he was going home from there, without dropping in on the boy's grandfather. I wanted the boy to feel that his father was coming to see him, and that he wasn't just a part of a visit to his grandfather.*
>
> *When my own son was studying in a yeshiva in a Haifa suburb, I would periodically take the bus, a two-and-a-half-hour trip, in order to visit him. I could only spend an hour or so with him, as I had a night position in Jerusalem. After the hour, I would begin the return trip — a total of five hours of*

---

12. This is why it is important to "go to bat" for them. When children get into hot water with their school, parents should speak up on their behalf. Not to blindly defend them, as sometimes it is beneficial for a child to pay a price for misbehavior or irresponsibility, but to present him or her in a more favorable light; to mitigate, if possible, the full thrust of the repercussions. Parents often say, "Your teacher is right," and leave it at that. While it's true that parents cannot undermine a teacher, their child must know that his parents will go to great lengths to provide him with as good a representation as possible.
Over the years, I have seen children who closed up to their parents because they felt that the parents did not make enough of an effort to see their side of things. Whether the parents are successful or not in their negotiations with the teacher/school is almost immaterial. It's the effort put out that matters most. The *Seforno* on *Bemidbar* 11:12 tells us that children love a father even when they have differences of opinion, if they feel that the father will put out his very best effort for them.

traveling in order to spend an hour with him. There is no doubt in my mind that this was a nonverbal message to him of how much he meant to me, and that made my traveling even more worthwhile.

Remembering What They Tell You

Listening is not a one-time affair, but a process. Children will often test us, to see if we really hear what they're saying without jumping to conclusions or issuing one-sided judgments. Only then will they be encouraged to come back and add a bit more. Children want guidance, or just someone to hear them out. This is generally true of any human being, regardless of age.

Since listening is an ongoing process, there will — we hope — be more than one conversation on any particular point. We can show our children, nonverbally, that they and, by extension, what they say, are important to us by remembering what they have said in a previous conversation. (I hope the reader remembers that I have said this before!) Sometimes parents can even tie in a point made by the child about a different subject when it's pertinent to the topic on hand.

Quiet Time

It is very important to find a place and a time where you can offer each one of your children your undivided attention. If this is difficult because of the size of your family or your home, then the planning needs more imagination. Sometimes you can meet your child outside the home for a half hour or so. Take him for some ice cream,[13] and then take some time to hear what's happening in his life.

---

13. The Gemara in *Sanhedrin* 103b tells us that food is an important agent in drawing people close to you.

One of the fundamental principles of this book is that we cannot compete with a dominant culture and fight its negative influences on its turf, but only on our own. We must compete in the areas where our strengths lie. The street, the society at large, cannot compete with parents when it comes to lending a listening, caring ear. *Parents are irreplaceable and children do not normally seek to replace them.* We must make the most of our strengths in the uneven battle for our child's soul, and listening and conversing are among our most prized parental powers, if we will only harness them properly.

❦ Points to Remember

HUMAN beings bond with, and understand each other, through speech.

WISDOM can be measured by the ability to identify function.

SILENCE is, or should be, the time when we are speaking to ourselves – when we understand and polish our inner world.

LISTENING conveys respect. When we listen, we are giving the speaker our minds.

CHILDREN need to know that they are an important, perhaps the most important, priority in our lives.

PARENTS are irreplaceable, and children do not normally seek to replace them.

CHAPTER NINE

Talking to Children

We have seen that maturity is the balance between intellect and emotion, and that as a child matures — and the intellect has correspondingly more and more input — then the person is held increasingly responsible for understanding the consequences of his actions.

We have also seen that respect toward a child is manifested by carefully considering and remembering what that child has told us about what he thinks, hopes for, and considers important.

We have also seen that emotion is communicated primarily on a nonverbal level, and that children are more affected by emotional input than by verbal, intellectual, input.

> *A parent who was having problems with his six-year old once approached me. I asked what he had tried before seeing me, and he replied that he always explained to his son, in no uncertain terms, what he was doing wrong. I asked if parental lecturing such as this had helped when he himself was a child, and he said no, it hadn't. Then he admitted it wasn't working with his child either. When I asked, "Then why do you keep on doing it?" he said, "I don't know what else to do."*

We need to talk with our children even when they're very young — even when they're still infants. But throughout the greater portion of their childhoods, words won't be our primary mode of communication, *especially when we're conveying our most important messages.* Even our verbal communication needs to have strong nonverbal components.

Rav Shlomo Wolbe, *shlita*, in a remarkable exposition on speech, refers to proper speech as a harp. (Words, arising as they do from our vocal chords, are indeed similar to the chords of a harp.) Just as many factors combine to give the harp its proper resonance and effect, so, too, is proper speech a combination of words, emotion and character.[1] Emotion, together with the character of the speaker, are nonverbal components that lend our words their full meaning.

Whether we're speaking with children or with fellow adults, our words are most effective when the nonverbal parts of speech are well utilized. It is important, therefore, to enumerate the major nonverbal parts of speech, which convey our true meanings and give power to our words.

1. **Tone of Voice.** The Gemara[2] tells us that family members accept authority when words are spoken softly. People are highly unlikely to want to be led by someone who can't even control himself. A person may shout hysterically that he *is* in control of himself, but the nonverbal message has already left its mark.

A soft tone of voice suggests self-control.

2. **Eye Contact.** Rav Yitzchok Hutner, *zt"l*, tells us[3] that a person's reality is present in his eyes, as has been said, "The eyes are the

---

1. *Felach HaShetikah VeHahodayah, Hilchos Dibbur U'Shetikah.*
2. *Gittin* 6b–7a; *Shabbos* 34a.
3. *Letters*, Letter #136. Rav Hutner (1906–1981) was Rosh Yeshiva of Yeshivas Rabbeinu Chaim Berlin and one of America's foremost disseminators of Torah. An ingenious *mechanech*, he plumbed the deepest recesses of his students' souls, molding each one according to his unique capabilities. As a student of Yeshivas Rabbeinu Chaim Berlin, this author remains forever indebted to him.

window of the soul." When we make eye contact, we are accessing the deepest recesses of the person. It is for this reason that to look into someone's eyes is considered an emotional message, whether of love or of hatred. Indeed, in some cultures it's considered an act of aggression, as is obvious from this true story:

> *While walking down a street in Manhattan, Mordechai made eye contact with someone sitting on a stoop. The man immediately jumped up and said, "I could kill you right now and everybody would understand me." Mordechai said earnestly "I'm sorry." (And did he mean it!) A miracle happened and the New Yorker "forgave" Mordechai's act of aggression and let him pass.*

There is no question that the same holds true in a positive sense. Many times I have found that a short, warm look into someone's eyes is a harbinger of a productive and happy meeting. I suggest that you try to engender within yourself a feeling of love or respect for some positive aspect about that person before you make eye contact. If you are meeting a stranger, realize that he or she has a pure, God-given soul, and is worthy of love and respect.

3. Touch. The Vilna Gaon[4] teaches us that touch is a primary means of conveying emotion. When used together with earnest words, it has an enormous effect. Touch is so powerful an emotional tool, in fact, that the Torah has placed special stress on where and how it can be used, but this is beyond the scope of this work.[5]

---

4. *Berachos* 6a. The Vilna Gaon points out that the *Tefillin shel Rosh* (the head *tefillin*) mirror the four senses that are in the head. Since each sense has its own opening (mouth, eyes, ears and nose), the *tefillin* have four separate compartments. The *Tefillin shel Yad* (the hand *tefillin*), however, parallel the sense of touch, which has no specific opening, but is all over the body, on the skin. Therefore these *tefillin* have only one compartment. The hand *tefillin*, the Vilna Gaon points out, point toward the heart, the center of emotion. The sense of touch is what awakens our emotions most of all.
5. *The Magic Touch*, by Mrs. Gila Manolson (Targum Press: Southfield, Michigan), is an excellent presentation of the rationale behind how the Torah views touch between men and women.

Teachers need to learn how to use this tool appropriately, just as parents do. If with an older child, however, the relationship has been strained, then touch must be used only with extreme caution. It's very personal and can be experienced as invasive when employed by someone to whom the child doesn't feel close.

4. **Sincerity.** There's a famous saying: *"Devarim ha-yotzim min ha-lev nichnasim el ha-lev,"* "Words from the heart can enter the heart."[6] In the same vein, when people ask me what they should speak about in a presentation I reply, "Something that's important to you. Something you sincerely believe in."

In one of my earliest positions as a *menahel ruchani* in *yeshivos*, I asked Rav Shlomo Wolbe, *shlita*, which sources I should draw on most frequently. His reply was, "The ones that speak most to you." When a person is inspired by a certain book or idea, then he is most likely to deliver an inspired presentation.

Children can sense very quickly how sincere you are. This has to do with honesty — whether you really believe in what you're saying — and also with whether you're prepared to back up your words. The most eloquent words will be ineffectual if the child senses that you're not prepared to stand behind them, or if necessary, to enforce them. In either case, your words will be flouted with impunity, and worse, you'll look like a hypocrite in your child's eyes.

Before speaking with a child about an important matter, sometimes it's useful to take a moment to *feel* what you're about to say.[7]

---

6. Although this saying is not found in the Gemara (it is brought in the book *Shiras Yisroel*, by Rav Moshe ibn Ezra, p. 156), it seems to have its root in the teaching (*Berachos* 6b), *"Kol mi sheyesh bo yiras Shamayim, devarav nishmaim,"* that whoever has fear of Heaven his words are heard.
7. See *Felach HaShetikah V'Hahodayah*, ibid.; and Rambam, *Hilchos De'os* 2:6.

Rav Moshe Feinstein, *zt"l*,[8] expressed the idea that we ourselves must be true models of what we want our children to become. He deduced this from the fact that when Hashem demanded of us that we be a holy nation, He said, "because I am holy."[9] Hashem is saying, "I can demand this of you, because that's what I am Myself.[10]

Although our own actions fall short sometimes of the ideals to which we aspire, our hearts[11] must be sincere, and the words we say to our children must be consistent with those aspirations. Otherwise we are role-modeling hypocrisy and are sure to eventually lose their respect.

5. **Facial Expression.** The prophet Yeshayahu[12] tells us that facial expression is a guide to the emotions behind a person's spoken word. The Hebrew word for face, *panim*, is related to the word *p'nim*, "inside," for the face tells us what is happening within.

The Gemara[13] teaches us that it is better to show a person "the white of your teeth" (to give them a smile) than to give them a drink of milk. Rav Avigdor Miller, *zt"l*, says that this is the case even if the person has just come in after a long trek on a hot day.

---

8. 1895–1986, one of the great world Torah leaders, who gained special prominence during the forty years following World War II.
9. *Vayikra* 11:44, 19:2.
10. *Dorash Moshe, Kedoshim*, p. 95.
11. See *Sefas Emes, Shemos*, p. 26, paragraph beginning "*Vayedabber*," where this dichotomy between the way we behave, where perfection is impossible, and where we want to be, where perfection is a praiseworthy goal, is beautifully elucidated.
12. *Yeshayahu* 3:9. See the Malbim ad loc. See also Rav Tzadok HaKohen, *Tzidkas HaTzaddik*, #205, where he uses this concept to explain how it is possible, for great men, to see a person's face and understand what lies within that human being (*Zohar*, vol. 1, 190a). [Rav Tzadok HaKohen of Lublin (1823–1900) was one of the greatest Chassidic thinkers and most prolific writers in modern Jewish history.]
13. *Kesubos* 111b.

Your smile is still of more value, and does more for him than a cold drink ever could.[14]

Young children are especially sensitive to our facial expressions. They respond to what they see on our faces long before they comprehend what we're saying.[15] The sense of sight touches their emotions even before the words we say to them make any sense at all.

It has been told that Rav Yosef Chaim Sonnenfeld, *zt"l*,[16] would make sure to go in person if something important needed to be said, for he considered a written letter insufficient.[17] The nonverbal components — the expression on his face, the tone of his voice — gave the message its truest meaning.

---

14. The simple explanation of this, I think, is that the smile addresses itself to the spirit of the person, while the milk (which you should also give him!) is answering a physical need. Spiritual needs are far more powerful in human beings than physical ones, for the spiritual component of the person is dominant. Parents who forget this principle, and address their children's physical needs totally, but neglect the child's spiritual needs — on the emotional level as well as in the domain of Torah — will pay a heavy price indeed, for their children will be far more likely to look to the enticements of the street to fill the void within them.
15. The Vilna Gaon points out (*Esther* 5:14, *Tikkunei Zohar* 89b) that the sense of sight touches the emotion. This is probably what our Sages meant when they said (*Avodah Zarah* 29b, *Zohar*, part 3, p. 289a), "Shuraiki d'eina be'uvanta deliba talya," that the muscles of the eye are connected to the understanding of the heart, for there is a connection between the eyes and the heart's instinctive understanding. There is a world of Torah, which we call *sod*, the Hidden Torah, which requires not only an intellectual understanding, but an emotional grasp of what is being taught. A full treatment of this idea is beyond the scope of this work. I would refer the reader to the Vilna Gaon's work, *Aderes Eliyahu*, on *Devarim* 32:7, and to his commentary on *Mishlei* 24:30; and to *Michtav Me'Eliyahu*, vol.1, pp. 218–223, in which the connection between heart, emotion, and a deep understanding of Torah's "secrets" is elucidated.
16. 1848–1931. He was the great leader of Jerusalem Jewry during the turbulent period before and following World War I. There is a beautiful biography of him entitled *Guardian of Jerusalem* (New York: Mesorah Publications, 1983).
17. See *Guardian of Jerusalem*, pp. 136–7 and p. 250.

OTHER FACTORS

In addition to the five elements mentioned above, there are other factors that can affect the success or failure of your communication with your child. They are also nonverbal, and deeply influence how your words will be taken. For instance:

1. **The Setting.** Our surroundings affect what goes on in our heads.[18] Just as a child is more likely to "open up" to a principal if they've gone out for pizza together than if they're on opposite sides of a huge mahogany desk, so, too, will a child open up to a parent more in one environment than in another.

Not only is the child affected by where he's being spoken to, but the parent is affected as well. A parent can easily be distracted by what's going on at home, and if he or she doesn't give the child his fully sustained attention, that's a profoundly felt nonverbal message. When a child is given full attention, the respect this conveys will encourage him or her to speak more freely.

Take a child out when you need to speak about something sensitive. Turn off your cellphone, if you have one, making sure that your child sees you turn it off. He needs to see that you consider the time with him so important that you don't want to be disturbed.

Private outings with just the two of you should not be reserved only for such occasions, otherwise the child will get uneasy every time you suggest going out. He'll think you're going out for another one of your "little talks."

To sum up, make the environment as relaxing and enjoyable as possible when you need to have a private talk with your child.

---

18. Rav Dessler, *zt"l*, in *Michtav Me'Eliyahu*, vol. 3, p. 129, explains that a person is enjoined to maintain a regular place where he prays (*Berachos* 6b) because in a place where a person prayed well once, there is a greater chance, by association with what had happened before, to pray well again.

2. **Being Calm.** Put all other matters out of your mind when talking to your child. This helps you see things in a better perspective. Being calm makes you into a good listener, which, ironically, is what you need to be if you want to be a candidate for the title "good conversationalist." *One of the greatest compliments we can give our children is to make a sincere effort to understand them. Then there is great reason to hope that they'll do the same for us.* While it is certainly a child's obligation to do his utmost to understand and honor his parents, it would do us well to try and make it as easy as possible for them to do this.

❧ Exercises

1. Remind yourself of the attitude that expresses love and respect: "If it's important to you, it's important to me."

2. Find a quiet, private moment, and talk softly to your child, using touch.

    If you have a good connection with him, use soft and caring eye contact, but if this is not the case, then the eye contact needs to be introduced at a later stage, when trust has been established and deepened. Eye contact is a very personal matter, a powerful tool, and therefore needs to be used judiciously.

    The initial subjects should be a sincere interest as to how that child's day went, both positively and negatively. Just listen, don't criticize or opine. Simply have genuine interest in what he or she has to say, and, through your eyes and short interjections, reaffirm the child's feelings, showing that what he or she has to say is important to you. In addition, remembering what the child has said on previous days is a nonverbal message that you hear what is being said.

3. If you cannot find a quiet, private moment, then this is in itself a problem that needs tackling. Sometimes going out for twenty minutes or so is a solution, if the home is too small or if there are too many distractions.

❧ Points to Remember

RESPECT toward a child is manifested by carefully considering and remembering what that child has told us about what he thinks, hopes for, and considers important.

WHEN a child is given full attention, the respect this conveys will encourage him or her to speak more freely.

ONE OF the greatest compliments we can give our children is to make a sincere effort to understand them. Then there is great reason to hope that they'll do the same for us.

CHILDREN can sense very quickly how sincere you are.

A SOFT tone of voice suggests self-control.

WHEN we make eye contact, we are accessing the deepest recesses of the person.

TOUCH is a primary means of conveying emotion. It must be used with extreme caution.

PART THREE

TACKLING LIFE'S CHALLENGES

CHAPTER TEN

Quiet Time and Renewal: Principles for Life

At the beginning of *Parashas Mikeitz*,[1] the *Sefas Emes* gives us a principle we would do well to heed if we are to lead the successful lives we pray for.

The *Sefas Emes* is speaking about the fact that there were seven years of plenty in Egypt before the years of hunger began.[2] These years of plenty were meant to be used, he tells us, as preparation for the years of hunger. This was true not only in Egypt as a nation, but also in the personal life of every individual.

Each person is given intervals of "plenty," during which he is meant to internalize the truths of life. From these quiet periods, he can develop direction and strength for life's inevitable trials. If he

---

1. The paragraph beginning *"U'mizeh sheyesh."* Written by the Gerrer Rebbe, Rav Yehudah Aryeh Leib Alter, *zt"l* (1847–1905), the *Sefas Emes* is an awe-inspiring work of immense scope and depth. This idea appears in the *Sefas Emes* many times. See *Bereishis*, pp. 90, 136; *Shemos*, pp. 66, 123; and *Devarim*, p. 90.
2. *Bereishis* 41:29–30.

doesn't prepare himself beforehand, but waits until the "years of hunger" arrive, then his intellect may not be sufficiently at peace to work problems out.³

I believe this principle holds not only on a lifelong timeline, but on a daily one as well. In each person's day there are going to be moments of quiet and moments of transition. The transitions will test one's patience, understanding, and physical and emotional fortitude. In keeping with this is the advice I give young men and women before they marry:

> *Young man, before entering your new home, pause for a few moments.⁴ You've formed a picture in your mind. You imagine that on the other side of that door you're going to find a neat home, a delicious supper prepared, and a wife who's delighted to see you.*
>
> *If you're sold on this picture, and then open the door to find none of the above, you could well feel like flying into a rage. Anger is the surprise and frustration at the gap between the way you think things should be and the way they really are. Take time, quiet time, to realize that what awaits on the other side may be a disappointment. Resolve not only to contain your anger, but also to give your wife the smile she needs and deserves.*

---

3. It goes without saying that it is never too late to learn to utilize quiet moments, and indeed, to create them.
4. This advice is based on what I learned over thirty years ago from Rav Avigdor Miller, *zt"l*, who said that a newlywed man should place a nameplate on his door and before entering his home, consciously recognize that it's his name and he is responsible for what goes on in that home. In addition, Rav Miller advised that when a person places his hands on the door handle to his home he should be firm in his resolve that no matter what scene will greet him he will not utter a word before seeking to understand the situation. Rav Miller's passing, in 5761 (2001), left a terrible void in the leadership of the Jewish People. His influence on this author, beginning in 1964 and continuing for the next thirty-seven years, is incalculable.

Actually, it would be better not to wait until you've already reached your doorstep. Give this matter some thought on the way home.

∼

Young woman, I suggest that you prepare for two important "transition times" each day: one, when the children arrive home, and the other, when your husband walks through the door. Prepare yourself for everyone's arrival while it's still quiet. Eat some fruit; put on a smile. Children especially will remember how it felt to come home. Make your husband and children feel wanted. Demonstrate nonverbally that you're glad to see them.

Quiet is the condition under which the intellect functions best. If parental decisions about children are to be rooted in the intellect, a parent must take and make these quiet moments a part of his daily life. Surprise is the enemy of our emotions, because it throws us off and causes us to react without due thought. The intellect needs quiet, and it proceeds more slowly than emotion. We need an early start, while it's still quiet within and without, to prepare for the surprises that can impede our judgment.

CARRY YOUR QUIET AROUND WITH YOU

The principle of the *Sefas Emes* has several other applications. Before we make decisions, we need quiet time to think. If sound — be it shouting, daily household noises, or even beautiful music — stimulates the emotion, then quiet is the natural element in which the intellect functions best.

I often define the ability to concentrate as "the ability to carry your quiet around with you." That's when you can shut out the noise of the world, concentrate on the truths of life, and put matters in their proper perspective.[5] Being able to ignore the distractions of your surroundings is a key element in making proper decisions, because decision-making depends upon correctly weighing the implications of your actions. This is the domain of the intellect.

BEFORE PRAYER

Perhaps the most important transition we make during the day is when we prepare ourselves for prayer. We are going to meet the King. Indeed, we should be so full of trepidation that we should be unable to mouth a single word, and we ask, before beginning the Silent Devotion (*Shemoneh Esreh*), that Hashem open our lips.

It is in keeping with this that certain pious people, known in the Gemara as *Chassidim HaRishonim*, spent a full hour in contemplation of what lay before them before beginning to pray. Even today Rav Shlomo Wolbe, *shlita*, urges his disciples to spend at least a few moments contemplating the fact that they are about to pray to Hashem.[6]

---

5. See *The Bridge of Life*, p. 59 (*Gesher HaChayim*, vol. 3, in Hebrew), in which he quotes *Yoma* 20b as stating that if not for the hubbub of the street, we would be able to hear the solar orb turn, that is, we would be able to concentrate and feel the fundamental truths of life and live accordingly. This is why, the *Gesher HaChayim* suggests, we feel uplifted and inspired when we see a sunset on a quiet evening. *Gesher HaChayim* is a three-volume masterpiece written by Rav Yechiel Michel Tukatchinsky, *zt"l* (1871–1954), of Jerusalem. The third volume deals with the meaning of life from the perspective of Eternity. It is truly an amazing and uplifting experience to read this book, in either Hebrew or English.
Rav Avigdor Miller, *zt"l*, suggests that the letters of the word *rasha*, evil person, are the same as *ra'ash*, noise, because the *rasha* is a victim of his emotions, and thus acts with only the moment in mind. When the rush of passion passes, his intellect takes over, and he is full of regrets. But his regrets are short-lived, for soon enough his emotions regain control and he lives, once again, only for the desires of the moment. The Vilna Gaon, in his commentary on *Mishlei* 10:20, suggests as well, that the intellect of the *rasha* is clear, but he is only affected to improve temporarily, as he is the prisoner of his emotions.
6. See *Alei Shur*, vol. 2, p. 349.

Indeed, prayer is in itself a means of learning to "carry your quiet around with you," for prayer demands of us to leave the manifold thoughts that crowd our minds and to focus on the truths of life that are expressed in prayer.[7]

THE KING — IN QUIET

A Gemara in *Maseches Berachos* is a beautiful example of the principle that the intellect, which should lead us, functions best in quiet. It goes as follows:

> *Rav Sheshes was blind, but wanted to recite the blessing uttered in the presence of a king. An enemy of the Sages, standing near him in the crowd of onlookers, tried to trick him into reciting the blessing at the wrong time. With each passing contingent of boisterous and trumpeting soldiers, this man told Rav Sheshes that the king was riding with that troop. Each time the Sage refused to recite the blessing, for he understood that the king had not yet appeared.*
>
> *Suddenly it fell silent — there were no blaring trumpets, no music of any kind, just quiet. Then Rav Sheshes recited the blessing, for he knew that the king was present.[8]*

The king, leader of his people, functions in silence. Indeed, our Sages are called kings[9] because they rule over their own minds,[10] and hence are worthy and capable of leading their people.

---

7. See *Chochmah U'Mussar*, vol. 1, *ma'amar* 152, where he says that prayer teaches us to concentrate and and achieve peace of mind.
8. *Berachos* 58a. Rav Sheshes based his insight on the fact that the King of kings appeared in the "still, small voice" (*I Melachim* 19:12,13).
9. *Gittin* 62a.
10. Heard from Rav Shlomo Wolbe, *shlita*.

Yaakov — In the Yeshiva of Shem and Ever

Yaakov, who serves as our paradigm for successful parenting in exile, went to the yeshiva of Shem[11] and Ever before going to Lavan's house. Yaakov's father, Yitzchak, had explicitly told him to go to the house of Lavan in order to flee from Esav's wrath, but Yaakov stayed at the yeshiva for fourteen years before continuing on. The Torah does not consider this detour a violation of his father's command. Indeed, the Torah explicitly states[12] that Yaakov complied with his father's command. How can this be?

It must be that when Yitzchak told Yaakov to go to Lavan's home, he meant that Yaakov must first stop off at the yeshiva of Shem and Ever. *It was in the quiet of those years that Yaakov prepared himself spiritually for the trials of living in an alien, hostile environment, and indeed, of raising his children there.*

As Rav Yaakov Kamenetsky, *zt"l*,[13] so beautifully observed, when it states that Yaakov taught Torah especially to Yosef, it was referring to what he had studied in the yeshiva of Shem and Ever.[14] For Yaakov had foreseen that Yosef, too, would endure the trials of exile and would have to raise a Torah-true family in the worst of environments.

---

11. Shem was the son of Noach. He was the king of Shalem (later known as Yerushalayim), and was the man who came to greet Avraham after his victory over the four kings (*Bereishis* 14:18-20). He founded an academy, which he later headed together with his great-grandson Ever.
I think that this meeting with Avraham was epochal, for it was the meeting between Shem, who was responsible for bearing the tradition of Noach, and Avraham, the self-made man who with his own intellect discovered the existence of the One God. They represent the two ways we must know Hashem: as *Elokeinu*, our God, Whom we have discovered by dint of our own work, and *Elokei avoseinu*, the God Whom we know from tradition, from our forefathers. See *Sefas Emes, Bereishis*, p. 56, the paragraph beginning *"B'midrash vehayah."*
12. *Bereishis* 28:7.
13. 1891–1986. He was one of the great Torah leaders of the second half of the twentieth century. He himself was a teacher of and adviser to some of our generation's greatest scholars and leaders.
14. Rashi, *Bereishis* 37:3.

SUCCESS AT THE END REQUIRES A PLAN IN THE BEGINNING

In most cases, the success of any undertaking will be in direct proportion to the comprehensiveness of thought invested beforehand. The Vilna Gaon[15] gives us the building of a table as an example. He observes that there are four things the table-maker will need to consider:

1. What the table will be used for
2. Which material to use
3. Which artisan to employ
4. What shape or form the table will take

The table's actual use comes at the end of the story, but it had to be the first thing in the mind of the builder: for all the other decisions regarding the material, the artisan, and the shape, depend upon the table's ultimate function.[16]

> *Mori VeRabi, zt"l, used to say that when we make a decision regarding children or embark upon a certain course in their upbringing, we need to bear in mind what effects it will have twenty years from now.*

To people who claim that they cannot project twenty years in the future, I give the following advice:

> *When considering a course of action whose outcome twenty years hence is unclear, look for someone who took a similar step or made a similar decision twenty years ago, and see how they, or their children, look today.*

---

15. Commentary to *Berachos* 61a.
16. See the commentary of the Vilna Gaon on *Mishlei* 1:1, in which he explains that this is what is meant by *sof ma'aseh*: that what *happens* last, is *bemachashavah techilah*, first in *thought*.

> *This also involves asking people about their past choices. Listen to their accounts of what went right and what went wrong. Although it is undeniable that no two circumstances are exactly the same, still, many important guidelines can be gleaned from such a discussion.*

About this there can be no doubt: we must invest quiet time for planning what steps we're going to take in the *chinuch* of our children. It is the intellect that can project into the future, and the intellect needs time and quiet.

RENEWING AND RE-CONFIRMING OUR GOALS AND IDEALS

Another function of quiet time is to provide us with an opportunity to renew ourselves and our commitment to our goals. Occasionally we need to reconsider what our ultimate goals should be, because it is our goals that determine our direction in life. If we conclude that these goals are still valid, we need to see if we are in fact moving toward them.

At other times, we may have to reaffirm our commitment to our goals, emotionally and intellectually.

EVERYTHING NEEDS RENEWAL

The Maharal teaches us that one of the four principles embodied in the Essential Name of Hashem (the *Shem Havaya*, i.e., *yud-kei-vav-kei*) is that Hashem constantly renews His world.[17] Indeed, each day in the Morning Service we say that Hashem, in His goodness, renews His Creation.

---

17. See *Nesivos Olam*, vol. 1, *Nesiv HaChessed*, end of the first chapter.

On a bus ride from the Western Wall, I heard the following profound thought from Rav Shemuel Betzalel, *shlita*:[18]

> The Midrash[19] states that there is one bird that refused Chavah's offer of the forbidden fruit of the Tree of Knowledge, and therefore is not condemned to death. Once every thousand years, a self-generated fire consumes it, leaving it the size of an egg. From that egg the bird regenerates itself. We see, then, that all living things, even those that live forever, need to renew themselves.

This need for renewal was one of the reasons Hashem commanded His People to go three times a year to Jerusalem. There, together with the rest of his people, the Jew could renew himself intellectually and emotionally. It was his chance to commit himself anew to a life of eternal meaning.

These three joyous times of the year — the holidays of Pesach, Shavuos and Sukkos — annually renew our emotional commitment to our goals. Then, in private, silent moments throughout the rest of the year, we can reflect, as individuals, on the bigger things in life.

It is the ability of the Jewish People to renew itself that is at the root of being the Eternal People.[20] Similarly, we would do well to spend a few moments a day renewing our commitment to all that is precious to us. And every once in a while, we need to take a bit more time to make sure that our relationships and day-to-day living are consistent with these goals and ideals. Then, and only then, can we hope to be successful in passing on these ideals to our children.

---

18. One of the heads of Jerusalem's Yeshivat Porat Yosef.
19. *Bereishis Rabbah* 19:9.
20. The Jewish calendar is primarily lunar, which also symbolizes renewal. For just as the moon wanes but returns again to its former glory, so do the Jewish People.

Deepening Relationships during "Quiet Times"

Emotions fluctuate. Our closest relationships need to be renewed and deepened if we are to prevent their bonds from becoming stale.

Perhaps the most important reason for having quiet time with our children is that such time spent with our children, individually or with the siblings together, sets the foundation for open, sincere, and productive communication. There are moments when we need our own private quiet time, and there are times when we should "share" the quiet with our children.

Almost no problem in a child's life, whether it be familial, personal, societal, or school-oriented, gets full-blown overnight. Lasting hurt feelings and deep disappointments don't arise from a single incident. Therefore, open, honest conversations with a parent should be a frequent occurrence, as close to daily as possible. That way, a problem is usually revealed before it becomes so deep-seated as to seem unresolvable.

Stay in Touch with Your Child's Reality

Human beings, especially the young, for whom so much in life is new, are in a constant state of change. This is because so many things are unfamiliar, and hence enthralling. Their imaginations are quickly excited.

In addition, they still don't have (as adults hopefully do) a well-worked-out inner sense of reality and values — the fruit of many years of learning and experience. The young are open prey to the ongoing input that all the myriad parts of their world impart, an enchanting world of material pleasures and fantasies that beckon. Especially in modern society, there are temptations for which a young person has not yet developed "antibodies." Many are the tests to which a young mind (and soul) are subjected today.

Now, more than ever, when our children are under such a massive barrage of spiritually lethal influences, is it incumbent upon us to maintain an ongoing dialogue in order to know what's on their minds and in their hearts. This relationship requires quiet time, and the sort of surroundings that enhance the desire to focus on each other. This time need not always be full of talk, for the act of spending time together, even in silence, is a sign of love. It implies: *I enjoy your company.* The talk need not always be full of meaning, either — quite the contrary. Small talk is a sign that simply being in each other's presence is wonderful in itself. We don't always have to be talking about something of monumental importance, it's being together that counts.[21]

BE PREPARED FOR SLOW CHANGE

If this quiet time has not been the rule, then it may be a good idea to start slowly. A sudden heart-to-heart "summit meeting" may find your child confused or, worse, suspicious, and can lead to frustrated feelings and expectations on the part of the parent. After all, the child may not want to "open up" so quickly in light of the past. In such a case, it would be better to take your child out for pizza, or to engage in some other activity you both enjoy, and forget about the "important" conversation. This is not unlike dating, wherein really personal or sensitive issues are not fare for the initial meetings. Develop a good feeling, and eventually you'll be better able to find out where your child really is.

Which brings us to the next important point…

---

21. The Hebrew word that epitomizes this type of speaking is called *sichah*. See *Tzidkas HaTzaddik*, #213, and the *Siach Yitzchok*, in the *Siddur HaGra*, at the beginning of the Evening Service.

Spend the Time Listening

The function of this quiet time with your child is not to impress upon him or her what you consider important in life, or what you feel he should be doing. On the contrary, *most of the time should be spent listening.* Show interest — with your facial expressions, your interjections, your questions to make sure you understand, and, as much as possible, with your affirmations of where that child is and what he or she is feeling. Sometimes you can simply be empathetic. Sometimes you can agree with the stated feelings or opinions. The main thing, however, is that you *listen*. And then listen some more. Listen nonjudgmentally. I'd like to say, again, that love means: "If it's important to you it's important to me." If the subject at hand is important to your child, then it must always be important to you.

We can often find precious keys to child-raising in the natural reactions of mothers. When a child comes with a minor bruise, or even an imagined one, the good mother knows not to say, "It's nothing." Instead, she kisses the "wound."

Never make light of what your child tells you.

Quiet Time as a Sign of Love

As stated above, we don't always have to have an "important" conversation when we're with the people we love. Small talk is a sign that just being together is what matters. Sometimes, little need be said. When walking with a younger child to shul, sometimes I take his hand and give it a gentle squeeze as we walk. This is a nonverbal message: *I enjoy just walking with you.* Sometimes this can be expressed verbally, telling the child how much you prefer *davening* with him to *davening* alone.

It is, of course, obvious that this tool can be used anywhere, anytime.

Song

If you are at all partial to singing, the value of singing with your child cannot be overemphasized. It may not be that quiet, but there's a quiet bond being formed.

> *I was once told by Rav Shlomo Wolbe, shlita, about a young man, son of an illustrious Jew, whose commitment to Judaism was faltering. The father sent his son to the famous Mirrer Yeshiva in Lithuania.*
>
> *One year later, the young man returned a changed person, with renewed idealism for all things Jewish. When his father asked him if he could point to something specific that brought about this remarkable turnabout, the boy replied that there were two experiences that towered above the rest. One was the Adon Olam song that the Yeshiva sang in unison at the conclusion of the Morning Service on Shavuos, which had followed an entire night of Torah study. The other was Simchas Torah, when the entire Yeshiva broke out in singing and dancing.*

I think that in large groups such at these, it's the sense of connecting with all the people with whom one is singing that gives the song its incredible effect.

Singing gives joy to the soul, which is one of the most important elements of a healthy mind, as we shall now see.

Happiness

There's something else the intellect needs in order to function optimally: happiness. The Beis Aharon[22] says that the letters in the

---

22. Rav Aharon Karliner (1802–1872), one the Torah giants of his time. This thought appears in *Beis Aharon*, Chanukah.

Hebrew word for thought, *machashavah* — מחשבה, can be rearranged to spell בשמחה — *besimchah*, "happily." A despairing or depressed mind cannot be relied upon to draw correct conclusions or to anticipate future outcomes realistically.

Happiness doesn't mean lightheadedness. It means that the mind is joyful because it trusts in Hashem, and trusts in the basic goodness of oneself and one's loved ones.

To summarize, quiet time is necessary for us to use our minds optimally. Quiet time helps us bond intimately with our children. And finally, quiet time helps us focus on the reality that Hashem, and His world, are intrinsically good, which is cause for happiness.

> *Rabbi Yehudah exuded a happy, radiant countenance. A Roman matron, seeing his happy face, thought he was drunk. He told her that wine made him ill, but that "The wisdom of a person lights up his face." (Koheles 8:1)*[23]

It is wisdom, which is rooted in quiet time, that truly brightens the life of the wise and sets the stage for a happy family.

---

23. *Nedarim* 49b.

🌹 EXERCISES

1. Take quiet time on your way home to imagine how your happy demeanor is going to affect the atmosphere at home.

   Imagine how you would like things to be when you arrive home, then change your picture to one that's less "perfect." Prepare yourself for the possibility that it will be the second scenario you may find upon opening the door, or maybe something worse!

2. Share with your spouse how you felt when you took some quiet time in the course of the day.

3. Before Shabbos ends, take a few moments to reflect on the coming week. Put into your heart the goals you wish to accomplish. See *Sefas Emes, Bemidbar,* p. 135.

❧ Points to Remember

Occasionally, we need to reconsider what our ultimate goals should be, because our goals determine our direction in life.

Each person is given intervals of "plenty," during which he is meant to internalize the truths of life and develop direction and strength for life's inevitable trials.

Transitions test one's patience, understanding, and physical and emotional fortitude.

The ability to concentrate is the ability to "carry your quiet around with you."

The success of any undertaking will be in direct proportion to the comprehensiveness of thought invested beforehand.

Most of the time with your child should be spent listening.

Never make light of what your child tells you.

Small talk is a sign that simply being in each other's presence is wonderful in itself.

Happiness results when the mind is joyful because it trusts in Hashem, and trusts in the basic goodness of oneself and one's loved ones.

CHAPTER ELEVEN

Taking Responsibility for Our Attitudes

Defining "Responsibility"

Before we can discuss the main topic of this chapter, three principles have to be set forth: The first two are as follows:

1. The Hebrew word for "life," *chayim*, is always in the plural, because life is infinitely varied and constantly changing. One of the hallmarks of this world is that things are in constant flux.

2. The Hebrew word for truth, *emes*, on the other hand, is always singular, because all principles, if they are true, flow from a single Source.

What the above means, on a practical level for each of us as individuals, is this: Since the world out there is always changing, if I "plug into" that outside world as my primary source of information, knowledge, and values, then I myself am always going to be changing and unstable. It follows then, that the only true stability available to me as a human being must be one that is based upon eternal truths. (In English, of course, the word can be used in the plural.) The capacity of these truths to sustain me will be in proportion to how completely I have internalized them. My personal stability as a human being depends upon the degree to which I have made eternal truths into a reality in my own mind.

3. One of the three Crowns mentioned in the Mishnah[1] is the Crown of Torah. This Crown refers to the perfection of mind that Torah study bestows upon a person, which can be expressed through his capacity to think — to use his mind.[2]

Perfection of mind enables a person to internalize truth. Internalizing truth makes one stable, and therefore capable of taking responsibility — literally, to be *capable of responding*. Responsibility is the ability of the mind to take what life brings our way, interpret it objectively, and to react to it in accordance with inner truths.

It is this ability to respond which will determine whether or not, at the end of the day, our lives are happy and productive. I think this is why the Hebrew word for responsibility is *achrayus*, a derivative of the word *achris*, meaning, "end."

What We Are Most Responsible For

Human beings cannot always influence how things turn out, so their responsibility is limited. A person can only be held responsible for what is under his or her control.

There are, however, two factors almost totally under a person's control, and which therefore fall squarely within the domain of personal responsibility. These are *attitude* and *desire*. To explain:

1. **Attitude.** *Although I may not be able to affect the material outcome of events, I am in control as to how I view them.* When our

---

1. *Pirkei Avos* 4:16.
2. See Maharal, *Derech Chayim*, p. 188.

Sages say that only someone occupied with Torah is truly free,[3] what they mean is that I may be totally deprived of my ability to use my body or wealth, but no one can force me to view a situation in any manner other than the way I choose to view it.

Attitude is one aspect of perfection of mind, which is the sphere affected by engagement in Torah study.[4] When someone is actively engaged in the labor of understanding Torah, he acquires a totally different perspective on life. *Torah frees the person to look at life correctly, and correct perception leads to happiness.*

2. **Desire.** In addition to our intellectual perception, although we may not be able to affect how things turn out, *we are in a position to control what it is we want.*

The Hebrew word for desire or want is *ratzon*, which, as Rashi[5] points out, refers to the essence of who you are. "If it is in your *nefesh*"[6] means, "Do you desire?"[7] The word *nefesh* refers to the facet of the soul in which emotion rests. We can discern the quality of a person's emotion by taking his pulse, which measures the rapidity of blood circulation. Hence, *ki nefesh kol basar damo hu*, "...for the *nefesh* of all flesh is its blood."[8] The emotional quotient of the person arises from the *nefesh*, where the blood is. This is why the intellect is said to originate in the mind, while the emotion has as its source the heart (where the blood is pumped).[9]

---

3. *Pirkei Avos* 6:3.
4. *Derech Chayim*, p. 288.
5. The all-time premier Torah commentator (1040–1104).
6. *Bereishis* 23:8.
7. The *Sefas Emes, Bereishis*, p. 195, the paragraph beginning "*U'v'midrash*," says this even more clearly, that who you are is basically what you want, what you yearn for. In addition, he says, the word *ratzon* is also related to the word *rootz*, run, for we run to that which we truly desire.
8. *Vayikra* 17:14.
9. This is why we have both hand and head *tefillin*, to express the subjugation of both our emotional self (the heart, where the hand *tefillin* face) and our intellect (head) to Hashem's will.

How I choose to look at things (my intellectual attitude) and what I want (on an emotional level) are the two things most under my control, and are therefore what I am most responsible for.

RESPONSIBILITY FOR MY HAPPINESS

A primary source of problems in relationships is thinking you would be happy if only some other person were to do such and such a thing, or (infinitely worse) if only the other person *were* someone else.

I'm not saying that how others behave toward us isn't an important element in our happiness. The closer someone is to us, the more he or she will affect us. There can be no question that this gives the other person a greater responsibility to treat us in a manner conducive to our happiness. But the *final responsibility* for how we experience our lives, with or without that person's support, is totally ours.

I DEFINE MY OWN ROLE

Related to these twin concepts of attitude and desire is how I define my own role within a given relationship. Rav Dessler[10] wrote eloquently that the world is divided into "givers" and "takers." Either a person is primarily motivated to bestow kindness on others, or perceives the value of others primarily in terms of what he receives from them.

This has little to do with whether you're actually receiving or giving, but rather, what your primary motivation is. One can give in order to get, as, for example, when a man holds a sale in order to make a profit. He'd rather have the other person's money without

---

10. *Michtav Me'Eliyahu*, vol. 1, pp. 32–54.

surrendering anything, but alas, he can't get it legally unless he gives something in exchange for the cash. Or one can get in order to give, as, for example, when a man who enjoys providing people with good merchandise holds a sale. He, too, wants to make a profit, yet deep down he keeps his clients' best interests in mind. He needs to earn a living, so he sells the merchandise, but if he could, he would give it away.

In any successful, healthy relationship, Rav Dessler says, each party is concerned about the other. When they each live that way, the relationship is a blessing for both. If, however, each is concerned with his or her "rights" vis-à-vis the other, then the relationship will be anything but happy.

Mori VeRabi, zt"l, put this idea into beautiful, lucid focus.

> *When Mori VeRabi, zt"l, was young, socialism was taking the world by storm, swallowing up millions of dedicated, idealistic young men and women. Mori VeRabi thought to himself: What's the problem? After all, the socialists are preaching equality in all areas of life, such as the sharing of wealth, etc.*
>
> *Mori VeRabi then thought of the law of the Jewish slave, whose Jewish master was obligated to treat him especially well. The master was not permitted to give the slave work that was actually unnecessary, just to keep him busy. On the other hand, the slave was obligated to put in a full day's work and be as productive and honest as possible.*[11]
>
> *What would happen, Mori VeRabi said to himself, if the slave were to remind the master of his obligations, and the master to chastise the slave for not working hard enough? Things wouldn't work. Only when each one kept his own*

---

11. Rambam, *Hilchos Avadim* 1:6,9.

responsibility uppermost in mind, then, and only then, could the relationship succeed for both.

In the entire Communist Manifesto, Mori VeRabi noted, mention was made only of the rights pertaining to the workers of the world, and what their employers were obligated to do for them. No mention was made of the obligations of the workers toward their employers — not a word about honest work and well-earned wages. Therefore, Mori VeRabi concluded, socialism could not be a Torah concept.

The same, *Mori VeRabi* said, applied to marriage. Each partner must bear in mind his or her *own* responsibilities.

I remember a poignant example of how vital this principle can be in families:

Mrs. G. had lost her son under tragic circumstances. Understandably broken, she began to withdraw more and more into herself.

In a meeting, it was pointed out to her that her remaining family desperately needed her wisdom, insight and fortitude. She was (is!) a very special lady, with a deep capacity for caring and giving.

Instead of focusing on how difficult things were for her, and how she wasn't getting what she needed, she shifted her focus to those around her, who needed her strength and hope for a renewed life.

She became a giver, and a very good one at that.

Our Children — And Us

How we choose to view the people in our lives — the talents, mistakes, actions, abilities, disabilities, virtues and faults of ourselves and others — is what makes it possible for us and our children to be happy and productive. May all of us learn to view life's challenges from the best perspective possible, and *b'ezras Hashem*, deal with those problems correctly and be blessed with good results. First, as parents, we must be able to recognize, and joyfully accept the responsibility for that which is most under our control. Then, and only then, can we raise responsible children.

To sum up, no one can make us happy — it's a decision that only we can make. *Our happiness is dependent on one thing and one thing only: how we choose to view the events of life.* This truth comes from within.

Truth is not subject to the constantly changing whirlwind we call life. If we anchor ourselves to eternal truths, we will be able to maintain our calm and happiness. Then we will truly be able to inspire our children to want to emulate our life ideals.

❧ EXERCISES

1. Make a list of what you feel you are most responsible for. Divide the list into areas which are completely self-contained, i.e., attitudes, states of mind, etc., and areas where you interact with others, such as your spouse or your children. Which list is longer and contains more areas of your life?

    Ask yourself: In those areas where I have more control, am I being more responsible, day to day, than in the areas where I have less control? Or, am I pushing hard in areas where I have less control?

    Ask yourself: Does added responsibility make me happier or sadder? Would I prefer that other people take responsibility or am I glad to shoulder those responsibilities which I seem the most capable of handling?

    Ask yourself: Do I tend to take responsibility for matters which are outside of my control? What are the results of my shouldering these responsibilities?

    Ask yourself: Am I happily transferring responsibility for things to my children? Am I educating them to be more and more responsible for how they look at things and react to others, besides whether they do their particular chores or not?

2. Savor the happiness of giving to others.

🌺 Points to Remember

The only true stability available to us as human beings is one that is based upon eternal truths.

Responsibility is the ability to take what life brings our way, interpret it objectively, and react to it in accordance with inner truths.

The final responsibility for how we experience our lives is totally ours.

CHAPTER TWELVE

Change: How Much, How Fast

Raising children requires enormous flexibility. We must be aware of the fact that our environment, our children, and indeed we ourselves, are subject to change. Certainly, the truths of life are constant, but often their application varies with different situations and personalities.

As stated, change is part and parcel of our lives. Each of us must develop the flexibility to make changes, whenever necessary, to bring about new, happier situations. However, each proposed change needs to be carefully examined. We have to determine how likely it is that a prospective change will have a positive outcome.

CHANGE — A HALLMARK OF THIS WORLD

One of the outstanding hallmarks of the physical world is that things are constantly in flux.[1] The entire universe is made of combinations of entities and substances, and all of these combinations are engaged in a constant process of breaking apart and breaking

---

1. Rav Yeruchem Levovitz, *Da'as Torah, Vayikra*, p. 148.

down. The rate of this breakdown is related, to some extent, to the ability of these combinations to stay "stuck" together.[2]

Man, at the center of Creation, is also subject to constant change. In fact, change is part of his identity. The name that man gave himself, Adam, refers to the earth, the very essence of which is that it can nurture new life and generate change.[3]

Man cannot help but change, as it is written: "For the successful one, the way to a successful life is upwards."[4] The Vilna Gaon explains this verse as follows:

> Man is described as "one who goes,"[5] who **must** [emphasis mine] constantly progress from one level to another. If he does not progress upward, then he must fall way down, heaven forbid, for it is **impossible** [emphasis mine] for him to remain at one level.[6]

Rav Aharon Kotler, *zt"l*,[7] explains this phenomenon in the following manner:

> Whoever remains at his spiritual level, without progressing from level to level, is considered as one who has become habituated to something. Once this habituation sets in, he is no longer expending effort in his service of Hashem, and this is then an automatic deterioration from his level.

---

2. See *Sefas Emes*, Shavuos, p. 46, the section beginning *"Issah Atzeres."*
3. Maharal, *Derush al HaTorah*, chapter 1.
4. *Mishlei* 24:16.
5. See *Zechariah* 3:7, in which man is referred to as "one who goes," one who still can grow, and in which the angels are called "standers," those who cannot progress, but rather, remain forever on the level of perfection with which Hashem created them.
6. Commentary of the Vilna Gaon on *Mishlei*, ibid.
7. *Mishnas Rabbi Aharon*, vol. 2, section entitled *Likras Yom HaDin*. Rabbi Aharon Kotler (1892-1962), one of the Torah giants of the twentieth century, paved the way for America's miraculous transformation into a country which could produce a pure and outstanding Torah individual — indeed, a community of them.

Resistance to change must, necessarily, be an exercise in frustration, for it works in opposition to the very core of our existence. The Gemara[8] tells us that part of the happiness of the righteous in the Next World is that they merit to continue growing even there, proceeding from one level to the next.

The Maharal writes as follows: "...for the greatness of the intellect is that it can never come to its completion, for there is no end to what can be understood."[9]

Change is not just a basic human *need*; it's also a basic human *right*. The recognition and acceptance of this right in others is an important key to vibrant, healthy relationships.

> *I was once asked how to maintain freshness in a marriage. I replied that accepting and adjusting to whatever changes one's spouse undergoes are not only a sign of respect for him or her as an individual, but are a sure way of keeping the marriage truly alive.*

There are, however, on the opposite end of the continuum, people who constantly desire change, and seek it incessantly.

How can we tell if someone's desire for change is positive or negative?

THE BIG PICTURE

When trying to assess whether or not a particular trait is a healthy one, it's good to look at the larger picture. We can ask ourselves if, generally speaking, the person in question is a healthy, functioning individual.

---

8. *Berachos* 64a.
9. *Nesivos Olam, Nesiv HaTorah*, chapter 9, p. 40. See also the commentary of the Vilna Gaon on *Berachos* 64a.

This approach can be applied, as well, to the subject at hand. If the general life situation is positive, then there's a good chance that any specific desire for change is coming from a healthy place.

This isn't a foolproof barometer, for even the most effective, emotionally healthy people have their defects — that's part of the weakness, and greatness, of being human. But at least the bigger picture will give us our first clue as to whether the desire is arising from strength or weakness.

When assessing if change is positive or not, one should answer three important questions:

1. **How total is the change?** When change is proposed, how drastic is the new solution? How much change does it call for? If the proposed change is too global, too all-encompassing, then be suspicious. A desire for change such as this could indicate an inability to see what is appropriate in this situation. It may be that too much is being perceived as wrong.

Even when the desire for a wide-ranging change does have validity, most changes need to take place slowly and progressively in order to be most effective.

2. **Is it change from within?** The next question to ask is, how much responsibility is the person seeking to change willing to take for the problems that exist? Does the person point to the environment, to those around him or her, or to various external circumstances, as the source of most of his or her problems? Is the person willing to investigate the possibility that the problem lies within? Or is the person only willing to consider something external as the cause?

If the parties involved in a problematic situation believe that only some outer change will solve the problem, then this solution is suspect. Although it's true that external changes are often important, they're rarely at the root of any problem and, by extension, they're rarely the solution.

Most of our problems arise from within: from our reactions, attitudes and assumptions.

3. How often is change sought? Another barometer of whether or not the sought-after change would be positive is how often the person feels the need for change. If it is a frequent occurrence, then it's quite possible that there's a tendency to seek change without paying enough attention to and appreciation for the way things are.

❧ Exercises

1. When presented with a problem, first take time to see what's right in the situation.

2. Examine your solutions — are they all-encompassing, and do they introduce many radical changes?

3. Examine, with a friend or loved one, how great, in general, is your need for constant change and variety in other areas of life.

❧ Points to Remember

CHANGE is not just a basic human *need*; it's also a basic human *right*.

RESISTANCE to change must necessarily be an exercise in frustration, for it works in opposition to the very core of man's existence.

MOST CHANGES need to take place slowly and progressively in order to be most effective.

MOST PROBLEMS arise from within: from our reactions, attitudes, and assumptions.

CHAPTER THIRTEEN

Tackling Overwhelming Problems: Principles of Problem-Solving

People are often beset by problems that appear to be overwhelming. They stand powerless, paralyzed by an apparently insurmountable situation. In fact, they're often right: the situation may indeed be "impossible," and does elude solution. Several important truths, which are clearly expressed in Torah tradition, need to be borne in mind here. In this chapter and the next, we will be discussing the kind of problems that relate to the deepest levels of human relationships, those that surface in the family between spouses, between parents and children, and between siblings.

In this chapter we will be discussing how to approach problems in general, and then, in the next chapter, we will apply these principles to childraising. How we regard, and address ourselves to, the serious problems that come up in the most "normal" of households will greatly affect the atmosphere in the home, and, by extension, the home's ability to inculcate in the children a desire to share their parents' values and ideals.

The Source of Our Behavior

Underlying attitudes are the ground out of which our behavior arises, whether the behavior is positive or negative.[1]

Which attitudes toward problems are productive, and which will make it harder to arrive at workable solutions?

"Emotional Temperature"

Our attitudes are formed from the merging of our intellects and our emotions. Before we can begin learning effective problem-solving, we must realize that it is the intellect which must ultimately make the decisions, for only the intellect can foresee the possible consequences of a given course of action. Emotion knows only the present. *The intellect certainly must consider the person's emotional reality, but decision-making is in the intellect's domain.*

Therefore a person must lower what I call his "emotional temperature," that is, the heat of the emotion, for this has a great deal to do with whether his intellect will prevail. An elevated emotional temperature can undo many an intellectual decision, so a person must be at peace in order to make levelheaded decisions for himself and others.

The Intellect Can "Talk" to the Emotion

As stated, the intellect needs to take the person's emotional perception and emotional reality into consideration before making a

---

1. See, for example, the commentary of the Vilna Gaon on *Mishlei* 15:1, in which he outlines the "anatomy of anger": It begins in the mind, proceeds to speech, and is completed in deed. This sequence, first of *machashavah* (thought), then *dibbur* (speech), and, finally, *ma'aseh* (deed), appears in many places. A deeper discussion of this is beyond the scope of this work.

rational decision. Sometimes, as Rav Avigdor Miller, *zt"l,* says, the intellect must "talk" to the emotion. There are several examples of this in the *Tanach.*[2] To name just two, *"Shuvi, nafshi, limenuchaichi,"* "Return, my *nefesh,*[3] to your tranquility"; and, *"Halleli, nafshi, es Hashem,"* "My *nefesh,* praise Hashem with excitement."[4]

ATTITUDES THAT LOWER EMOTIONAL TEMPERATURE

There are certain attitudes that will help to lower one's emotional temperature. To name two of them:

1. **Problems Are Not a Sign of Pathology.** Problems are an integral part of life. Since humans are imperfect, we will make mistakes in our actions, judgments, and conclusions. In addition, it is normal for different people to have conflicting, yet legitimate, agendas, goals, and priorities. When we see problems as a normal aspect of human existence, as occurrences simply to be expected, we can react less emotionally to them. Remember, *surprise* is the adversary of constructive emotion, much as *laziness* is the adversary of intellect. *The less surprised we are by our problems, the better chance we have at dealing with them from a position of emotional strength.*

2. **Problems Are Not "Unnecessary".** Rav Boruch Eliyahu Goldshmidt, *zt"l,*[5] clarifies another aspect of the way we view problems. He says that we see problems as *unnecessary impediments* to

---

2. See *Bereishis Rabbah* 34:10, where there are many examples of this idea, that the righteous talk to and are in control of their heart. For instance, "Now, Chanah was speaking to her heart" (*I Shemuel* 1:13) and "And David said to his heart" (ibid. 27:1).
3. *Tehillim* 116:7. The *nefesh* is the part of the soul that has the emotional component.
4. *Tehillim* 146:1. See Rav Avigdor Miller, *Praise, My Soul* (New York: Bais Yisroel of Rugby, 1982), p. 154.
5. The late *mashgiach* of the Yeshiva of South Fallsburg, New York, and a close student of the renowned Rav Aharon Kotler, *zt"l.* His untimely passing in Elul 5760 was a deep loss to the Jewish People. His book, *Seichel Tov Yitein Chen,* on marital harmony, is one of the finest works on the subject I have ever seen.

the achievement of our goals. Therefore, we have no patience for them. He gives the following beautiful example:

> *Many people are willing to drive great distances daily, and are on the road for long periods of time. The length of a particular journey does not disturb them, as long as they know that it takes such and such an amount of time to get from point A to point B.*
>
> *Should there, however, be a ten-minute delay that is perceived as unnecessary, then they have no patience for it.*[6]

In the same vein, if we bear in mind that problems are a predictable and integral part of life, we'll be less surprised when they come along. It's when we're surprised, when we expect things to "go our way," that we get upset and irritated. Indeed, part of the pleasure of this world is that we have mountains to climb, the higher and more intimidating the better.[7] We are taught that "Man was born to toil,"[8] and that this is an expression of Hashem's kindness, as are all things in our world.[9]

Where there's no toil there's no pleasure, and, above all, no feeling of self-worth.

The *Sefer HaYoshor*[10] says as follows:

> *A person must develop a strong and brave heart to be able to accept [all sorts of possibly negative or painful] occurrences.*

---

6. *Seichel Tov Yitein Chen*, p. 14. His rationale is based on the words of the *Nimukei Yosef* (an important medieval commentator), in his commentary on the Rif, *Moed Katan* 6b.
7. See *Mishlei* 14:10, "The heart knows the bitterness of its soul. So, too, will no stranger share in her [the heart's] joy." The Vilna Gaon ad loc. explains that there is a connection between the extent of one's pain over a given situation and the joy over its resolution. The same idea appears in Rav Tzadok HaKohen, *Resisei Lailah*, section 17.
8. *Iyov* 5:7.
9. See *Tehillim* 89:3, "*Olam chessed yibaneh*," "the world was created with kindness."
10. Sixth Gate, pp. 66–7 (Eshkol ed.).

> *He should think about them before they come, and should await [their possible arrival] at any time, and he should say to himself, "If they have not come today they will come tomorrow, and if not tomorrow, then the next day." If he will do this, both intellectually and emotionally, then when these events do transpire, they will not disturb him and they will not cause him to forget his service [of Hashem].*

It should be noted that *Sefer HaYoshor* is not a book that preaches a pessimistic, "prophet-of-doom" outlook on life. The entire book is replete with positive attitudes and ideas of self-appreciation, and encourages us to develop a sense of fulfillment.[11]

Rather, the *Sefer HaYoshor* is teaching us that this world is a place where difficult times are to be expected, for such is the nature of this world. It calls this world *Gei HaTelohos*, the Valley of Misfortune, for it is with this attitude that the righteous are able to maintain their equilibrium. It is the person who views the world as a place where things should always go well who will be thrown off balance when misfortune does strike.

The world is a place of infinite opportunities for happiness, yet one of its chief hallmarks is conflict. Problems needn't throw us off balance, nor cause us to throw our hands up in defeat. A problem is not a sign that something is basically wrong. We can't expect this world to be so "efficient" on our behalf as to erase problematic situations or personalities. Nor should we be so arrogant as to expect the world to live up to our specifications as to how things "should" be.

---

11. See pp. 60, 64, 74, 83, 116 (Eshkol ed.), to name a few. It is a book full of wonderful advice for successful living. My hope is that one day it will be translated into English.

Bringing Down Emotional Temperature

What are some of the ways to bring down one's "emotional temperature?"

1. Expect to Have Some Failures. Parents need to develop the attitude that there will be times we fail in our role, either because the problem doesn't lend itself to a simple, immediate solution, or because we've used the wrong approach, or because of more deeply embedded causes.

Rav Samson Raphael Hirsch, of blessed memory, said that children are like the arrows of a marksman.[12] Just as a marksman doesn't score a "bull's-eye" every time he shoots, so, too, when it comes to children — there will be mistakes. This is vital for us to know, since our ability to bounce back is enhanced by our knowing that failures are par for the course. This concept will go a long way in keeping our "emotional temperature" down.

2. Take Quiet Time. It is imperative to take quiet time to understand that we will make mistakes, and that this should not upset our emotional equanimity. This quiet time should be reserved for a conversation in which our intellect (or our spouse!) talks softly and reassuringly to our emotional self and prepares it for the surprises that can throw us off.

There are specific attitudes that raise our emotional temperature, and we should address these before we enter an emotionally charged situation. Some things we can tell ourselves are as follows:

3. Think: "I Am a Good Person Even if I Fail to Solve this Problem." People often cannot separate how well they do from

---

12. *Tehillim* 127:4. See *Sefas Emes, Shemos*, p. 26, paragraph beginning *"Vayedabber,"* where the author, *zt"l*, expounds beautifully upon the fact that it is part and parcel of the "World of Deed" *(Olam HaMa'aseh)* to be imperfect. Only in the "World of Thought" *(Olam HaMachashavah)* can there be perfection. See also *Sefas Emes, Bereishis*, p. 8.

how good they are. It is one of the basic tenets of Judaism that the soul is inherently pure, and that one's goodness is immutable.

When a person realizes that his basic goodness is never in question, he can calm down more easily.

4. Think: "Can We Live with It — At Least Temporarily?" Sometimes people feel an intense pressure to eliminate a problem — immediately. Few problems can or must be solved totally and immediately. This is usually not a realistic possibility.

When a person realizes this, not only will his emotional temperature drop, but he can then begin the path of true problem-solving. Eventually, *b'ezras Hashem,* the problem will be solved.

5. Get Proper Sleep and Diet. Proper sleep and diet are integral parts of a calm, optimistic individual.

> *Mori VeRabi HaGaon Rav Chaim Pinchas Scheinberg, shlita,*[13] *sometimes tells deeply overwhelmed or bitter people who come to him for advice, "Gei shloff zich oys," "Go get the sleep you need."*

6. Ask: "Is this Really the Problem?" Sometimes a problem really stems from a different, more emotion-laden source. For example, there can be a strong disagreement between spouses, but the high emotional temperature stems not from the problem itself, but from the perceived "battle" between them, with all the baggage they may be carrying along with it.

Alternatively, in a disagreement between parent and child, if a parent sees the conflict as determining who is "stronger," and who will "win" this confrontation, then an unnecessary emotional

---

13. Rosh Yeshiva of Yeshivas Torah Ore, Jerusalem, and one of the foremost authorities in the Torah world today, especially in the areas of Torah Law and education. He has been, and continues to be, this author's guide in all areas of life.

atmosphere will be injected into the situation and emotional temperatures will rise.

7. **Ask: "Is It Really Our Problem?"** We parents are prone to assume ownership, or responsibility, for problems that are the child's, not ours. We are here to help the child with his or her problem. *Mori VeRabi, zt"l,* was very clear about this and emphasized it to people who wanted to be successful in *chinuch*. If, for instance, a child is *chutzpahdik, Mori VeRabi, zt"l,* said that the child has a problem, and that we are here to help him stop that behavior.

8. **Ask: "Where's Our Focus?"** People often tend to notice only the negative, for when things go well, we take it for granted, often attributing it to our skill at handling things. When a problem presents itself, we tend to focus on the specific behavior, without looking at the person as a totality. We tend to look away from his or her many redeeming traits. Emotion overwhelms us, and there is little room for perspective.

See the person as a whole, and his or her behavior as only a part of that whole.

Don't Look for Who Is to Blame

Seeking to determine who is at fault can be highly counterproductive. Doing so makes people go on the defensive and cast blame in return. Those who are accused tend not to offer solutions, lest they be seen in the atmosphere of animosity as thereby confirming, somehow, their responsibility for the mistake — and thus coming off as even more incompetent or guilty. Problems do need to be traced to their source, but this must be done without any connotations of blame whatsoever.

People are more up front about where they might have gone wrong, and more open to advice on how to prevent such things in the future, when discussions are oriented toward problem-solving, not blaming.

This principle is especially true when it comes to children, who are arguably the most precious people in our lives. Parents facing a problem with a child can easily slip into finding fault with each other, and special care must be taken to ensure that this does not occur. When parents consider themselves as one unit, there's less blaming. Just as the right hand doesn't blame the left for its poorer penmanship, so, too, should couples never blame each other for mistakes.

If this is an ongoing problem in the dynamic between the parents, then it's part of a larger issue and needs to be dealt with, much as other issues of domestic tranquility need to be addressed before the home atmosphere can be improved.

In short, when parents stop looking for who is at fault, whether at home, school or on the street, then the true source of the problem can be more easily identified and dealt with.

Parents need to be clear about where they want everyone to end up, if they want to find a path that will eventually get them there. Be it a short-term or long-term solution, clarity about the destination makes it easier to see if a certain route will take us closer to our goal or farther away.

APPROACH PROBLEMS TECHNICALLY, NOT EMOTIONALLY

A good way of putting this principle into use is to *regard problems from a technical vantage point, rather than an emotional one.* Emotions cool when things are put into a technical perspective, since we tend to blame less when things are presented in a more impersonal manner.

Problems May Require Long-term Solutions

Many problems stem from long-term neglect or misjudgment, and their resolution will not necessarily be swift. Difficulties that are rooted in the realities of family, school, or society, often require attention on a fundamental level, and this can take time.

The realization that a problem isn't going to disappear quickly is an important step in minimizing frustration and allowing the intellect to give the problem its full input. We are not frustrated with an airline when a flight from Israel to New York hasn't arrived after five hours in the air, since we know such a flight takes much longer. Parents must realize that an integral aspect of a real solution is the time it takes.

The Beis HaLevi[14] teaches us that there are two meanings to the word *amal*, labor. First is the difficulty of doing something which takes a long time, and of seeing the fruits of our labors only after some delay. This is the kind of difficulty we have just been discussing. The second is doing something that in itself is an arduous task. This is our next point, the truism that:

All Beginnings Are Difficult

Our Sages have taught[15] that all beginnings are difficult. When a person knows that problem-solving is especially difficult right at the start, it allows him to rein in his discouragement.

> *Mori VeRabi HaGaon Rav Chaim Pinchas Scheinberg, shlita,* once said, "If the beginning isn't difficult, then you haven't begun."

---

14. Rav Yosef Ber Soloveitchik (1820–1892), Rosh Yeshiva of the yeshiva of Volozhin and later a *rav* in Brisk. He is the founder of the Brisker Soloveitchik dynasty. See *Beis HaLevi* on *Shemos*, page 5a, the paragraph beginning *"Issah B'miarash."*
15. *Mechilta, Shemos* 19:5. This piece is brought by Rashi on the verse.

There are several beautiful interpretations of this idea, and I will bring those that are appropriate to problem-solving.

1. Beginnings Are Fateful. The beginning is the basis for all that follows.[16] "Difficult" in this context means fateful, for the direction that you face at the outset will determine where you will end up.

2. Finding the Right Place to Begin. When faced with a troublesome problem, it's good to inject some initial success into the situation to encourage everyone involved. Finding the spot where a breakthrough might be made most easily isn't always simple. This is so especially if the problem seems insurmountable and monolithic. "Difficult" in this context means "difficult to locate."

3. Our Responsibility. Taking a different tack, the *Beis HaLevi* says that it's our responsibility at least to begin. Perhaps solving the problem totally is beyond our ability, but let us at least start![17] In a similar vein, the *Sefas Emes* tells us that all true beginnings, beginnings that lead to permanent change, need at the outset our earnest, pure-hearted work.[18]

We must, at the beginning of our search for a solution to a vexing and painful problem, purify our hearts, and set out with the humility and prayer that will bring help from Hashem.

---

16. I think that the Hebrew word *kivun* (direction) stems from the word *kein* (base), for one's direction is determined by one's destination. In the same vein, the word for intent is *kavanah*, for it is intention which forms the basis of whether an act is good or bad. Similarly, the word for "yes" is also *kein*, meaning that there is a basis in fact; that this thing is correct.
17. *Beis HaLevi* on *Bereishis*, dealing with the sin of Kayin. The same concept, that we are held more responsible at least to begin, appears in *Michtav Me'Eliyahu*, vol.1, p. 257.
18. *Sefas Emes, Shemos*, p. 89, the paragraph beginning "*B'midrash olisah.*" All beginnings, he writes, are scrutinized by the Attribute of Hashem known as Divine Justice, and are hence difficult to achieve. The *Sefas Emes, Bereishis*, p. 25, paragraph beginning "*B'Rashi Noach – 5637,*" emphasizes that achievements that begin with the work of man, known in kabbalistic terms as *Issarusa D'Lisata* (an Awakening from below), and without the aid of Divine Inspiration (*Issarusa D'Liaila*), are more often permanent achievements. This is an enormously important subject, but beyond the scope of this work.

This brings us to another attitude which, as we have said, we must have firmly in mind before beginning to problem-solve:

THERE WILL BE PROBLEMS THAT SEEM TO DEFY SOLUTION

As we have said at the beginning of this chapter, some problems seem to defy even partial solutions. Our attitude toward these must reflect the following idea, as stated by the *Bnei Yissoschor*:[19]

> *There is a well-known theological problem: How can we have free will when God, at the same time, foresees our actions? We know of no completely viable answer to this question. What, then, is the function (in a world in which every part of the Creation is masterfully functional) of a question for which there is no answer? It is to teach us that in this life, we will encounter questions and problems for which we have no resolution. This is an intrinsic part of our human condition, and while we can try to resolve our problems, we must never imagine that all of them will lend themselves to resolution.*[20]

The truth of the matter is that problems which totally and permanently defy solution are relatively few. We'll see in the next chapter that when we find even a partial remedy to even one small part of a seemingly insurmountable dilemma, the entire picture can undergo a shift. Not the least significant reason for this is that our attitude toward the problem, and toward ourselves, changes dramatically when we see any manner of successful change. Therefore our attitude toward apparently unsolvable problems must be twofold:

1. **To accept the fact that such problems exist and that they're a normal part of life.**

---

19. Rav Tzvi Elimelech Shapira (1783–1840), one of the early giants of the Chassidic Movement.
20. *Bnei Yissoschor, Likkutim*, at the end.

2. To continue to look for some small part of the problem which might be subject to some kind of change, even a tiny one.

This brings us to the final attitude that I would like to set forth, before giving any advice on the practical side of problem-solving. It is, perhaps, one of the most important attitudes, and is an indispensable ingredient in a generally happy, stable life.

Getting Pleasure Out of Small Changes

Sadly enough, we live in a world in which people can be stingy when it comes to encouraging others. To renew our energy and determination during what can be the long and painful process of true problem-solving, sometimes we must *learn how to encourage ourselves.* One of the best ways to accomplish this is to derive pleasure, satisfaction, joy, and, above all, hope, by taking conscious notice of small changes. How we measure these small changes will be discussed in the next chapter.

> *Rav Wolbe, shlita, says that when he flew to Egypt to address the soldiers during the Yom Kippur War, the plane he was in suddenly descended to such a low altitude that it was almost hugging the ground. When asked if this signaled engine trouble, the reply was that the plane was flying low in order to avoid detection by Egyptian radar.*
>
> *From this, Rav Wolbe extrapolated that the Evil Inclination isn't interested in "low-flying planes," i.e., people who seek small changes. He only becomes alarmed, and oppositional, when a person embarks on a full frontal attack against him by trying to affect quick and drastic change.*[21]

---

21. *Alei Shur*, vol. 2, p. 190.

THE GREATNESS OF EACH SMALL CHANGE FOR THE BETTER

The *Sefas Emes*[22] says that the greater a person becomes, the more he recognizes the importance of each small change. As I like to put it, "Small change isn't small change." On a spiritual level, there are several important reasons for this:

1. In the spiritual world, there is no such thing as a small change. Each level attained is a completely new one.[23]

2. The payback — even for a small act — is of incalculable value, since it is rewarded forever.[24]

There is, however, a simpler explanation: *Big accomplishments are made up of a succession of small ones.*

Rav Mendel Kaplan, *zt"l*, is quoted as follows:

> *Every minute is precious. The Wrigley Building in Chicago was built with the profits from selling millions of pieces of chewing gum at a penny each. From this we see that every small thing is precious.*[25]

---

22. *Bemidbar*, p. 113, paragraph beginning *"V'al pi."* The *yetzer ha-ra* is called a *ksil*, a fool, for he does not bother to oppose you when you seek to make only a small change.
23. See *Chochmah U'Mussar*, vol. 2, pp. 341–3, the section entitled *Alitos HaMa'alos*, and *Michtav Me'Eliyahu*, vol. III, pp. 105–6, section entitled *Erkei HaMa'asim*.
24. I once heard the following explanation, based on the *Baruch she'amar* blessing: the proximity of the words "and He pays goodly reward" (which is seemingly redundant, since all reward is by definition good) to the words "the One who lives forever," is because since Hashem continues paying forever, His reward is indeed good. For even the tiniest reward, if compounded forever, is of incalculable value.
25. Rav Yisroel Greenwald, *Rav Mendel* (New York: Mesorah Publications, 1994), p. 94.

Being Prepared for Surprises

Life can be compared to a golf course: the sand traps, high grass, and sudden winds are all to be expected. The fact that they're there doesn't make us feel that something has gone horribly wrong, because we know that that's how golf courses are designed. The game would be no fun without them. Nor do such obstacles deter us from striving to achieve our goal, to finally get that golf ball where it's supposed to go.

Look at the totality of the life that Hashem has bestowed upon us, with its manifold joys, when preparing to solve with equanimity whatever serious problems we've been given.

Plan a Response

As in a fire drill, we'll be calmer if we know that there is a certain plan of action available to meet the requirements of a given situation, should it arise. This plan should be clear enough to be implemented efficiently and, if necessary, quickly.

Express Your Anger or Solve the Problem — Which Do You Want?

Mori VeRabi, zt"l, used to say that you can get angry or you can solve the problem, but you can't do both.

We are responsible, as adults, to harness our emotions and reign them in. Then we will have the presence of mind to become the parents our children truly need, and create a home environment which our children will want to live in and, eventually, emulate.

"My Child Is Good!"

Another mindset which should be stressed is that each parent is obligated to know — in his heart, not just intellectually — that each child is inherently pure and good, and that this will never change. The parent must always, no matter what, feel and display this attitude: "My child is immutably good, no matter where he or she has gone or how far he or she has strayed."

Every day of our lives we are enjoined to begin our day with the declaration, *"Neshamah she'nasata be tehorah he,"* "The soul that You have placed in me is pure." This statement carries two messages:

1. Hashem Himself has placed our souls in us.

2. We are immutably, essentially pure, and this essence (like any essence) is unchanging. Hence, no matter how far we may have strayed, we can return. It is for this reason that the Hebrew for penitence, *teshuvah*, refers to coming back, returning. It is a return to what always was and always will be.

Hope, Perseverance, and Encouragement

1. **Hope.** The Zohar[26] says that as long as a parent has not lost hope for a child, then the Divine Awakening from Above, *Issarusa D'Liaila*, remains. But if the parents give up hope, then along with this impediment to the Awakening from below, *Issarusa D'Lisata*, will come a loss of Heavenly help as well. In simpler terms, the special help we receive from Heaven is weakened or forfeited when we lose hope here below on Earth. Judaism teaches us that the physical

---

26. The classic work of what has been called Jewish mysticism, the *Kabbalah*, which was written some two thousand years ago. The idea expressed here appears in *Vayikra* 32b.

and spiritual worlds are inextricably intertwined, and one affects the other.

The knowledge that our child is irrevocably pure is an important ingredient in a parent's hope.

2. **Perseverance.** When we persevere in the correct manner, with wisdom and without undue pressure, results will eventually be forthcoming. There is a story about the Emperor Napoleon which expresses this:

> *Once, on the Ninth of Av, the day when Jewry tearfully mourns the loss of the Beis HaMikdash, Napoleon passed by a synagogue and heard the mournful crying. Upon asking what the crying was about, he was told that the Jews were mourning their destroyed Sanctuary. Napoleon expressed surprise, for he had not heard of such a thing happening. When informed that it had occurred 1750 years earlier, he exclaimed, "Mourning for something that was lost 1750 years ago! There is no doubt that they will someday regain it!"*

The Jewish People have retained their identity through the ages. It is this stubborn perseverance, with its source in the knowledge that Hashem has an indelible love for them, that allows parents to continue working on their relationship with, and loving, an estranged son or daughter. Certainly this ability to continue, no matter what, is indispensable. Our children are pure, and thus we are never permitted to give up on them.

Sometimes, because of the emotional pain a given problem is causing us, we must temporarily remove ourselves from it, but give up? *Never.*

3. **Encouragement.** If we believe in the immutable goodness of our children — and ourselves — then we can be a source of encouragement throughout any kind of estrangement, or other difficulty. Every small step along the way will renew hope for an eventual resolution of the problem in the best manner possible.

Noticing Your Child's Strengths

The ability to find a child's strengths is one of the major strategies of problem-solving. It brings the possibility of success much, much closer.

These strengths could be in an area of character, scholarship, or in relation to a particular individual. Since some victory right at the outset is so important, his or her first efforts, small though they may be, should be crowned with success.

Many young parents notice what's wrong with their child, and think that education consists of catching them doing something wrong and correcting them. This is especially true of the firstborn, whose parents are usually younger and have more time to devote to their child. When younger siblings come along, the oldest one seems so "big," and thus in need of more intense "education," i.e., correction. I call this *makkas bechoros*, the "plague of the firstborn."

> *I remember coming home one day and my wife told me that a mother had called with a question. Should she insist that her two-year-old son pronounce his words correctly? I told my wife that this son must certainly be her first child, and it was.*

I would suggest a simple exercise:

Take a few moments each day to notice, and get down in writing, something that someone has done right. *Feel pleasure from it.*

Then proceed to your child and spouse. When you can find five things your child has done right, and five for your spouse, and have felt pleasure over these things, then spend a few moments thinking about each one's strengths and taking pleasure in them.

Now you are ready, in a happy frame of mind, to figure out where to start problem-solving with a child whom you respect and in whom you can see much good and potential.

One more point, the most vital of all, needs to be made before we proceed to the practical side of problem-solving:

The Happiness of Being Dependent on Hashem

Before taking any action, feel the happiness of being dependent on Hashem. Understand the privilege of asking Him for help. Without Hashem's help, nothing can be accomplished.

Feeling Dependent — Feeling Close

The righteous do not *want* to be independent of Hashem. They want to feel the need for Him, the need to trust Him, and the need to be held by Him. The sin of the Generation of the Tower was that they wanted to be totally independent of Hashem, something equivalent to taking out an insurance policy on your insurance policy.[27]

This idea is also evident in Yitzchak's blessing to Yaakov: "And God will [continually] give you from the dew of heaven and the fat of the earth."[28] Rashi comments that He will continue to do so, to give us what we need in small "parcels." He is certainly capable of satisfying all our long-term needs all at once, but that would deprive us of the closeness we feel toward Him by receiving things often from His Hand, and the good feeling of being dependent on Him.[29]

---

27. See the *Shiurei Da'as, Dor HaFlogah*, by the Telsher Rav, Rav Yosef Leib Bloch (1860–1930), for a beautiful in-depth treatment of this subject.
28. *Bereishis* 27:28.
29. This idea is expressed in the *Sefas Emes, Bereishis*, p. 111, and in the *Shem MiShemuel*, vol. 1, p. 291.

The Beauty of the Land of Israel

Indeed, the beauty of Eretz Yisrael is expressed in the Torah as being the place where we are dependent on rainwater for crops, while in Egypt the Nile rises annually to water the lush soil of the Nile Delta. Israel's pronounced need for rain, the Ramban explains, is to ensure that we live according to Hashem's will. When we stray from His ways, He will "turn off the tap."[30] It is a great happiness to be humbled by the constant need for Hashem's kindness. This idea was beautifully expressed by the *Beis Elokim*:[31]

> *This idea [that Hashem takes personal interest in Eretz Yisrael] can be compared to a great emperor who rules the entire world. To his far-flung provinces he sends one annual expedition with supplies, so as not to have to send several shipments. To those who live in his palace, however, he gives a daily allotment, since they are close to him, and he can fulfill their needs as they arise.*[32]

This principle is beautifully expressed by the following true story:

> *Rav Yechezkel Levenstein, zt"l,*[33] *was known for his stern demeanor. One day, people noticed that he had an uncharacteristically happy countenance. When asked the reason for his joy, he related that before and during the war years, the yeshiva, both when it was in Mir and later in Shanghai, China, was poor, and that even his meager salary was often late in coming. He was, therefore, forced to rely on Hashem. What a great happiness!*

---

30. See the Ramban, *Devarim* 11:10.
31. *Sha'ar HaTefillah*, chapter 5. Written by the Mabit, Rabbi Moshe of Tirnai (d.1580), one the great scholars and thinkers of his generation.
32. Indeed, the original name of the Land of Israel was Canaan, which denotes *hachna'ah*, humility. See *Be'er Moshe* (*Devarim*, p. 721), by the Ozhorover Rebbe, zt"l, one of our generation's great Torah leaders.
33. 1884–1974. He was the illustrious *mashgiach* of the *yeshivos* of Mir and Ponevezh.

> *Now, however, the head of the Ponevezh Yeshiva, Rav Kahaneman, was always punctual and reliable about paying the salaries of all the staff members. This lessened the feeling of dependence on Hashem, and took away the happiness of feeling close to and dependent on Him. Lately, however, the yeshiva had had some difficulty paying salaries on time, and so now everything was back in the Hands of our Heavenly Father, Who indeed cares for all of our needs.*[34]

To sum up this chapter: *Our attitude to problems is the most important first step in dealing with them.* This includes an appreciation for small gains, and the perceptiveness to see where these small gains are most likely to be achieved. Problems are a part and parcel of life, and are Hashem's way of giving us both the pleasure of meeting challenges and the happiness of needing His help.

Let us now begin dealing with problems on a more practical level, bearing all of the above in mind. There will, by necessity, be some overlapping of material, since active problem-solving has its roots in the attitudes cited in this chapter; repetition, couched in different words and examples, will bring these points home. Only when the principles mentioned here become a part of the parents' emotional reality will there be, with Hashem's help, consistent progress in solving even the most difficult of problems.

---

34. See Rabbi Avrohom Chaim Feuer, *Tehillim Treasury* (New York: Mesorah Publications, 1993), p. 141.

❧ Exercises

1. Check your diet and try to cut down or eliminate caffeine, sugar, and other substances that can give you a "high," then a "low."

2. Keep a diary of events that you thought would be tragic and turned out for the best. (Rav Shlomo Brevda, *shlita*, in the name of Rav Yechezkel Levenstein, *zt"l*.)

3. Keep a record to determine when you're most prone to becoming overly emotional in a negative sense. Plan quiet time beforehand to reflect on how to prevent it, or at least to have an awareness of what may lie ahead.

4. When you see an emotional outburst by someone else, think about whether you want to behave that way.

5. When you become overwhelmed and angered by someone's misbehavior, find something good that that person has done, and take pleasure in it.

🌺 POINTS TO REMEMBER

PROBLEMS are an integral part of life.

OUR ATTITUDE to problems is the most important first step in dealing with them.

A PERSON must lower his "emotional temperature" in order to make levelheaded decisions for himself and others.

FEW problems can or must be solved totally and immediately.

BIG accomplishments are made up of a succession of small ones.

WHERE there's no toil, there's no pleasure, and, above all, no feeling of self-worth.

THERE will be mistakes.

PROPER sleep and diet are integral parts of a calm, optimistic individual.

THE PARENT must always feel and display this attitude: "My child is immutably good, no matter what he or she has done."

PEOPLE will be more open to advice on how to prevent errors in the future if the discussions are oriented toward problem-solving, not blaming.

BEFORE taking any action, feel the happiness and humility of being dependent on Hashem.

CHAPTER FOURTEEN

Practical Problem-Solving

One of the most important questions we can ask in life is, "Why?" If we can trace a problem back to its source, then a resolution — or at least the beginning of a resolution — becomes visible.

SOME "WHY'S" WHEN DEALING WITH VARIOUS CHILDREN'S ISSUES

What follows are some common sources for a child's misbehavior:

1. Fatigue. One condition that commonly causes parents concern is simple tiredness, and it's something we do need to take seriously. It's usually related to problems with weekend sleep patterns and late bedtime habits. Sleep is one of the factors in a good emotional attitude. In addition, the ability to study properly is inextricably tied up with it.[1] It's safe to assume that many school-related

---

1. See *Shulchan Aruch, Even HaEzer,* section 25, in the commentary of the Taz, where this point is eloquently presented. *Mori VeRabi* Rav Chaim Pinchas Scheinberg, *shlita,* has mentioned this Taz innumerable times in the over thirty years that I have been privileged to know him.

problems begin with sleep irregularities. Indeed, one of the examples we will be dealing with in this chapter is the universal challenge of how to get children to bed, and to sleep, on time.[2]

Poor sleep patterns are at the root of a number of problems.

> *I once had the privilege of bringing a group of seventeen-year olds to HaGaon Rav Shach, zt"l, the Ponevezher Rosh Yeshiva. He spoke to them for a total of fifteen minutes,* twelve of which *were devoted to the importance of a good night's sleep.*

2. Food. Sometimes certain foods can cause misbehavior, either because there is an undetected allergy present, or because some food item is causing hyperactivity or sleepiness. Sometimes hunger produces an inability to control one's emotions and behavior, which of course causes all kinds of problems.

3. Social Issues. Often a child will be unruly or feel down because of social problems at school or in the neighborhood.

4. Academia. Academia, or a problematic relationship with a teacher, can also weigh heavily on a child's mind. New teachers can frequently be over-aggressive or strict, at least in the eyes of a sensitive, young child.

This brings us to the next point in our search for the "why" behind a problematic situation. Amazingly enough, this effective tool is often disregarded by distraught parents. I recommend that the parents…

---

2. See chapter 1 of *To Kindle a Soul*, by Rabbi Lawrence Kelemen, *shlita* (Jerusalem: Targum Press, 2001), where he cites sleep as being at the root of many problems, even ADD, Attention Deficit Disorder, which can cause a child untold problems in school.

ASK THE CHILD WHAT HE OR SHE THINKS

I usually ask parents *what the child thinks is going on*. What does he see as the source of the problem? Too often the parents' reply will begin with the words, "Well, I think…".

There are several good reasons for consulting the child. Among them:

1. An observer usually can't see a situation in its entirety. He needs the input of the person himself, who's directly involved. This is not to say that the picture this person provides will be totally *accurate*, or that it will give an objective view of the bigger picture, but there will be a clearer perspective of what's going on. Moreover, the person involved can tell you what *his* truth is. While people who are personally involved in situations can sometimes be so overwhelmed by their emotions, or by the circumstances, that they lose perspective, they often possess a vivid clarity that others can't possibly have.[3]

2. We earn their cooperation. *When people are listened to, and feel understood, they are far more likely to cooperate with even uncomfortable conclusions.* There is no question that hearing what the child thinks should help us to formulate a plan of action. *If children see that their thoughts are an integral part of our response, they'll be far more likely to respect and work toward the successful resolution of the problem.*

---

3. This concept is graphically portrayed in *halachah*, whereby a person who is ill on Yom Kippur, the Day of Atonement, and says that he feels he needs to eat, is given greater credence than the doctors who say that he can forego food. See *Shulchan Aruch, Orach Chayim*, section 618:1, for a fuller treatment of this issue. The great Rosh Yeshiva, Rav Yisroel Zev Gustman, *zt"l*, once said that before you answer a question — in fact, even before understanding the question — you have to understand the questioner. Who is he? What does he think or feel?

Recall what Has Been Already Tried

It is important to check back in one's mind for anything that might have helped in the past to resolve such a problem. Invaluable insights can be gleaned from seeing what has worked before, even in part, as well as what hasn't worked. Details about a partial success, or lack thereof, can be of value, for it is often possible to incorporate them into a new response.[4] Just as we don't want to regard problems monolithically, that is, as solvable on an all-or-nothing basis, so, too, should we refrain from looking at solutions as all-or-nothing affairs. We're glad to learn from solutions that have been either failures or incomplete successes. Partial remedies can often lead to complete solutions.

Look for a Pattern

Sometimes it's a good idea to postpone any serious attempt to resolve a situation for a certain period of time, during which we can try to detect some kind of pattern. This pattern can include:

When — Is there a time of the day or week when the problem seems most likely to surface?

Where — Is there some place where things most frequently go wrong?

Who — Is there a person or persons who seem to act as a catalyst for the misbehavior, or whatever the problem may be?

---

4. This idea is applied in *halachah*, when an idea that was rejected by the Gemara, or by an earlier commentary *(Rishon)*, will often be applied in other areas, where the reason for the previous rejection does not apply.

See what Resources — Especially People — You Have at Your Disposal

Know what you can — and cannot — do. Sometimes we overlook help from sources we wouldn't usually think of, such as a family friend, or a teacher from a previous, more successful, school year. It's worthwhile to take a few moments to consider, together with one's child, those individuals who might have had a hand in previous good experiences in relation to him and to seek their help. We often forget about people simply because they're not in our immediate geographical area, or because they haven't been involved with the child or with our family for a while.

Certainly there are material resources (such as moving the child to a different school, or finding a tutor, etc.) we can employ in the effort to help our children, and these are important. But material resources pale in comparison to certain people who know your child and have enjoyed a good rapport with him in the past. As in so many other areas of life, we need to build on the good as much as possible, and this includes those individuals who were able to access our children's strong points even on only one occasion.

We must, however, recognize our limitations. Sometimes we need to seek a partial solution because we lack the ability, in terms of our relationship with our child or our lack of material resources, to affect more far-ranging changes.

Then we can hope and pray that one success will lead to another.

Find the "Weak Link"

When we try to solve a problem, we'd like to be able to achieve some initial successes. Therefore we'd do well to break down the problem into its various components and start work on one portion of it — we'll call it the "weak link" — which would most appear to lend itself to some immediate manipulation.

If there is no one particular weak link, then we may have to scale down our definition of, and grand expectations for, "success," and start working from that altered perspective.

When we look at a problem, it may seem insurmountable. We would do well to pick a specific type of behavior we'd like to change, or a specific timeline for achieving it, or a particular setting — such as the home or the school — where we'd like to see it happen.

An Example

It would be helpful to offer as an example of these principles a true story about how some thorny issues were resolved. This story involved several issues and problems, but it had a happy ending.

> *A parent called me to complain about her child, a twelve-year old boy. There was a lot of pain over the child's behavior, both within the home and outside of it. Disinterest and misbehavior in school, not getting up on time, not going to shul, poor relations with his siblings, a generally uncaring attitude in regard to sharing family responsibilities, in addition to being generally undisciplined — these were among the points of conflict that she enumerated.*
>
> *Numerous reminders, said the mother, were of no avail. It could take ten reminders or a shouted command to evoke the desired reaction.*
>
> *Everything seemed wrong.*

Break the Problem Down into Its Parts

People often regard problems with the attitude, "How can I solve it?" The situation is regarded monolithically, with consideration given only to whether a total solution is possible.

In the above case, a total solution at that point was not feasible, and regarding the problem from that vantage point was just discouraging to everybody involved.

I asked the mother to pick one area of behavior that she wanted to begin turning around, taking the following points into consideration:

1. It should be specific.

2. Progress should be defined and measurable. The behavior should lend itself to small, concrete incentives.

3. It should be in an area in which the child's strengths lie.

Since it was before Pesach, the mother proposed that the child should willingly participate in preparations for the holiday. She wanted him to do this without all the nagging and frustration that usually accompanied requests for help at that time of year.

We proceeded to build a program whereby the child could participate in choosing which chores would be his. These were to involve a minimum of supervision from the mother (to avoid what the child perceived as nagging) and were to be tangibly rewarded upon completion.[5]

This stage was a success. It set a precedent for future cooperation between mother and son.

---

5. I proposed, in addition, that as much as possible, the chores this child was assigned at the outset should involve tasks that don't take a long time, and whose completion produces immediate gratification. An example of such a chore is polishing the silver candelabra, because of the satisfaction one feels looking at the beautiful results of one's efforts. Since there are often several children in a home, and they would all prefer certain tasks, I recommend that the parents draw up a detailed list of the chores that need to get done, and divide them up, together with the children, with consideration being given to which are more difficult and/or less enjoyable. When one of the children is particularly problematic, as in our example, then I believe that that child should *temporarily* be granted his preference, if it's within reason.

I think that if we analyze this case we will see several important principles regarding problem-solving in general, and the parent–child dynamic in particular.

Establishing Where to Begin

A long list of problems can be disheartening to all concerned. If the parent, and the child, can be persuaded that there is value, *great value*, in even slight signs of progress, then the process of finding the beachhead can begin.

The first point to consider is that there should be a good chance of short-term success in whatever approach you choose at the outset, even if such success would look small when measured against the enormity of the entire problem. So ask yourselves: *In which area can we expect the least resistance?* This is generally the area in which a child's strengths lie, for it is precisely here that he or she has most likely tasted the sweetness of success in the past.

What area would seem to lend itself to the measuring of accomplishment and progress? This means finding a tangible, visible kind of behavior that can elicit positive feedback and encouragement, both by way of verbal expressions of satisfaction from other members of the family, and by way of small but pleasing incentives. This potential for encouragement is vital. Parents and children both may be pessimistic by now regarding any possibility for a real turnaround in the child's behavior and parent-child relations. A more positive attitude, and the belief in the eventual solvability of the problem, is one of the biggest advantages to be gained by taking that first small step in the right direction.

In our example, the child was allowed to give some input about which chores he felt were best suited to him. Upon the successful completion of each day's job, points were given which eventually led to a reward.[6]

LOWERING THE EMOTIONAL TEMPERATURE

The completion of these specific chores, with a minimum of parental direction, allowed for a calming of the atmosphere in the home and set the stage for the mother becoming less intense and anxious about the future of her relationship with her son. Now she could start interacting with him more calmly.[7] This in itself was the achievement of a major goal, for children not only detest constant parental criticism and directives, but learn to "tune out" and ignore their parents' words altogether, at which point we'll start hearing those familiar vague refrains on the child's part: "Yeah. Okay... I'll do it later... Yeah... Okay..." If the parent starts getting frantic from frustration, this further increases the level and intensity of the parent–child dialogue, which in turn causes the child to turn off even more.

Parents often complain, "I have to tell him ten times before he does it!" or, "Unless I scream I don't get anywhere." It is of the utmost importance for a parent to absorb this fact of life: *if you repeat yourself ten times to a child, then the first nine times you didn't say anything.* And furthermore: if you consistently resort to screaming, then until you reach a certain decibel level, there's no real need

---

6. I recommend, when possible, that the reward involve the child's choosing a family game or activity. This teaches the child the value of giving, and helps improve sibling relationships.
7. I strongly believe that the worst time to ask children to do chores is when the parent is desperate for their help. Doing chores is a normal part of being a family member, and should be regarded as part of family life. It is part of training our children to be givers, and should not, therefore, be invoked mainly when the mother is having a mini-crisis of exhaustion or time-pressure. At pressured moments, there will be an undercurrent of demanding and negative emotion that the child may rebel against. If in general there is a difficult situation of this nature in the home, then domestic help should be hired to supplement the contributions of family members.

on the child's part to listen, since — happily enough for him — you haven't yet reached the boiling point.

Tell your child to take his pick: you can repeat yourself either once, twice, or three times. You will not be repeating things more than that. *If he needs more repetition, no problem. He can repeat your words to himself as many times as necessary before compliance. But compliance must occur, and within a reasonable period of time.*[8]

DERIVING PLEASURE FROM SMALL SUCCESSES

As mentioned above, the *Sefas Emes*[9] tells us that it is the hallmark of a great person to value the smallest accomplishment. It is vital that we encourage ourselves and our children for every "little" success.

The *Sefer HaYoshor* states (regarding maintaining an even temper):

> *If he succeeds at this even for two months, that is, if he will endure, with a smile, various infuriating situations, he should know, and regard himself, as a great and successful warrior [emphasis mine].*[10]

SMALL BEGINNINGS

The *Divrei Yehoshua*[11] gives a wonderful paradigm:

---

8. You should, of course, carefully choose which area you wish to enforce, bearing in mind its likelihood of success and the firmness of your intention to truly follow through.
9. *Bemidbar*, p. 113: "It is the way of a person who is straight in his service of God, that the higher his level [of righteousness] becomes, the more he knows the value of each small thing."
10. Sixth Gate, paragraph beginning *"VeDa"* (p. 64 in the Eshkol ed.).
11. Written by Rav Yehoshua Heller, zt"l (1814–1880), the *Divrei Yehoshua* is a masterpiece on understanding the human psyche. He was one of the first students of Rav Yisroel Salanter, zt"l.

> *A tiny worm looks at a giant cedar tree, and wants to fell it. The worm is so tiny and the tree so powerful and majestic. But the worm chooses* one specific point *[emphasis mine] and begins to chew with its puny mouth. It does not look at the entire tree, just at the point at which he is working.*

We should just look, as we work, at the portion of the problem that's right at hand, that spot where we can make some kind of dent.

The *Divrei Yehoshua* continues:

> *If we continue to follow the worm in his efforts to fell the tree, we will find that the effect he has on the tree is not the same with each passing day. The first day, the entire progress that the worm makes is the amount that he chews away. By the next day, however, the area around where the worm has eaten is a bit dried out, and it becomes easier to chew away a greater area, both in circumference and in depth. The worm's progress on the second and third days becomes increasingly greater, and the same effort yields more results. Eventually, the tree eats away at itself more than the worm does.*

Initial successes, even "small" ones, engender increasingly greater strides toward solving a problem.

LEARNING TO LOOK AT A PROBLEM IN ITS SMALL COMPONENTS

Related to the idea that we should cherish even small beginnings is the ability to continue to value, as we go along, every small accomplishment. Often we need to focus on the smallest of short-term goals, and not look so carefully at what lies ahead, lest we become discouraged at the seemingly impossible tasks that lay before us. An extreme and painful, but stark, example of this comes from the Holocaust.

> *During the death marches that the Nazis forced concentration camp inmates to endure, the aching, tortured survivors of the marches say that had they thought about having to continue marching even another hour, they would have died. They thought only of the next step, and then the step after that.*

Rav Shlomo Brevda, *shlita*, once told a story that depicts this lesson most graphically:

> *Many people, among them yeshiva boys who had never held an ax in their lives, were brought to a Siberian forest. They were taken to a place in the forest where the trees were several feet wide and were ordered to cut them down. It seemed that no person had cut down a tree in this part of the forest in a millennium. Some people passed out, and died, just from looking at the trees. Those who survived were those who only thought about the next blow of the ax, and not a second beyond it.*

There is no doubt that when part of a problem is solved, we can then look at the whole problem differently. We start feeling that perhaps we can make it after all, to a greater extent than we had dared hope for. But something else happens, too. We look at ourselves differently. We begin to believe that perhaps we can, after all, conquer a challenge we had previously deemed impossible.

A noted educator, Rav Hillel Mandel, *shlita*, gives a brilliant example of this:

> *Roger Bannister became a sports legend when he succeeded in running a mile in four minutes. Today, almost fifty years later, if you applied to an Olympic committee and presented as your credentials your ability to run a four-minute mile, you'd be laughed out of the room. That record has been broken many times since Bannister first set it.*
>
> *What happened? From an achievement that once seemed impossible, the four-minute mile has now become*

commonplace. Until Roger Bannister made his run, people thought such an achievement was humanly impossible; but once it was done, people began believing in their own ability to do it as well. The four-minute mile lost its "impossible" status.[12]

Succinctly put, *Mori VeRabi, zt"l,* said that effective problem-solving can be likened to a cat unraveling a ball of yarn — a little at a time.

Finding the "Weak Link"

As mentioned regarding to the twelve-year old who was "doing everything wrong," we must look around for a "weak link." Evaluating where it might be would involve:

1. **What:** What is the child is doing that we want to stop, such as being unresponsive to repeated requests.

2. **Where:** Where does the problematic behavior occur: in the home, with siblings or parents, or outside, in school or social situations? In the above case it was both in the home and at school.

3. **Who:** Is there one parent who's having more trouble? Is it the mother, who is too easily manipulated, or the father, whose sternness has invited mindless resistance on the part of his children?

---

12. I believe the same idea can be applied to the function of Yom Kippur and particularly that day's *Ne'ilah* (closing) Service. Even if a person does not retain the same lofty heights that he or she achieved on Yom Kippur, the realization of having once attained them, even temporarily, makes it easier to achieve them again. Not only is it easier to achieve something already reached once, but we also can look at ourselves differently forever. Once we have achieved the heights of *Ne'ilah*, we can believe that we will do so once again.

4. **When:** Is there a time of the day, week, or year that the problem especially rears its head? Does the mother lose her patience Friday afternoon? Does the father often arrive home at night exhausted and irritable?

When a problem is appearing both at home and in school, it is generally better to start at home since the parents naturally have more control over what happens in their own domain. In addition, teachers can sometimes have conflicting or crowded agendas, while parents will be more motivated to zero in on the situation.

If, however, the home dynamic is so complicated that an initial success there is unlikely, school can certainly be the place to begin. In addition, schools may not be able to wait until an issue is resolved at home, and progress may have to be shown more quickly.

How to Define the "Weak Link"

The *Divrei Yehoshua*[13] tells us that our actions are determined by three categories of contributing factors: Inborn, Environmental, and Habitual.

1. **Inborn.** There is little that can be done about our genetic component. We must regard any disabilities that we may have as part of Hashem's "game plan," to give our lives special meaning by challenging us to overcome those handicaps. Sometimes, these very handicaps are the key to a successful life. Young people stricken with diabetes, for instance, develop self-control, which will serve them well throughout life. Persons with a lower native intelligence are often great successes because they learned early to work hard and not be deterred by difficulties. However, it is clear that our main efforts at change must take place in the other two areas of our

---

13. Part 2, chapter 1.

lives: the environment in which we live, and the habits we develop. They are the "weak links" where our efforts need to be directed.

2. Environmental. While there is little that can be done to change the outside environment, short of moving, much can be done to change the environment in our homes. Suffice it, at this point, to say that the more our children see the contrast between their homes and the society beyond — with the home being a happy, warm, nurturing place — the greater the chance we can inculcate and transmit to our children the ideals that are precious to us.

3. Habitual. Habits are usually the area of life that is most subject to our control. This is not to suggest, however, that bad habits are easy to change.

Poor habits are best changed by adopting new, positive ones.

In *Sefer HaYoshor*,[14] it is written that although starting a new habit is difficult, it can quickly become part of a person's lifestyle. Then it is no longer such a challenge.

SPECIFIC PROBLEMS: BEDTIME

All three factors cited in the *Divrei Yehoshua* come into play when dealing with a common problem: the almost universal challenge of getting children to bed on time.

The Torah tells us, "And it was evening and it was day."[15] I use that verse as a paradigm for, "The day begins with the night before." Dealing with bedtime disciplinary problems is a key to solving many other problems that are engendered by poor sleep patterns.

---

14. Sixth Gate, p. 77 (Eshkol ed.).
15. *Bereishis* 1:5.

Many a diligent student is affected by sleep-related problems. In fifteen years as a *mashgiach* in *yeshivos* for students of junior high school age and up, several ideas have worked for me. We will be applying these ideas to the question of why some children have a harder time getting to bed on time. Following the framework of the *Divrei Yehoshua*, there seem to be three basic causative factors:

Inborn Tendencies. Some people are what we call "night people." That is, they don't get sleepy until much later on. This has a physical, neurological component, and is not merely the result of habit. In a similar vein, some people are more affected than others by caffeine and other stimulants. They get results from a smaller dose, and the effects can last longer, even if the stimulant was taken at an early hour of the day.

A person needs to listen to his own nature, and not fight it. There's often little we can do, in the long term, to counteract it. Our approach to a problem must include recognition of intrinsic tendencies, and on that basis to construct a solution. It seems unwise to set up a situation whereby we're constantly battling something which is an inherent part of who we are. If a child seems to have an inborn tendency to go to bed late, then his habits and environment must be dealt with more carefully. If everything is set up appropriately, then even "night children" can learn to unwind at night, wake up rested, and get ready for a successful day.

What seems very important in helping a "night child" succeed in the daytime world of school is to make sure that there is a set wake-up hour that is adhered to consistently, both during the school week and on weekends. There are experts who are specially trained to help people with inborn sleep problems, but I don't think that's usually necessary. Most of the time, in my experience, it's the other two components, environment and habit, that are at the root of problems in getting our children to bed at an appropriate hour.

Let us, then, examine these two factors:

Environment. If the home is a noisy, busy, active, interesting place to be, then it will be difficult for a child to go to bed, much less fall asleep. If the home is relatively small, the problem will be compounded. If there are several children in a given room, of various ages, each with different sleep patterns, then this, too, obviously, will contribute to the difficulty.

Sleep will be more difficult if there's an atmosphere of tension or worry in the home, even if it's not high profile; children are uncannily sensitive to emotional nuances.

Once the environmental elements are identified, parents and children can pool their ideas on how to make the home an easier place in which to fall asleep. This can involve changing the timing of certain home activities, allowing a younger child to fall asleep in the parents' room, and making a conscious effort to reduce tensions in the home.

One consequence of identifying the environmental reasons for bedtime problems is that parents will tend to blame the child less, and stop referring to the problem as a lack of discipline on his part. Instead, they'll seek to eliminate, as much as possible, the factors in the environment that are at the root of the problem. Ceasing to blame the child is in itself an important step in healing the parent–child relationship and sets the stage for an atmosphere of constructive cooperation. *Creating this atmosphere of cooperation is, in any case, of more urgent importance than solving any particular problem on the practical level.*

Habit. Counterproductive habits before bedtime can take many forms, from eating stimulating foods to engaging in activities that raise the energy level. People often need to wind down, and we can't expect our children to switch within a few minutes from activities that stimulate them, to falling asleep.

Often people are caught in a vicious cycle, whereby late bedtimes engender daytime naps, which in turn can lead to later bedtimes.

Professional sleep counselors caution against tossing and turning in bed, for tossing and turning tends to become habitual. Rather, a person should only go to bed when very tired, and thus be more likely to fall asleep relatively soon.

A hot bath, for twenty minutes, has often been found to induce drowsiness. It can be made part of the bedtime routine.

Small Steps. Let's take a look at each step in the process of getting children to bed. We want them asleep in bed with the lights out, but first we've got to get them into the room. Once they're in there with their pajamas on, it's often beneficial to let them play a relaxing game. Then they can read in bed. Afterwards, they don't need to go to sleep right away, but the light should be turned off.

By breaking the process down we avoid confrontation, because the child is being led along in stages. If the process gradually becomes routine, the routine itself can induce drowsiness. Remember, we do not look at a problem monolithically, but rather, as *parts*, or, as in the case of bedtime, *steps*. Getting the child into the room without getting into bed; getting him into bed without the lights out; getting the lights out without his falling asleep. Each step should bring encouragement in its wake.

An Ideal Bonding Time. Bedtime can be an ideal time for parents to bond with their children, either by talking, or listening, or by reading a story. This time can be quite enjoyable for a child, and can in itself serve as an incentive for keeping to a reasonable timetable in going to sleep.

Ideally, the unwanted consequence for not following the routine surrounding bedtime can be the loss of this pleasant, comfortable, happy interlude with the parent. When it does get forfeited due to misbehavior, it can be made up the following night, if the next evening the child follows the bedtime ritual properly.

In such a way, bedtime can eventually start operating less confrontationally and more automatically.

To sum up, I recommend the following:

~ Find out whether the main problematic factor is innate, environmental, or habitual. Make sure that the home, diet, and evening activities do not contribute to sleeplessness.

~ Establish an automatic (no pestering or nagging) pattern for going to sleep that begins well before bedtime and proceeds in gradual stages, with the road to bed consisting of many small steps.

~ Reward good sleep habits with more parental attention.

SPECIFIC PROBLEMS: HOMEWORK

Another common problem that parents confront is the child's inability or unwillingness to do homework. By using the principles outlined above, we can help solve this frequent source of parent-child conflict.

Pinpointing the Source. As a first step, we need to see where the problem seems to be stemming from. Is it a new problem that just began this year, or is it perennial? Is it with all subjects, or only some? Is the problem stemming from the home, or is it school-oriented?

Some school-oriented reasons why homework can be a problem include:

~ Lack of clarity and understanding, either about the topic to be studied or the homework assignment itself.

~ A dislike, on the part of the child, for either subject or teacher.

~ Lack of teacher follow-up as to whether or not the homework was done.

Sometimes the function of homework is not to help the child review, or to improve his understanding of the subject material, or to develop relevant skills — but to keep him busy and off the street. Although this is sometimes a valid reason for giving homework, ingenuity is called for in order to make the assignment interesting, since the student will eventually sense that the homework isn't really needed for mastery of the subject.

Parents can't usually control whether or not a teacher follows up to make sure assignments get done, but they can nonetheless have an impact on the teacher-child relationship. For instance, a parent can address, in the home if necessary, the child's lack of understanding of the subject or the assignment. What's important, at this point in the problem-solving process, is to pinpoint where the problem seems to be stemming from.

Often, however, there is also a home component. Some examples of this are:

~ A noisy, busy, or otherwise distracting home atmosphere. This can include a home where there is a TV.

~ A home in which the parents are unavailable to help, or incapable of helping, the child with his or her homework.

~ Parents who, sadly, do not regard the teacher or the schoolwork as being that important, an attitude which easily rubs off on the child.

~ A child's natural desire, when he comes home, to escape the pressures of schoolwork, and to relax and enjoy the home environment. The child is, basically, trading in his "student hat" for his "child hat." This impulse is justified, especially if the child has had a long day and needs to unwind emotionally or physically.

Parents would do well to put their major efforts into correcting these home-oriented factors, for these are more directly under their control. Remember, the more control you have over a situation, the more it becomes your responsibility to effect whatever changes are possible to improve the situation.

The same factors that affect bedtime are sometimes present regarding difficulties staying on task with homework. Children can be naturally, innately vulnerable to distractions, or they can tend, by nature, to be disorganized. This has an impact on their ability to concentrate. Sometimes, as we've pointed out, it is the home environment that is contributing to poor homework performance. Sometimes a child is simply not yet accustomed to a routine by which homework gets done as a matter of course, in which case it's a matter of developing the habit.

Once again, by treating this problem part by part, as opposed to monolithically, we can find a successful resolution. A good solution is one that allows us to treat the problem on a technical level, *blaming no one.*

Begin Where Success Is Most Likely. Start the child off doing homework in the areas of least resistance, in those topics at which he or she is most likely to succeed. The resistance or likelihood of success are in relation to the subject, the homework's level of difficulty, and the child's relationship with the teacher.

Begin the Homework in School. Usually a child wants time off from school-related work when he arrives home. A possible solution is to organize getting some of the work done in school, after school hours. Car pools can be set up with interested parents participating. The school will need to have a teacher or aide on hand to supervise, and perhaps to help explain the homework when necessary. Even if not all the work gets done in school, it is much easier finishing an assignment at home than to start it from scratch.

In Boca Raton, Florida, Rabbi Kenneth Brander has, in the past, set up a homework "hot line," whereby members of the Kollel are available at certain hours of the evening to answer homework questions. In some communities this could help children over some of the homework rough spots.

PROBLEMS HAVE SOLUTIONS

Problems have solutions. *What's important, however, is not as much the difficulty itself as our attitudes toward it.* Remember, a happy home is the greatest single factor in problem resolution.

✣ EXERCISES

1. EVALUATING YOUR CHILD'S STRENGTHS:

   Make a list of your children's strengths.

   Evaluate which strengths are dominant.

   Try to utilize this strength or strengths in helping begin the resolution of a household or individual problem.

2. BREAKING A PROBLEM DOWN INTO ITS PARTS:

   Break a problem down into its elements.

   See which part of the problem lends itself to a more immediate solution, and is most likely to succeed.

   Feel pleasure and optimism at a small change.

3. KEEPING TRACK:

   Keep a diary of "heavy" problems that eventually were solved, either wholly or in part.

   Keep a record of what was done to help solve those problems.

   Once again, feel the satisfaction that you felt when those problems were resolved.

❧Points to Remember

PROBLEMS have solutions.

ASK the child what he or she thinks.

CREATING an atmosphere of cooperation is of more urgent importance than solving any particular problem on the practical level.

BUILD on the good as much as possible.

PARTIAL remedies can often lead to complete solutions.

IF, AS A RULE, you repeat yourself ten times to a child, then the first nine times you didn't say anything.

A HAPPY home is the greatest single factor in problem resolution.

PART FOUR

BUILDING A WARM HOME IN A COLD ENVIRONMENT

CHAPTER FIFTEEN

The Two Dynamics of Love

Love is complete when two seemingly opposed dynamics are present. No loving relationship is complete without them. They are:

1. **The amount of trouble I go to,** and the effort I make, to understand you.

2. **The trust I place in you,** by virtue of which you need not explain yourself and I don't need to understand everything.

I believe that these two manifestations of love are expressed in the verse: "It is the honor of God when the matter is kept hidden and it is the honor of the King when the matter is examined."[1] The Midrash[2] explains that the first part of the verse, "when the matter is hidden," refers to the six days of the Creation. The second part of the verse refers to the all the days of history that follow Creation. This means that the Creation itself is hidden from us but how

---

1. *Mishlei* 25:2.
2. *Vayikra Rabbah* 89:1; see also *Yalkut Mishlei*, section 961.

Hashem guides this world should be examined.[3] Rav Hutner, *zt"l*, commenting on this *midrash*, says that genuine honor comes about when things that should be hidden are kept secret and things that should be understood are examined.

These two aspects of our relationship with Hashem, the effort to understand and the ability to trust, are eminently applicable to our relationships with other human beings. This is especially so when we are engaged in relationships involving both an emotional and an intellectual bond, and the connection between parents and their children is no exception.

"For I Know Him"

When referring to Avraham Avinu, Hashem said, "For I know him."[4] Rashi explains that "knowing" is a way of expressing love, for you cannot totally love someone whom you don't know. By

---

3. *Pachad Yitzchok,* Rosh Hashanah, *ma'amar* 1. I once suggested to Rav Shlomo Wolbe, *shlita,* that the following *midrash* explains why (as is Rav Wolbe's opinion), we should neither advocate nor discourage a *shidduch* too forcefully:
The Midrash (*Bereishis Rabbah* 68:4) says that a Roman matron once asked Rabbi Yosi bar Chalafta what Hashem has been doing ever since the completion of the first six days of Creation. Rabbi Yosi's reply was that Hashem has been making matches. What could this mean, *what has He been doing?* He's running the world! Perhaps the matron's question meant, rather: What is Hashem doing today that is similar to the Creation? To this, Rabbi Yosi replied that Hashem has been making matches — a kind of creation of new worlds. If, then — as it is expressed in the *midrash* to which we are referring — the original Creation is beyond our ken, and we would do well to keep a humble profile in regard to understanding it, then so, too, in regard to matches. We can help clarify issues, but shouldn't dare to push too much, nor try to impose the force of our own personalities upon the prospective spouses.
4. *Bereishis* 18:19.

extension, the effort you make trying to understand someone is a powerful expression of love.[5]

There's no question that there are different ways of "knowing" a person. For some it is an intellectual feat. We learn about someone, begin to understand and respect where he or she is coming from, and eventually love the person. For when you trouble yourself to understand someone, you get a glimpse of his innate nobility of soul, the trials and tribulations that are uniquely his, and you begin to perceive the Divine spark that glows within each of us.

For others, however, and especially for children, "knowing" can be far more subtle and nonverbal. Children, even the very young,

---

5. See also *Sifri, Devarim* 6:6, in which the relationship between understanding and love is discussed. It is for this reason, I believe, that the study of Torah is considered to be one of the supreme ways in which we can express love for Hashem. It is also the prototype of the father–son relationship, as we say in *Shemoneh Esreh*, "Return us, our Father, to Your Torah." (When it comes to *service* of Hashem, the term "King" is used in regard to the fulfillment of mitzvos, as in: "and bring us close, our King, to Your mitzvos.") Torah study is essentially the effort we invest in understanding how Hashem regards His world. This is why, I think, there is a qualitative difference between Torah studied with toil and Torah studied without toil, for effort is an integral part of any expression of love. The more effort I put into it, the greater the indication of love.

When it comes to other mitzvos, although there is a reward for effort — "According to the pain, is the reward" (*Pirkei Avos*, chapter 5) — the mitzvah is still intrinsically the same, whether or not it involves effort. With Torah study, the mitzvah itself is intrinsically transformed when undertaken with toil. In regard to mitzvos in general, the effort we expend fulfilling the mitzvah is not necessarily an intrinsic part of the mitzvah itself. For example, a Jew living somewhere from which he must travel great distances and pay huge sums of money in order to obtain an *esrog* for Sukkos will certainly be rewarded for his efforts, while the Jew living in Meah Shearim, who pays a much smaller price for an *esrog* purchased just a few yards from his door, receives no such reward. However, when each of these Jews takes the *esrog* in hand on Sukkos, there is no qualitative difference between their mitzvos.

With regard to Torah study, the qualitative difference between Torah that is not studied with sacrifice and toil, and Torah which is, lies, I believe, in the latter's being an act of love. It is my effort to understand what is important to the *Ribbono shel Olam*. It is sort of similar to this: If I know my wife likes cheesecake and I travel a mile to buy it, it is a greater expression of love than if I need to just cross the street to get it.

can sense who truly loves them. This form of "knowing" is by no means inferior to an intellectual realization; quite the contrary, such instinct often proves to be better grounds for the cultivation of emotion than the conclusions of the intellect.

When we speak about nurturing a caring relationship, we are speaking of the effort expended, on a conscious level, to understand another person. This is accomplished primarily by way of sensitive listening, and by careful, noninvasive, nonthreatening questions.[6]

TRUST

The other dynamic that gives love its powerful ability to reach others is trust. Instead of questioning and investigating, one conveys, either verbally or nonverbally, "It's okay, you don't have to explain yourself. I trust you."

Which should come first, understanding or trust? It's a good question, and like many good questions, I think both answers are valid. Trust certainly can exist *before* understanding, as indeed is the case with children. But trust is a far more powerful expression of love when it *follows* understanding, for then it's based on something more stable, a foundation upon which more sublime levels of trust can be built.

Trust implies a deep relationship, one that transcends the need for understanding. But it is far greater and more mature when built upon the foundation of understanding.[7] The truth is that this is a

---

6. See Part 2, chapter 1, for an expansion of this vital subject.
7. The exclamation of the Jewish People before the giving of the Torah, "We shall do and we shall [then] listen [i.e., seek to understand]," while expressing the desire to *do* before we understand, came as a culmination of the many lessons and tests undergone during the Exodus. These lessons were enough to convince the intellect of the wisdom of following Hashem, and also to engender such a love for Hashem that we will follow Him even when we do not grasp the meaning of His commandments. The *chukim*, the laws of the Torah whose meaning we do not comprehend, are therefore an indication of our unique relationship, built on trust, that we have with Hashem (see Rashi, *Bemidbar* 19:2).

never-ending cycle: as we trust Hashem more and more deeply, He rewards us with greater and greater levels of understanding.[8]

Trust is at the root of all relationships, especially those in which the emotional component is of great importance — of which parenting, of course, is a prime example. Indeed, the word for trust has its roots in the parent–child relationship, as we will now see.

THE ROOTS OF TRUST — EMUNAH AND BITACHON

It has been taught that *emunah*, belief in Hashem, and *bitachon*, trust in Him, are one and the same, with *emunah* being likened to the tree and *bitachon* to the fruit.[9] If we examine the root of the word *emunah*, we discover one of the best ways to establish trust.

EMUNAH — "MOTHER"

The root of the word *emunah* is, according to Rav Yitzchok Hutner, *zt"l*, *eim*, אם, "mother,"[10] and means "the first one I trusted." It seems that this root is at the heart of many words in Hebrew referring to any deeply internalized knowledge. Internalized values are more stable than those that come to us from external influences, for the latter may change, while who we are internally endures. It is for this reason that the word *emunah* also refers to steadiness and dependability.[11] The word is also at the root of אמן, *omein*, which

---

8. See *Sefas Emes, Vayikra*, p. 41, in which he asks how could the "wise son" ask at the Seder to understand even the *chukim*, which by definition seem to defy human comprehension? The *Sefas Emes* replies that when one trusts Hashem totally, even the *chukim* can be understood. See also *Sefas Emes* on *Bemidbar*, pp. 135, 140 and 161, in which a similar idea is expressed.
9. Ramban (1194–1270), *Emunah U'Vitachon*, chapter 1.
10. *Pachad Yitzchok*, Sukkos, 17:2.
11. See *Shemos* 17:12, "And his [Moshe's] hands were steadfast (*emunah*)." Or, in *Bemidbar* 12:7, "In the whole of My House is he [Moshe] trustworthy (*ne'eman*)."

means to educate, because education, too, is a process of internalizing life values.[12]

The cultivation of trust, and even more so, teaching a child to trust on a deep level, is very much a parental function, especially on the part of the mother. It is in this relationship that a child learns what it means to rely on someone, to not be alone, and to feel loved *unconditionally*.[13] We instinctively understand this principle.

We cannot live happy, productive lives without an ability to trust. Damaging a human being's capacity for trust is tantamount to destroying some of his humanity.

Trust Is a Two-Way Street

We as parents must therefore make sure not to betray the trust our child places in us. We must erase from our vocabulary the words, "I promise," and replace them with "I will do my best," and the child should learn that such words are deeply meaningful.

> *I remember only once ever using the word "promise" to my children. My eight-year-old daughter had been taunted by her ten-year-old brother, who had told her that she was adopted. Upon hearing this, she ran into her room, threw*

---

12. *Esther* 2:7. I think that the word (אומן, *ooman*), artisan, also refers to an internalized knowledge. Watch a carpenter wielding his hammer. He doesn't seem to be thinking much about how to use his tool, because he is not; the skill has already been internalized. Or consider the modern Hebrew word אימונים, *eemunim*, which refers to army training maneuvers. This training is meant to so deeply internalize certain reactions that they become second nature, and as such can be activated even under a sudden stress, such as an ambush.
13. This is not to imply that people who were young when their parents divorced, or who were orphaned early on in life, cannot, Heaven forbid, develop the ability to trust. Their route, however, may be a longer one and, by necessity, more calculated. It often happens, in fact, that the very fact that so much effort on their part had to be invested in learning basic trust — an admittedly "artificial" process — results in their becoming the most wonderful of marriage partners, friends, and, of course, parents.

herself on her bed, and began to cry hysterically. After all, she had thought that she had a family, and now it had all "disappeared" in one fell swoop. I sat down next to her and comforted her, telling her that there was nothing wrong with being adopted, but it just happened to be that she wasn't.

It was no use; she just kept bawling and screaming. Then I said to her, "I promise you that you are not adopted." She had never heard that word from her father in her entire life. Immediately, she got up, and went about her day normally, as if nothing had happened. In the thirty-odd years that I have been blessed with children, I have never before — or since — used the word "promise."

We, in turn, must trust our children — not a naive trust born of being too lazy to see where they're holding emotionally or religiously, but one whereby a trust betrayed is the most heinous of crimes. When children know that a betrayed trust will hurt their parents more than anything else can, and when they know that our love for them is unconditional, they are far more likely to tell us about themselves and their lives. This is especially so when it comes to teenagers. If they'd rather do things behind our backs and thereby risk losing our trust, then such "trust" is, in any case, tenuous and fragile.

When it comes to training children to have the confidence to perform various physical tasks, we help them to grow in their abilities by giving them more and more responsibility, micromanaging them less, and giving positive feedback. When parents show trust, children try hard to make sure that trust is justified.

The same goes for matters of the spirit and for values. When children think that their parents are suspicious of their every move, they will be less motivated to prove their trustworthiness.

The following true story points this out, in the words of the child herself:

My father was a rav in a town in prewar Hungary. I had begun to show interest in the local youth group, which had a strong secular Zionistic leaning. One evening at home, I overheard one of the townspeople telling my father: "Your daughter has joined the Zionist youth." My father's reply was instant and firm. "My daughter would never do such a thing. She is loyal to me and to the Torah ideals that I stand for." Upon hearing those words, I resolved never again to attend those youth meetings, for I loved my father so much and would never betray the trust he had placed in me.

An important point must be made here. Unconditional love and trust do not imply that anything goes. On the contrary, love is sometimes expressed with sternness. This is how Hashem also treats us; He always loves us, but that love is not always manifested by way of encouragement, tacit or otherwise, for what we are doing.

Building a trustful relationship with a child also has another, vital offshoot:

Trusting Hashem

Trust in parents is a prelude to trusting Hashem. As stated previously, Rav Yitzchok Hutner, *zt"l*, said that the word אם, mother, translates as "the first one whom I trusted." He goes on to say that the letter *nuhn* (ן) that extends the word אם, mother, to form the word אמן, Amen, is the root of the word *emunah*, אמונה, and is translated as, "The trust which I originally had in my mother, I was able to elevate to include Hashem, and the greater spiritual world, when I matured."[14]

This is a sobering thought. *If we wish to impart to our children the happiness of trusting Hashem, we must first be examples of that*

---

14. *Pachad Yitzchok*, ibid.

trust ourselves. In our children's eyes, parents are a paradigm for God Himself.

When Moshe Rabbeinu entered Pharaoh's chambers and declared *"Bni bechori Yisrael,"*[15] "Israel is my firstborn son!" he was making an epochal pronouncement. Never before in history had a human being been audacious enough to declare a child–parent relationship with Hashem. Never before had a human being, no matter how beloved to Hashem, dared contemplate eating from a sacrifice that he had brought before God. All the great men of antiquity, from Adam, the first man, all the way through history to the Patriarchs, had brought the *olah* sacrifice to Hashem and burned it completely on the altar, with nary a bite for the human being who had so lovingly brought it before Hashem. Now there was going to be a change. The Jewish People were being designated as God's children, and as such would be able to partake of the *korban Pesach*. It was an offering that they were bringing to their Father.[16]

One of the things that changed in the wake of the Exodus was that the Jewish People were now expected to trust Hashem. The lessons of the Exodus and the year of miracles leading up to it were meant to create a close enough feeling to Hashem that the Jewish People would trust, and follow, what to the human mind seemed like an irrational set of commandments. Until then, they had been expected, like all the nations of the world, to use their intellect to live correctly.[17]

For example, Shabbos, the celebration of Creation, was a holiday belonging to all mankind, yet was given to the Jewish People in

---

15. *Shemos* 4:22.
16. *Shem MiShemuel, Bemidbar,* p. 57
17. See Rav Nissim Gaon (d. 1050) at the beginning of the Talmud, and the Ramban at the beginning of *Parashas Noach* (*Bereishis* 6:12), and *Toras Avrohom*, p. 130. The Jewish People's observance of the *chukim*, commandments whose comprehension is beyond human intellect, were, for this reason, a prime source of the world's ridicule of the Chosen People. See Rashi, *Bemidbar* 19:2. There are many sources for this important principle, which is beyond the scope of this book.

memory of the Exodus. This, says the *Meshech Chochmah*,[18] was because only the Jewish People could be expected — indeed, commanded — to do the irrational: to keep a day of rest, to close their stores, to leave their fields, and to trust in Hashem's bounty and benevolence. Only they had learned the lessons of the Exodus, and could thus be crowned with the title "son," with all the rights and obligations that this entailed.

Shabbos — A Lesson in Trust

Certainly, Shabbos is one of the vehicles whereby we can begin teaching our children to trust Hashem. Indeed, one of the major messages of Shabbos is to trust that Hashem will provide for you, that you needn't work on the seventh day in order to earn a living. Shabbos is the weekly celebration of the special relationship we enjoy with our Creator.

When we assume a calm and joyous demeanor on Shabbos, this is not lost on our children. Shabbos can truly become the day our children look forward to most, for then their parents are at their best, and are delightfully relaxed and accessible.

A Small Starting Point

Indeed, I tell people who wish to begin the long road of acquiring trust in Hashem to begin at the most propitious moment of the week, when the Shabbos table is set with delicacies. Reflect on all the bountiful happiness that Hashem has bestowed upon you, and then, while *Shalom Aleichem* is being sung and the Kiddush recited, just "hand over the keys." Say, "All right, Hashem, You take over now. I'm letting You run the world for five whole minutes."

---

18. *Devarim* 10:20, paragraph beginning "*Vehineh.*"

Then, for those five magical minutes, savor the joy of being held in the strong and loving arms of Hashem.

When the five minutes are up, go ahead and "take back the keys." Remain convinced, as usual, that you run the world.

As time goes on, you will be able, with Hashem's help, to "hand Hashem the keys" more often and even during moments more tense than those before the Friday evening meal.

With the Exodus the Jewish People were expected, for the first time in human history, to form an emotional relationship with their Creator. The commandment to stand in awe of Him[19] and to love Him was the hallmark of that emotional relationship. Indeed, the commandment to study Torah for its own sake is the most powerful expression of this love, for Torah study is the effort to understand Hashem and what is important to Him. Love is a declaration of the principle, "What is important to you is important to me." Parents need to behave in such a way that their children can trust them totally, if they hope to instill in them a trust in Hashem. This will be, *b'ezras Hashem,* one of the most important elements in raising a child successfully in today's world.

TRUST IS GREATER THAN UNDERSTANDING

We have discussed two expressions of love: understanding and trust. There is no doubt that both understanding and trust are nec-

---

19. Regarding the fear which arises from the fear of punishment, see Rav Tzadok HaKohen, *Pri Tzaddik,* vol. 1, *Ma'amar Kedushas HaShabbos* (*ma'amar* 3), paragraph beginning "*Vechal.*" The fear arising from fear of punishment is understandable intellectually. The non-Jew, too, since he is obligated to use his intellect, is expected to feel this fear. It is for this reason that Avraham Avinu commented on the people of Gerar, that there was no fear of *Elokim* in the place, *Elokim* referring to the aspect of Hashem that punishes. The nations were enjoined to remain sexually moral, and a breach of this, in the face of God Who could, and had indeed, punished them, was a breach of intellect. This was an ominous sign to Avraham as to what type of people he was dealing with. See *Bereishis* 20:1–11.

essary to a mature, stable relationship, but the closeness which we seek with our children, the closeness that bespeaks a special relationship, requires trust, above all. Real trust is something we reserve for those closest to us. It is both fragile and powerful. It can transform all our relationships, lifting them to an exalted level to which understanding alone cannot propel us.

Trust is also the earliest aspect of the relationship a child experiences or, God forbid, fails to experience. Those first impressions, all having to do with trusting his parents, are etched so deeply into his innermost psyche that they will profoundly influence not only his view of us, but of life itself. We must therefore guard this precious trust with every power we have at our disposal, never succumbing to any short-term gain that might seem to be gotten from even a slight betrayal of that trust.

May our children perceive and sense real trust. May they rely on our truthfulness and loyalty even under trying situations when their trust is most strongly tested.

Today's world can be bewildering to a young soul. It can also be seductive, fatally so. Our children need a safe harbor, a warm, secure, loving environment in which the emotional climate mirrors that first and foremost parent–child relationship alluded to in Moshe Rabbeinu's immortal words, *"Bni bechori Yisrael!"* "My child, My firstborn, Israel!"

❧ Exercises

1. Review the chapter on listening, or read other books that teach you how to be a better listener, to convey to your child your desire to understand him or her.

2. Try to find opportunities during the day when you can convey trust to your children. This can be when they express their need for something, or their version of some incident. Tell them, "Fine, I trust you," or, "It's okay, you don't have to explain why you need the extra money. I trust you." Of course, you must truly feel this way. If indeed there is no trust, then find small things to trust in, and try to build an open enough relationship where eventually you can trust about bigger things as well.

🌺 Points to Remember

WHEN you trouble yourself to understand someone, you get a glimpse of his innate nobility of soul.

NURTURING a caring relationship means expending effort, on a conscious level, to understand another person.

TRUST is at the root of all relationships.

WHEN parents show trust, children try hard to make sure that trust is justified.

IN OUR children's eyes, parents are a paradigm for God Himself.

PARENTS need to behave in such a way that their children can trust them totally.

CHAPTER SIXTEEN

The "Triple A" — Attention, Appreciation and Affection

Rav Moshe Aharon Stern, *zt"l*, the beloved and sorely missed *mashgiach* of the Kaminetzer Yeshiva in Jerusalem, believed that the heart of a happy marriage could be expressed with the "Triple A": attention, appreciation, and affection. (The order is mine.) The importance of these three applies to all close relationships, and I would like to take the liberty of explaining at greater length what I believe each "A" stands for.

1. Attention

My definition of respect is: "You take up space on my hard drive." What this means is that when you say something, it matters to me, it makes a difference. Your feelings, ideas, and wishes are important to me and I remember them. Truly loving someone is deeply connected with knowing him, and knowing the child is contingent upon his being willing to let you know who he is. If you pay attention, people will talk. I have a simple example of this from my own family:

> *The first multisyllabic "word" that I heard from one of my children was "entigliaro." I remember it because it was his giant step forward into the world of human speech. However, since neither my wife nor I had any idea what he meant, he failed to get what he wanted, and he soon dropped "entigliaro" from his vocabulary. On the other hand, when my youngest son used the expression "nini" to mean pacifier, we understood him, and he got what he wanted. The word stuck, and our house became the only place in the Milky Way where the word "nini" was used instead of pacifier.*

It is painful to speak and not be heard. For this reason, people who are not heard stop talking, because healthy people, even young ones, stop doing things that hurt.

It goes without saying that if their own words are used against them in any way, children will close up. Sometimes they will cease to volunteer even their most superficial thoughts. This total shutdown of communication sets the stage for many problems, not the least of which are emotional illness and defiance of parents.

As is the case with all problem-solving, a small opening must be found from which to begin. The following situation, which, I am sorry to say is a true one, is a stark example:

> *An eleven-year-old girl, the youngest of several, had become completely closed. Her parents, who were older than the norm for a child of that age, had fallen out of tune with her age group and temperament, and had finally lost contact with her altogether. They efficiently, conscientiously and lovingly made all decisions on the girl's behalf without consulting her.*
>
> *They came to me for advice on how to get her to speak to them again. My advice was to consult her as to what she would like the family to buy or prepare for dessert on*

Shabbos. There was no question in the girl's mind that her words would have import, so she spoke.

This opening eventually led to greater levels of communication.

How "Closed Children" Get That Way

People are never born closed — they get that way. *When children speak and are not heard, they stop speaking.* As adults, we know we feel that way, too, but somehow we don't apply the same rules of human nature when it comes to our children.

We must make sure to listen to our children, just as we would do for anyone who is important to us.

What Attention Is — And Isn't

We must pay attention to what our children are saying. This does *not* mean that we will obey their every wish, nor that children should see their words causing immediate or total compliance on the part of those around them. What "getting attention" means, at the minimum, is that the child's words are accepted civilly, are empathized with, and, whenever possible, that something is done in response. It cannot be overemphasized that it is highly desirable when at all possible to make some change in response to the child's words, as it will encourage him to express himself again in the future.

2. Appreciation

Simply put, "appreciation" means noticing what's right about someone or something.

We all have a tendency to notice what's wrong. Basically, this stems from the notion that when everything turns out okay, that's just the way it's supposed to be. But when something goes wrong, we sit up and wonder, "What happened?"[1]

Overcoming this tendency calls for some hard work, but the fruits of our labor will make it all worthwhile.

Noticing What Is Right

It is easier to *take upon* a new habit than it is to *erase*, i.e., suppress, the old one. In other words, instead of just trying to refrain from a bad habit, rechannel that habitual behavior into some positive action, and start making *that* a habit.

I would suggest that when we notice something wrong, we should get into the habit of noticing something right as well. This will bring down our "emotional temperature," and give us a more balanced view of the situation. Since it is easier to do this with inanimate objects than with people — especially people to whom we're emotionally connected, as is the case with our children — when starting out on your new career of becoming less critical and less focused on the negative, try the following exercise:

> *If, for example, you see a painting that you don't think is worthy of the term "art," notice its beautiful frame. If the frame, too, in your opinion, is in poor taste, notice how nicely the picture is centered on the wall. And if it's not centered on the wall, at least appreciate how it covers up that gaping hole in back of it!*

---

1. This is why we don't appreciate being healthy, and are prone to taking precious few steps to prevent ill health. Rav Yechezkel Levenstein, *zt"l*, is quoted (by Rav Shlomo Brevda, *shlita*) as having said that the *Asher yatzar* blessing recited after using the bathroom, when uttered carefully, and with gratitude, augers good health. This blessing (and the others we recite each morning) can certainly be understood on more sublime levels, but it can also simply alert us to the fact that good health is something to be thankful for. It is not a given. Therefore, it needs to be preserved.

Only when we notice what's right can we give genuine verbal appreciation. The words we say to our children must come from our hearts. Before giving words of appreciation, we have to first adjust our critical mindset.

Appreciation encourages people to continue on in the good things they're doing. The Hebrew word for encouragement is *eedood*, and I believe that it is rooted in the word *ode*, Hebrew for "again." If we want something to be repeated, we must give encouragement. For many children, especially younger ones, the sweetest moments are those in which their parents show appreciation and encouragement. *If we only knew how precious our encouragement was, we would give of it more freely.*

3. Affection

The third "A" is affection, and in this section we use this word interchangeably with love. Affection can be expressed emotionally, verbally or with physical contact. Parental affection should be as close as possible to a parent's love for an infant, that is, as unconditional as possible. Just as Hashem's basic love for us is not predicated upon anything else, so, too, should our love for our children be as unconditional as possible.

Love and affection, while not blind, allows us to overlook, to some degree, the beloved one's defects, or even his misdeeds.[2] When people live in close proximity to one another for extended periods of time — such as in a family — this love allows them to overlook and forgive those traits that can rankle us.

Just as the chances of a plant surviving or even flourishing in the tundra increase if it is first given the chance to develop strong and healthy roots in a greenhouse, so, too, will our children survive

---

2. *Mishlei* 10:12.

and, indeed, flourish, in an alien environment, if they have the deep and healthy roots that an affectionate home gives to those who breathe its invigorating atmosphere. Then the attention and appreciation for each child's unique qualities will bring forth a rich harvest of delicious fruit.[3]

Affection is the fertile soil in which attention and appreciation can grow. With all three elements working together, a parent–child connection develops that cannot be found out on the street. This helps a child maintain his loyalty to home and all that it stands for, since that's where he gets attention, appreciation and affection in abundance, in ways he won't find anywhere else.

---

3. See Maharsha, *Ta'anis* 5b, where he writes that a person's good deeds are to be likened to the delicious fruit of a tree.

❧ EXERCISES

1. Ask your child how his day went, and pay special attention to any specifics that normally you may overlook, such as the normal disappointments or high moments that take place during an ordinary school day. When relevant, ask him about those points a few days later.

2. Take the time to notice something your child does and compliment him or her on it.

3. Take the time to praise the child sincerely for who he or she is, without it being linked to anything specific that he or she has done.

4. Express sincere affection in whatever way you feel most comfortable: verbally or nonverbally, or by buying your child a small gift for no apparent reason.

❧ Points to Remember

We must make sure to listen to our children, just as we would do for anyone important to us.

Truly loving someone is deeply connected with knowing him, and knowing a child is contingent upon his being willing to let you know who he is.

Parental affection should be as unconditional as possible.

It is easier to take upon a new habit than it is to erase or suppress an old one.

For many children, the sweetest moments are those in which their parents show appreciation and encouragement.

Only when we notice what's right can we give genuine verbal appreciation.

CHAPTER SEVENTEEN

Three Expressions of Love

The Torah accords great value to a person's giving of himself to the community,[1] either as a teacher and disseminator of Torah or as one who attends to the needs of the community's poor, sick or troubled. However, one of the common problems faced by such busy, altruistic people is that sometimes their children end up feeling that when it comes to them, attention and understanding are lacking. Looking back later on in life, many such children have said that they felt they were in competition for parental attention with the manifold good deeds of their parents. This does not auger well for their wanting to continue in their parents' righteous footsteps, nor does it make for a healthy parent–child relationship. One encounter with such a child stands out in my mind:

> *A young man in his late teens told me he couldn't even bring himself to open, much less study, any of his father's published works. He felt that these books had cost him his father.*

At the same time, many great, altruistic families have succeeded in raising beautifully dedicated and loving children. This success

---

1. See *Daniel* 12:3; *Bava Basra* 8b.

has been achieved, to some extent, not in spite of their being busy with community affairs but because of it. Their children have seen, and been inspired by, their parents' example.

There is no question that the feeling of being loved and respected by one's parents is one of the decisive elements that will cause the child to espouse their value system. If, therefore, we can discover how great, busy men or women communicate love and respect to their children, then the rest of us, even those of us not so burdened, can use that as a blueprint for inspiring our own children to emulate us and adhere to what we hold dear.

Rav Reuven Feinstein, *shlita*, once told Rav Paysach Krohn, *shlita*, how he knew as a young boy that his overwhelmingly busy father, Rav Moshe Feinstein, *zt"l*, had loved him dearly. Rav Krohn recorded these impressions in one of his wonderful "*Maggid*" stories.[2]

Rav Reuven mentioned three things his father did which conveyed, non-verbally, the message of love and respect which every child, and, indeed, every human being, needs. These three things, which remained engraved in Rav Reuven's memory, can serve as a paradigm for three fundamental rules, not only for parenting but for human relationships in general. I cannot know whether Rav Moshe, *zt"l*, consciously had in mind these three expressions of love, but for me, and hopefully for others, they will serve as an aid.

1. Caring for Physical Needs Without Being Asked

Rav Reuven remembers how on cold winter mornings in New York City, his father would enter his room and lay out his school clothes for him on the radiator. Reuven knew his father was taking special care of him, ensuring that his son would have the pleasure

---

2. *In the Footsteps of the Maggid* (New York: Mesorah Publications, 1992), p. 123.

of putting on warm clothes. In this original manner, Rav Moshe enabled his son to experience his parental concern for his well-being and comfort.[3]

This is in keeping with what Rav Moshe, *zt"l*, told his student, Rav Pinchas Weiner, *zt"l*,[4] about how to make a student believe that his teacher truly has his spiritual welfare in mind. A teacher, said Rav Moshe, must show concern for his student's *physical* welfare if he wishes to demonstrate concern for the student's *spiritual* welfare.

This concept brings to mind a beautiful story:

> *Rav Moshe Schneider, zt"l, tells of a famous, brilliant professor who refused to convert to Christianity, despite the fact that he was not at all observant and that conversion would greatly enhance his career prospects. When asked why he so stubbornly refused to leave the Jewish People, he related the following story:*
>
> *As a young boy he had come to Radin hoping to be accepted into the famous yeshiva of the Chofetz Chaim. It was right after Sukkos and many candidates were waiting to be tested. His first day in Radin went by without a test, and he was forced to sleep over. Having nowhere else to go, he decided to sleep on one of the benches in a local shul. It was cold. An elderly man entered the shul, and upon seeing the boy lying on a cold bench, removed his own coat and covered him. The entire night the old man paced the cold shul and learned*

---

3. Rav Yaakov Horowitz, *shlita*, mentioned that Rav Reuven thinks that the reason his father warmed his clothing in the morning (and dressed him under the covers!) was also to insure that his child would not develop a negative attitude toward waking up for a day of Torah study.
4. Beloved principal, in Toronto and Jerusalem, whose greatness in all matters, be they between man and God or between man and man, will long be remembered. I am personally indebted to him for believing in my potential as a classroom teacher and giving me my first position, even in the face of widespread skepticism as to the ability of an American to efficiently teach an elementary school grade in Israel.

with a sweet tune, and his coat warmed the sleeping boy. The old man was the Chofetz Chaim and the boy was that professor.

"Many times I was tempted to convert," said the professor, "but whenever I thought back to that memorable night, I would say to myself, with such a nation I cannot part ways."[5]

2. "What's Important to You Is Important to Me"

Rav Reuven recalls that during the summers, his family stayed on a farm in the Catskill Mountains. There wasn't that much for a little boy to do, but once a day, a farm worker would drive his truck to "town" to pick up supplies. The back of the truck was cushioned with hay, and the children would climb in for their daily ride. The roads were poorly paved, and the ride was blessedly bumpy.

Rav Reuven had a daily learning session with his father. If the truck was ready to leave during that learning period, Rav Moshe would stop and tell his son that they could continue later, but for now he should make sure he didn't miss the truck ride.[6]

3. Unvarying Love

The third thing Rav Reuven experienced as a child was that he almost never lost his place near his father at the Shabbos table,

---

5. S*efer HaZikoron l'Rav Moshe Schneider, zt"l*, p. 98 (Bnei Brak, 1965). This story was related to Rav Schneider by the Ponevezher Rav, Rav Yosef Kahaneman, *zt"l*.
6. In general, I advise fathers who are studying with their children to stop five minutes before the child wants to. That way, children have positive memories of the learning sessions, always remembering wanting to go on, never feeling it as a drag. This is analogous to selling a stock while it is still high. If the child wants to stop early, then this is a separate problem that needs addressing.

despite the fact that Rav Moshe was often host to important, world-famous guests. This, I believe is a paradigm for the third expression of parental love.

Children have a powerful sense of justice. If your behavior at home varies greatly when guests are present, your child will at some point cease to respect you.

We are generally respectful and accommodating to guests, but *our children are our most important guests.* They, too, will be moving out, in about fifteen years. While we need not (and perhaps must not) treat our children exactly the same way we treat other guests, we must remain as calm and good-natured and patient with them as with anyone else in our house. *If we are famous and held in high esteem by the community, but the child does not see our behavior in the home as deserving of the same respect, then the stage is set, God forbid, for the child to reject not only the father, but the society that so reveres him.*

Rav Reuven felt that his father's love for him was consistent, and it made no difference whether or not someone outside the family was there. It was the same wonderful, caring and nurturing relationship whether or not there were onlookers.

Our Sages have taught us[7] that Torah is acquired by our creating *simanim*, memory aids, by which we can retain the lessons we have learned. Perhaps these three pointers, given to us by one of our generation's greatest men, can help us remember some of the basic truths of child-rearing, and, indeed, of all human relationships.

---

7. *Eruvin* 54b.

❧ Exercises

1. Inquire after your child's material welfare, and try to make a change in his or her room that will make it more comfortable and inviting.

2. Find a special story you can tell your child.

3. Before Shabbos, ask your child, or children, what would make them enjoy the meal more. Is there a dessert they would like? A song? A story? Let them plan the *seudah* with you.

4. Pay special attention to your child or children at the Shabbos table. If you usually have guests, then have several Shabbos meals without any, so as to accustom your child to interacting with you at the table.

❧ Points to Remember

MANY children have said that they felt they were in competition for parental attention with the manifold good deeds of their parents.

A TEACHER (or parent) must show concern for his student's physical welfare if he wishes to demonstrate concern for the student's spiritual welfare.

CHILDREN are our most important guests.

IF YOUR behavior at home varies greatly when guests are present, your child will at some point cease to respect you.

CHAPTER EIGHTEEN

The Greatest Gift You Can Give Your Child

The greatest gift you can give your child is the knowledge that he is never alone. Hashem is always there with us, at all times.

Parents would do well to express, but even more, to feel, that Hashem is indeed with them and that they are never alone. When a difficulty arises, seize the opportunity to sincerely reaffirm our trust in Hashem, in front of our children. Indeed, Rav Shlomo Wolbe considers trust in Hashem the foundation of a successful home.[1]

Two of the gifts that we receive when we realize we are never alone are happiness and fearlessness.

Happiness

True happiness consists of being rooted in the truths of life — the greatest of which is that Hashem is the Source of all good, and

---

1. *Alei Shur*, vol. 1, p. 258.

that He is always present, loves us and is desirous of bestowing His goodness upon us.

The Chazon Ish writes, "In truth there is no sadness in the world for someone who recognizes the light of Truth."[2]

This light, even a little bit of it, can drive away a lot of darkness,[3] for the sadness of the darkness, the feeling of being alone and cut off, is false, while the light of Hashem's presence is true. A small amount of reality can, indeed, drive away a huge but unreal darkness.

Fearlessness

Rav Lazer Nannes[4] tells how he endured the twenty years of torture in Siberia:

> *When called for an interrogation by the KGB, I always had a picture in mind — that of my father, telling me not to fear them. They could do nothing to me.*

When Rav Lazer was asked what he was thinking during those hellish years when he had been tortured for no reason at all, his response was simple, but overwhelming. He was thinking, "This is none of my business." Rav Lazer's relationship to Hashem was that

---

2. *Letters*, vol. 1, letter #36.
3. *Chovos HaLevovos*, Gate Five, chapter 5.
4. Rav Lazer, *zt"l*, spent twenty years in a Siberian labor camp, "guilty" of observing Judaism. In his book, entitled *Subbota* (written under the pen name Avrohom Netzach), he depicts the unsuccessful attempts on the part of the KGB to tear him away from Shabbos observance, *kashrus*, and even from keeping his beard. Not only did he escape death on numerous occasions, but he earned the begrudging respect of his KGB tormentors. He passed away, in Jerusalem, right before Purim 1998, at the age of 100, fearless and full of trust in Hashem until his last day. His wife, of blessed memory, was indeed his life's helpmate. Before the eyes of this author, she inspired a girl — with whom she shared no common language except the language of the heart — to a lifelong commitment to Judaism, and to a deep conviction that Hashem does not do bad things to good people.

of a private to a general. In his view, he was here to do whatever job Hashem would give him. He knew how beloved he was to Him, and there was no question that he would follow His "orders" unquestioningly.

While most of us can only dream of such a level of closeness to Hashem, the source of Rav Lazer's greatness, and his ability to maintain himself as a decent human being even in Siberia, is of the utmost importance to us.

We are fortified, and made fearless, by the knowledge that we are never alone. We can always carry with us an awareness of Hashem's presence and, also, the words and faces of those who love us.

There are several basic things a person can do that nurture an awareness of Hashem, in himself and in his children.

Gratitude

The Vilna Gaon and the Maharal[5] both divide man's world into three realms: between man and God, between man and his fellow-man, and between man and himself. One of the sources both of them bring is the *gemara* in *Bava Kamma* 31a, in which three opinions are presented among the Sages as to how to achieve piety. One of them is to perfect oneself in the area of making *berachos*. This refers to the realm between man and God. It seems to indicate that gratitude, which is the catalyst for expressing praise of Hashem in the form of a *berachah*, is at the root of service of Hashem and becoming close to Him.

Aside from role-modeling gratitude, parents can train their children to feel gratitude toward Hashem in several ways:

---

5. *Aderes Eliyahu*, Devarim 32:5, and Maharal, *Derech Chayim*, in his introduction to *Pirkei Avos*.

BIRCHOS HASHACHAR — NOTHING IS TO BE TAKEN FOR GRANTED

The morning *berachos*, in which we thank Hashem for the gifts that He bestows upon mankind in general, and on the Jewish People in particular, are, in my opinion, an excellent means of increasing our awareness of the overwhelming gratitude we should feel toward Hashem. Vision, or being able to walk and to think, are not to be taken for granted. We even thank Hashem for having shoes *("she'asah li kol tzorki")*.

When a child realizes how much Hashem gives him, the stage is set for the child to feel that Hashem loves him, daily and forever.[6]

YOU ARE INHERENTLY GOOD

Every child must know that he is indeed deserving of Hashem's love, since he is inherently good. "The soul You have placed in me is pure," is a basic concept in Judaism, and is recited daily.

Parents should not even say "Good boy!" to a child when he does something good. A person's goodness is immutable and is not contingent on the good things he does, as important as actions are. "That was a great thing you did, son!" would be better.[7]

---

6. To go a step further, see *Toras Avrohom*, p. 218, by Rav Avrohom Grodzinsky, *hy"d*, the last *mashgiach* of Slobodka in Europe. Rav Avrohom says that when a person looks at what he has with a good eye, an *ayin tovah*, he will look differently not only at the *Ribbono shel Olam*, but at His world and other people in it. In my opinion, this is the foundation of giving and of setting up a home.
7. I believe that a perfectionist is someone who cannot separate how good he is from how well he does. Perfectionism is one of the great enemies of a happy home, and hampers the growth of happy children.

You Are Intrinsically Great

Not only are you inherently good; you are possessed of a noble soul, and are therefore intrinsically great. No one can deprive you of the intrinsic greatness with which Hashem has blessed you. Our greatness comes from Hashem; this is reiterated numerous times in the Torah, beginning with the epic statement of Moshe when he appeared before Pharaoh, "My child, my firstborn, Israel."[8] Being called Hashem's "child" is indicative of a great connection to Him.

Rav Yaakov Galinsky, *shlita*, one of today's great teachers and speakers, told the following story, drawn from his personal experience in a Siberian labor camp:

> *It was common knowledge that the more important you were on the "outside," the worse you were treated in the camp. In the same barracks as Reb Yaakov, was one non-Jew who was given the worst, most degrading jobs in camp. Once, during the night, Reb Yaakov saw this man get out of what passed for a bed, quickly put something on, walk back and forth, and then return to "bed."*
>
> *The next morning, Reb Yaakov made certain to stand next to him at the morning roll call. He asked him what he had done during the night, getting out of bed and all the rest of it. The man turned white with fear. Perhaps Reb Yaakov was a KGB "plant," and he would be severely punished. Reb Yaakov repeatedly assured him that he had nothing to fear, and finally the man relented and told him. He had been a general in the Latvian army before Stalin had decided to erase that country from the map. Anyone who was important in Latvia was either killed or exiled to Siberia.*
>
> *This general had done an amazing thing. He had smuggled into the camp a piece of his uniform, and during the night he*

---

8. *Shemos* 4:22.

would don it and march back and forth, doing a few military paces. Why was he doing this? After all, it was excruciatingly difficult to get up after a long day of backbreaking work, and rest was no small matter in Siberia. To use his words, "They want to make me forget I'm a general, they want to make me lose my self-respect. I am, and always will be, a general!"

At this point Reb Yaakov declared to his audience, "We are all generals. Let no one ever make us forget how special and important we are!"

When a person is aware of his intrinsic and immutable greatness, then it is easier to feel that Hashem is close to him, and will always be close to him. It goes without saying that parents must also feel the same way about themselves in order to be able to convey this to their children!

Protection from the Outside World

This knowledge is a vital anchor for our children. Today's world, as we have reiterated so many times, can be seductive as well as frightening. We, and certainly our children, need to be anchored in the eternal truths of life in order to grow and prosper in joy and security.

The knowledge that Hashem is close and loving, clearly conveyed to a child, is a tremendous deterrent against the possibility that he will, God forbid, bow to the pressures of the street. Usually a person succumbs because he or she seeks approval from the environment. To one who genuinely knows that Hashem is never far, His approval is more important.

🌺 Points to Remember

THE GREATEST gift you can give your child is the knowledge that he is never alone.

EVERY child must know that he is indeed deserving of Hashem's love, since he is inherently good.

WHEN a child realizes how much Hashem gives him, the stage is set for the child to feel that Hashem loves him, daily and forever.

HASHEM'S approval is more important than that of the surrounding environment, to one who genuinely knows that Hashem is never far.

CHAPTER NINETEEN

Building Self-Esteem in Children

THE CHALLENGE OF OUR TIME

The Hebrew word for "life," *chayim*, always appears in the plural. One of the reasons given for this is that life actually consists of two planes of existence, this world and the World to Come, with a true, well-lived life being one that prepares a person for success in both.[1] This, it seems, is what our Sages mean when they say that evil people, even in this world, are considered as if they were dead,[2] for the "life" they lead in this world is not leading them to success in the next.

Given that the purpose of parenthood can be generally defined as the preparation of a child for a successful life, and in light of the above definition of *chayim*, parenthood today is indeed a great challenge. This was put starkly by one of America's premier Torah educators:

> *Rav Yitzchok Hutner, zt"l, once told one of his students that when his, the student's, child goes to the neighborhood grocer*

---

1. *Sefer HaShoroshim*, quoted in the commentary *Kol Yehudah* on the *Kuzari*, at the beginning of the third section.
2. *Berachos* 18b.

> to buy a container of milk, he is subjected to more trials (in viewing immodesty) than his father's grandfather was subjected to in his entire life in the shtetl.

TECHNOLOGY

Another characteristic of modern times is that the assembly line has created people who really don't feel that they've done much. An autoworker, at the end of a long day, can only bend over and point to a screw in the car's fender and say, "That's my screw!"

> *Rav Shlomo Wolbe, shlita, once told me that one of the reasons people are so weak in their self-image and their ability to take criticism is that technology has created a world in which the person sees very little of his own effort in whatever is produced. He mentioned, in illustration, the case of a cardiologist who had created a computer program incorporating his criteria for diagnosis. Now his secretary was able to diagnose his patients.*

If modern life is so difficult, how can parents even begin helping their children cope with its seemingly impossible challenges?

I think that an example from our physical world can suggest a starting point:

> *All of us live under an ocean of air. The air pressure we endure is so powerful that we really should become as flat as pancakes. That's what would happen if we were under the deep sea without a diving suit. Why, then, are we not crushed? Because Hashem has provided us with an equal amount of pressure from within, and this outward push within us balances the pressure exerted upon us from the atmosphere.*

This is why building our children's self-image is so vitally important today, more than ever. Our children must feel good about who they are, and the ideals that they stand for. Only this will enable them to "push back," to be able to say "no" to a society which seeks to swallow them and frustrate their ability to build future happy lives, both in this world and the next.

At this point, let us find a working definition of self-esteem, and then understand why it's so often lacking in children. Then we will discuss what we can do about it.

Defining Self-Esteem

Self-esteem is a person's recognition of his or her innate, immutable goodness, based upon the fact that his or her soul was created by God and is forever tied to the Source of all goodness and purity. As we have often found reason to mention in earlier chapters, we state daily, "The soul that You have placed in me is pure." *This purity is based neither on my evaluation of myself, nor on other people's evaluation of me.* We are intrinsically good, we are children of Hashem, and His love for us is eternal. I know I am good because God told us so in His Torah. Although there is certainly retribution for sinfulness, this in no way contradicts the fact that I am intrinsically good, and that the path back to Hashem, *back to my natural self,* is therefore always open.

The Root of Permanent Self-Esteem

It must be noted that self-esteem is not built by effusive statements like "That was really great!" "What a terrific drawing!" for everything the child does. First, such statements are seen by the child as being affected and, in addition, they lose their value through overuse. What, then, is the root of true self-esteem?

We have learned that human beings function in three dimensions: in the relationships between man and God, man and his fellowman, and man and himself. I believe that all three are alluded to in the verse, "And you shall love your fellowman as yourself, for I am Hashem."[3]

What is interesting is that love for others is predicated upon love for yourself. "You shall love your fellowman as yourself." It is assumed that you will love yourself. Why? The verse ends: "I am Hashem." You love yourself, and, by extension, others, because Hashem said so.[4] That makes this love immutable.[5]

Love of self is therefore not an expression of haughtiness, but rather, a recognition of the intrinsic, God-given goodness which is shared by all of humanity.

WHY CHILDREN, ESPECIALLY, ARE AT RISK

The younger the child, the less he has developed a perspective upon his own self. Children look outside of themselves for a model on which to pattern their behavior and attitudes. As *Mori VeRabi, zt"l,* said, children are like new immigrants to a country. They look around and start behaving like everybody else.

This means that children are particularly susceptible to put-downs and to criticism of their abilities. If you tell a child that he's stupid, that child will believe you, and as a consequence, his actual mental capacities and self-image will not develop naturally or fully.

---

3. *Vayikra* 19:18.
4. What this seems to mean is that the Divine commandment to love yourself is then extended to include others. *That is, others are also included in your definition of self.* Those who have seen the intense caring that the great Torah leaders of the Jewish People displayed toward total strangers can testify that this is indeed a lofty yet achievable goal.
5. See Maharal, *Derush al HaTorah,* p. 31, the paragraph beginning *"Va'omar shuv,"* in which he shows that many times the last statement mentioned in a verse or pronouncement of the Sages is meant to cause the matter to endure. For instance, when we are told to make ourselves a teacher and "buy" a friend (*Pirkei Avos* 1:6), we are then told to judge all men favorably. If I cannot judge favorably, I will be unable to keep either the friend or the teacher, because eventually he will do something that irritates me.

Children are deeply affected, consciously and subconsciously, by how others regard them. The following is a true story of a young child in his second year of school.

> *A six-year old, well-behaved and obedient, developed severe pain in his leg. He would scream from pain during the night, and this would awaken him and his worried parents. When he was taken to the family doctor, a well-trained pediatrician, the doctor feared the onset of muscular dystrophy, or perhaps a rarer disease called dystonia.*
>
> *Over the following months many hospital tests were performed and they were all negative, but the pain continued. The doctors then suggested that perhaps there was a psychological factor at the root of the pain.*
>
> *A competent psychologist, Dr. Avigdor Bonchek, was consulted, and it came to light that the child's teacher was reprimanding this child for reading too quietly. Of course, to this sensitive child, this was the worst way to get him to read more loudly. Dr. Bonchek suggested waiting until the end of the term, which was due shortly, to see what would happen with the pain when there would be a change of teacher. Indeed, as soon as there was a new, gentler teacher, the pain went away, never to return.*

While we must indeed bring our children's mistakes to their attention, this cannot be done continually, as if we were watchdogs, but rather, only on those occasions that it is really necessary to do so. We must *never* say or suggest that the child is incompetent; rather, we should tell the child that a mistake has been made that needs correcting, and that it's not the end of the world.

Children look to us for their first sense of self-worth. We dare not betray this innocent trust.

From Home to School: The Perilous Transition

When a child enters school the potential for a worsening of self-image increases greatly.

> *In 1994, at a Torah Umesorah convention, I listened to a presentation on classroom discipline. I read the presenter's book, "Discipline With Dignity." It contained a frightening statistic. When children enter first grade, 80 percent have a high self-image, in fifth grade 20 percent have a high self-image, and by the time they finish high school, only 5 percent have a high self-image.*

Even if we claim that these statistics are based on the general public school system, and that the Torah day schools will not devastate self-image in the same manner, the fact remains that there must be something about school, in general, that affects a child's self-image negatively. We can safely assume that if this process is endemic to school systems in general, then a Torah-oriented school environment may well contain some of these elements, too. Identifying these elements is the first step in trying to alleviate or neutralize their effects.

Arguably one of the most difficult — and fateful — transitions in a child's life occurs when he leaves home to attend school. People have always been trying to figure out how best to react to the common crying and hysteria that children express when they're put into a classroom and their mothers turn and walk away. But it doesn't end there. School, with all its rules and societal and scholastic pressures, will from that point on continue to exert a greater and greater pressure and influence on that child, and will continue shaping his self-perception.

One of the main reasons that school can cause a worsening of self-image is that it isn't, *and cannot be,* as accepting an environment as the home. It is a rare teacher who finds the time and presence of mind to nurture and encourage her young charges as a mother would.

In addition, schools measure success by a different yardstick. Schools judge the child's ability to listen for relatively long periods of time, to obey certain rules, and to interact with other students amicably and respectfully. Schedules need to be kept and, as early as first grade, it is expected that homework will be done diligently and regularly. These skills, social and intellectual — so necessary for success in school — differ from those that are called for at home.

The greatest drop in self-esteem, in 60 percent of the students, occurs between first and fifth grades. I would therefore like to focus on what happens in these grades.

First through Fifth Grades

The school's focus undergoes a gradual, but inexorable, shift between first and fifth grades.

When seeking a first grade teacher, a principal will put far greater emphasis on the warmth of the applicant's personality than he would for a fifth grade teacher. Fifth grade pays more attention to the group's reaching a specific level of academic achievement, and the child finds himself on a conveyor belt, whereby academic failings are less likely to be overlooked or accepted with an encouraging attitude.

As the child becomes still older, there is a shift in how the learning is presented. In the earlier grades, especially the first two, there is (or should be) one person who does most of the teaching. A young child finds it difficult to establish a relationship of trust if there is a parade of "specialists" going through his classroom. As the years go on, however, many schools, especially in the secular disciplines, understandably shift to a departmentalized system, whereby each subject has someone else who is especially equipped for its instruction. The teacher–student relationship that had once been characterized by warmth is now structured on technicalities. The teachers aren't necessarily cold, but there is little quality time available for constructing any sort of emotional relationship.

In addition, the child's social awareness increases dramatically between first and fifth grades. For example, if a first grader is doing poorly in reading, he'll be far less likely to realize how poorly he's doing vis-à-vis the rest of the class. An older child, though, is painfully aware of his or her academic shortcomings.

What all this adds up to is that a child who may have done well in a nurturing, maternal environment — where there was much less need to keep to a specific schedule, learn specific material, obey rules and interact with a relatively large group of peers — finds himself in an environment which increasingly measures his success in areas of behavior with which he may have scant familiarity.

Parental Responsibility

What this means is that parents cannot relinquish responsibility for their child's sense of self when the child enters school. Parents must stay in touch with the teachers to see if there are any problems that can be nipped in the bud. Whenever possible this "checking in" should be:

1. **Positive.** Parents would do well to honestly emphasize their appreciation for the good work a teacher is doing. I encourage parents to send notes to the school, especially at the beginning of the week, stating, for example, how the child had repeated something the teacher had said, and, in general, to recognize the teacher's investment of time and effort in their child.

2. **Brief.** Parents shouldn't take up too much of the teacher's time during their regular "checkups." They don't want the teacher to regard them as a burden. Then, when time with a teacher really is needed, the teacher will be more likely to accommodate the parent.

3. **Solution-Oriented, Not Blame-Oriented.** Someone once told me that when the Japanese have a problem, they want to know how to solve it. Americans, on the other hand, want to know "who did it." The latter approach is generally not productive. Try to keep the discussion as solution-oriented as possible.

Generally speaking, the principal should be brought in only at the teacher's initiative. Parents who are quick to call in the principal are undermining the teacher's authority and sending him or her a distinct message of mistrust. In any event, it will ultimately be the teacher who implements the proposed solution.

THE HOME FRONT

While the school often measures "achievement" with an academic yardstick, the home is where the total person should be appreciated and valued for who he or she is.

One good way to enhance a child's self-esteem and good feeling at home is to give him more and more of a say about what goes on in the house — whether it be about where to go on an outing, what to have for supper, or the allocation of chores. When the child feels good about himself at home, a less-than-perfect academic record won't break him. And if there's any conflict regarding teachers or schoolwork, such snags won't make him reject the values which school (the same one that's giving him trouble!) is asking him to espouse. *The child knows that as important as academia is, it does not measure — nor is it even supposed to measure — his sense of self-worth.* A poor academic record then becomes a technical, not an emotional, problem. Lateness, a poor social record, or other problems, are examined in a similar light.

> *Once, during a panel discussion, someone in the audience posed a question: "What can I do when I feel that my child's teacher is undermining me?"*

> *My response was that if a parent is parenting as he should be, a teacher cannot undermine him. The parent should be spending more time with the child, over a longer period, than the teacher ever will. In addition, the parent obviously has a greater fiscal commitment to the child, whereby prizes and other incentives can be offered, beyond what the teacher can afford. Above all, the parent should have made himself or herself into a more admirable and beloved role model than the teacher can ever hope to be.*

What Parents Can Do

Parents should never forget that they have an enormous ability to affect their children's school life, both directly and indirectly. They must, however, start early enough and stay on top of things. *They must be aware of, and appreciate, their child's strengths.* The home must be a place where the child feels loved and respected and a part of things. And when necessary, parents need the humility to ask advice and seek counsel.

I would like to end this chapter with a discussion of the far-reaching ramifications of a healthy self-image, since the more aware we are of something's importance, the more will we consciously strive to achieve it.

Self-worth: Taking Care of Yourself and Serving Hashem

We have stated that the deepest kind of self-esteem is respect for oneself as God's handiwork. Taking care of one's own health is a natural expression of this feeling of self-worth. Yet it might seem as if this concept has no significant bearing on how one relates to God. This isn't the case, though, as the following story demonstrates:

> *A pious man, noted for abstinence and physical self-affliction, once approached Rav Yisroel Salanter[6] for guidance in serving Hashem. Rav Yisroel, who apparently knew the man's background, replied, "There is no greater ingratitude to Hashem, than one who disregards the needs of the body Hashem gave him."[7]*

Rabbi Yisroel Salanter himself practiced what he preached:

> *Dr. Badess, the head of a hospital, once stated that of all the thousands of people who came to him for medical care, only one, named Lipkin (Rav Yisroel Salanter's family name) ever totally followed his instructions.[8]*

A prophet,[9] when advising people who sought Heavenly advice on how to best fulfill their life's potential, would advise them, "According to their souls' root[10] *and their bodies' nature*" (emphasis mine).[11]

The Talmud itself enjoins us to regard ourselves "as if a holy man were living inside of us."[12] Provide your organs with proper nutrition and maintenance, to enable that holy being — you — to serve God.

---

6. 1810–1883. The founder of the *Mussar* Movement and one of the Nineteenth Century's great thinkers, who lived his life in total consistency with the ethical principles he taught.
7. *B'Tuv Yerushalayim,* by Rav Bentziyon Yadler, zt"l, p. 342.
8. *Meoros HaGedolim,* by Rav Chaim Zeitchik, zt"l (Jerusalem, 1969).
9. Whose primary function was to advise people on their unique path in serving Hashem.
10. A kabbalistic concept dealing with each particular soul's unique, innate nature. The *Sefas Emes* (*Bemidbar*, p. 120, paragraph beginning "*BaMishnah*") tells us that the Hillel's statement, "*Im ein ani li mi li,*" "If I am not for me who is for me?" (*Pirkei Avos* 1:14), refers to the fact that if I do not fulfill my life's unique mission, no one else will, or can.
11. Vilna Gaon, *Mishlei* 16:4.
12. *Ta'anis* 11a.

Taking care of your physical well-being is an expression of self-worth and is related to your service of Hashem. *I am worthy, hence my service is worthy.*

If this is the case regarding physical needs, how much more so when it comes to mental well-being. Our minds are the sanctuaries of our souls and need protection from physical — and spiritual — threats.

LOVE OF HASHEM — RECOGNITION OF THE GOOD WITH WHICH HE HAS BLESSED US

The relationship between self-worth and service of Hashem can be taken a step further.

We love something for one of four reasons. The first three are:

1. *Tov* — **good.** We are attracted to things that we recognize as possessing intrinsic goodness.

2. *Areiv* — **tasty.** The prospect of physical pleasure serves as an attraction.

3. *Mo'il* — **utilitarian.** Something that we perceive as helpful to us in the achievement of our goals will merit our attention.

The Vilna Gaon[13] uses food as a prototype to illustrate this point. Food can be a mitzvah (*tov*), such as eating of the Temple sacrifice or matzah on Pesach, it can be tasty (*areiv*), or it can be nutritious (*mo'il*).

The Vilna Gaon points out a fourth type of bond, that which is formed by the sense that someone cares for us. "As water reflects a face, so, too, does the heart of a man reflect [the heart of] his fel-

---

13. Vilna Gaon, *Shir HaShirim* 5:2.

lowman."[14] It is easiest to love for this reason. While the first three reasons require some appreciation of the person or object before we experience love for it, the fourth is simply an involuntary response. *When I feel your love, I love you in return.* This requires no introspection or thought, just the ability to receive and accept as real, someone else's love. This is what a child does. Even infants have an uncanny way of feeling who truly loves them, and they respond in kind.

> *A rav was once approached by a husband who was troubled by the feeling that his wife loved him more than he loved her. The situation had a serious potential for danger. In order to quell the sense of guilt that was consuming him, the husband would have to deny the reality of his wife's love.*
>
> *The advice given the husband was to let in his wife's feelings of love, and to accept them, to feel loved and simply enjoy feeling loved. That eternal principle, "As water reflects a face, so, too, does the heart of a man reflect [the heart of] his fellowman," would come to bear on this relationship and he would begin to feel love in return.*
>
> *Baruch Hashem, the idea worked.*

All this is predicated, however, on self-esteem. For if I feel that I myself am not deserving of love, then your love is misplaced and hence will not serve as a catalyst to my returning it. *I can feel loved by others and by Hashem only if I truly believe that I am intrinsically worthy of that love.*

THE FUNCTION OF LUXURIES

I believe that an important tool for developing love of Hashem is latent in the love to which we have just referred.

---

14. *Mishlei* 27:19.

In a utilitarian world, there seems to be no justification for luxuries. They don't seem functional. *On closer investigation, however, we can see luxuries as an expression of God's love for us.*[15] When we receive things that are vital for sustaining life, we don't feel loved. But when Hashem gives us things that exist solely for our pleasure, then we know He loves us. If we will let that love in, we will certainly love Him in return.

THE SECRET OF THE TZADDIK'S STRENGTH

When King Solomon drew a distinction between evil people and the righteous, he chose to emphasize not the fact that the righteous do good and the evil do bad, for that is merely the outcome of something else, something more basic. King Solomon tells us that "the righteous fall seven times[16] and the wicked fall… [even after one failure]."[17] In other words, *it's not that the tzaddik doesn't fall; he falls, even many times. What is important is that he gets up again.*

Where does the *tzaddik* derive this ability to continually rise again, even after countless failures? *One answer is that he knows he is intrinsically good, and is therefore always able to rely on Hashem to continue to help him.*

Again, we say daily, "The soul that You have placed in me is pure."

---

15. See Tosafos, *Berachos* 37a, where the *Borei nefashos* blessing is explained, and the words *al kol mah shebarasa* refers to luxuries, such as apples. See also *Maharal, Nesivos Olam, Nesiv Gemilus Chassadim*, in chapter 1, where he also expands on the idea of Hashem's creation of luxuries. Perhaps this is why our father, Avraham, sat his guests under a tree, for tree fruit, such as the apple, is the symbol — as the aforementioned Tosafos mentions — of luxury. Avraham wanted to impress upon his guests Hashem's love for them, which is symbolized by the luxuries that He bestows on them. (Indeed, Rav Avigdor Miller, *zt"l*, says that the English word "paradise" stems from the Hebrew word *pardes*, orchard, for indeed Paradise was an orchard.)
16. In the Written Law, "seven times" is symbolic of "many times," and does not mean seven in a literal sense.
17. *Mishlei* 24:16.

REAL AND IMAGINED STRENGTH

The only people who are truly strong are those who recognize that their strength is not rooted in their own abilities, but in their connectedness to Hashem. Haughty people limit their strength to their own personal abilities. No matter how highly they may view themselves, once they have reached the limits of their own perceived resources, they can go no further.[18]

Seeing ourselves as part of Hashem's handiwork, and as members of His beloved People, is at the root of any true knowledge of our intrinsic goodness. We know that we are never totally rejected by Hashem, Whose Hand is always outstretched to us. This is the source of the *tzaddik*'s stability,[19] that is, his ability to recover from failure and resume his loving relationship with Hashem. For that relationship is inviolate and benevolent.

The more we can inculcate our children with the knowledge that they are never alone and that Hashem has an immutable love for them, the higher will be their self-esteem and their ability to withstand societal pressures and disapproval.[20]

---

18. This ironic dichotomy, whereby the haughty are limited and the humble can avail themselves of Hashem's limitlessness, is dealt with by the Maharal in *Nesivos Olam, Nesiv HaTorah,* chapter 2.
19. It is interesting that the righteous are called a foundation, as it says, "And the *tzaddik* is the world's foundation" (*Mishlei* 10:25). The primary hallmark of a foundation is its stability.
20. I believe that the soul's immutable purity finds its expression in the fact that the soul's sojourn in *Gehinnom,* Hell, is limited, while the soul remains in *Gan Eden,* Heaven, forever. Just as when visiting a foreign country a person is limited to whatever visa he has, since he is not a citizen of that country and it is not his place, so too is the soul not a "citizen" of *Gehinnom,* but rather of *Gan Eden,* and therefore remains there forever.

🌹 Points to Remember

THE PURPOSE of parenthood can be defined as the preparation of a child for a successful life.

CHILDREN look outside of themselves for a model on which to pattern their behavior and attitudes.

LOVE for others is predicated upon love for oneself.

SELF-ESTEEM is a person's recognition of his or her innate, immutable goodness, based upon the fact that his or her soul was created by God and is forever tied to the Source of all goodness and purity.

PEOPLE who are truly strong are those who recognize that their strength is not rooted in their own abilities, but in their connectedness to Hashem.

TAKING care of your physical well-being is an expression of self-worth and is related to your service of Hashem.

LUXURIES are an expression of God's love for us.

PARENTS must be aware of, and appreciate, their child's strengths.

WHILE the school often measures "achievement" with an academic yardstick, the home is where the total person should be appreciated and valued for who he or she is.

WHEN I feel your love, I love you in return.

CHAPTER TWENTY

Sensitivity and Oversensitivity

Children are highly sensitive to all that goes on around them. People's words affect them intensely. Family atmosphere, positive or negative, is deeply felt. In addition, since their sense of self is not yet strong, they are vulnerable to disapproval and mockery from the dominant culture.

Let's discuss sensitivity, in general, before looking at what bearing it has upon children.

WHY PEOPLE TOLERATE PHYSICAL "SENSITIVITIES"

"At night it seems worse." This was the statement of a woman who, in a state of panic, faxed me from Los Angeles; by the time I called her the following day, she was considerably calmer. Had she been "just over sensitive"? Certainly not. Sometimes things hit us more at one time than another.

People understand and tolerate physical sensitivities. For example:

> *I remember the case of a boy from the Mirrer Yeshiva in Brooklyn, who easily could have been killed in a local hospital. One of the on-duty physicians was about to*

administer penicillin, when another doctor insisted on testing the patient for allergy first. The boy was highly allergic. No one would think of reprimanding the boy with, "You're just being too sensitive."

~

I've often been up late because I have had two cups of tea, and am sensitive to caffeine.

~

*Sensitivity works the other way as well. It has been found that Israeli soldiers need three times the dose of antibiotics that Egyptian soldiers do. Overuse has rendered the Israelis not sensitive **enough**.*

I think that the reason people are more tolerant of physical sensitivities is that they're not thought of as our "fault," while emotional sensitivities are seen as being under our control. Therefore we can be "blamed" for them.

What We Can and Cannot Do

To determine what is and is not under our control, we need to distinguish, first, between that which we can change and that which we have no power to change, and second, between what can be changed right now and what will have to wait.

Before starting on that process, however, there's one fact of life we would do well to recognize: *precious little can be done to change other people's perceptions or opinions,* at least in the short term. Sometimes we can change our own perceptions, and by doing so affect the perceptions of others, but almost always, change must begin from within ourselves, and this can often bring about change in others.

BEING SENSITIVE CAN ALSO BE POSITIVE

We began with the assumption that sensitivity is something to be dealt with, in other words, toned down, muted, or eliminated. This is not always warranted. The quality of relationships engaged in by sensitive people is often richer than those of the less sensitive. Such people often have a rare ability to attune themselves to others and to reach out, coming to know and understand people on a deeper level than is the norm.

> *Rav Chaim Shmuelevitz, zt"l, was noted not only for his great intellect, but also for his capacity to feel extreme emotion. Tears would come to his eyes when he saw a pair of infant shoes, imagining the happiness of the mother when her child takes his first steps.*

> *Mori VeRabi, zt"l, once broke down crying with emotion when he attended a celebration marking the completion of the study of Sefer HaChinuch by a group of students from Yeshivas Aish HaTorah. He was a powerful man, in control of his emotions and his ability to endure physical pain, but he gave free vent to his emotions when he deemed it right. It was my privilege to accompany him on his first visit to the Western Wall. On the road as we made our approach, he caught sight of the Dome and broke down sobbing.*

> *Rav Eliezer Ginsberg, shlita, rosh kollel of the Mirrer Yeshiva, tells that when Rav Elozor Shach, zt"l, was told that the general anesthetic that he would be receiving for a medical procedure would affect his ability to learn with a clear head for several days, he refused the anesthetic, even though it meant that he would need to be tied and held down during the operation. One of those present at the*

operation later related that Rav Shach did not utter a groan. But this same Rav Shach broke down sobbing upon hearing of the deaths of three Israeli soldiers, with whom he shared no direct connection of any sort.

But there is another kind of sensitivity, an oversensitivity that damages us and pulls us down. When it comes to our children, we need to help them deal with the fact that some people may make fun of them or may become angry with them. While they need to care about what other people might say or think, they cannot allow themselves to be drawn too quickly or deeply after the emotions of others. Children are also sensitive to what they see in their environment, such as anger or criticism directed at someone else. Last, but not least, they are sensitive to the input and influence of a dominant culture which may run counter to what we wish them to become as adults.

Where to Begin

The first step in any process of change is motivating yourself to begin. Were you more aware of how much there is to gain from modifying your sensitivities — thereby becoming less easily upset by others — you wouldn't be deterred by the difficulties involved in that process. Your desire for personal growth would make it all worthwhile.

This lack of motivation comes from two factors:

1. Progress is slow and irregular.

2. One must un-learn old habits and replace them with new ones.

Motivate yourself by looking around and seeing the benefits that accrue to those who seem to be in control of their sensitivities, and of their reactions to other people's behavior. Ask yourself what it might be like to have better relationships with those you love, with those with whom you're in frequent contact, and with whom you work and whose good will is something you dearly desire.

When it comes to getting yourself motivated, begin where it's easiest, and where the likelihood of success is greatest. Perhaps you can focus on one particular relationship that is troubling you, rather than setting out to change your sensitivities across the board. Measure your progress not in terms of totally eliminating the problem, but rather, of decreasing the frequency with which the problem occurs. You can even focus on controlling your sensitivities during a specific time of the day. Keep track of what happens and watch for a pattern to emerge, then take some quiet time to think it through, preparing yourself beforehand for those junctures at which things usually seem to go wrong.

WHERE PEOPLE ARE COMING FROM

We need to understand where people are coming from. When we misread people who cause us to overreact, it is often because we have mistakenly jumped to the conclusion that their behavior and feelings are directed against us. *If we see that the person manifests these attitudes and behaviors to everyone, then our "emotional temperature" goes down.*

> *Once when I was dealing with a man who was angry about his father-in-law's constant interference in his life, I was able to calm him down by showing him that this man was controlling with everybody, not just with him. In fact, the father-in-law had tried to control his daughter before she had even met her future husband.*

Developing Your Inner Self

The common denominator in all our responses is ourselves. When we can find quiet, stability and acceptance within ourselves, we become less vulnerable to whatever goes on around us. In other words, when we appreciate who we are and the goodness we have within us, we will be less sensitive to the non-acceptance or mockery of others.

Appreciating Who We Are and What We Possess

One of the primary functions of a Torah school today is to deal with the fact that the outside world mocks us, even as it beckons to our children. The only way we have of resisting that world is by giving ourselves and our children a healthy appreciation for who we are and the spiritual riches we possess.

> *Mori VeRabi, zt"l, once said, "The secular Jew gets enraged by a sign saying, 'No dogs or Jews allowed,' while I can pass by such a sign and not be disturbed in the slightest. Why is this so? Because the secular Jew feels that he is paying the price for being a Jew, but has no idea what he gains from it."*
>
> *Although blatant anti-Semitism such as this is, thank God, generally absent from modern Western society, the principle endures. As Mori VeRabi put it: The secular Jew is paying the price without getting the product.*

As with many other things in life, sometimes we must pay a price for what we have. What we have in this case is Torah and Jewish identity. If the price is not being admitted into a country club, so be it. Thinking in these terms will help us go far in eliminating feelings of anger and controlling our emotions.

Once when I was using my frequent flyer miles to go first class, the stewardess brought over the first class menu so I could see what I was missing, just to be sure.

Trust me, there was no pain over the fact that I couldn't order the bacon.

There is no escaping the fact that the only way to truly transcend the derision of others is to know that we are intrinsically worthy. Nothing else will really work.

There is, however, something that can help us while we're still in the process of attaining this lofty level, and it is to bear in mind that there are others — people whose opinion we value, such as our peers, our teachers, our rabbis and *rebbetzins* — who have recognized our intrinsic worth, and appreciate all that is noble in us, even as they recognize our deficiencies. We would do well to play back in our minds any recordings we may have of their remarks to us, and carry these thoughts with us. For those of us who are more visually inclined, we can call up the images of those who love and respect us.

Above all, the *Ribbono shel Olam* values and cherishes every Jew and Jewess. They are the beloved children of those who stood firmly and loyally by Him through thick and thin.

Turn to any page in the *siddur* and you will see the enormous love and connection we have with the Creator. *We are never alone.* There is always Someone up there cheering us on, showering us with love for withstanding tests that no other generation in Jewish history has ever had to endure.

Our children must know who they are. They must know how beloved they are to Hashem at all times, but especially when they must sustain their loyalty to Him in the face of ridicule, whether explicit or not.

❧ Points to Remember

CHILDREN are highly sensitive to all that goes on around them.

PRECIOUS little can be done to change other people's perceptions or opinions.

CHANGE must begin within ourselves.

WHEN we overreact, it is often because we have mistakenly jumped to the conclusion that the behavior and feelings of others are directed against us.

THE ONLY way to truly transcend the derision of others is to know that we are intrinsically worthy.

WHEN we find quiet, stability, and acceptance within ourselves, we become less vulnerable to whatever goes on around us.

PART FIVE

ENEMIES OF A HAPPY HOME

CHAPTER TWENTY-ONE

Sibling Rivalry

Sibling rivalry is one of the chief contributing factors to an unhealthy home atmosphere. It ranks high among the causes of discomfort and unhappiness at home, putting children at greater risk for getting drawn into the culture of the street.

While some level of sibling rivalry is normal, there are a number of things that need to be checked if the rivalry gets too intense, just as a doctor who finds several cases of pneumonia in a home will check the house for drafts. Some of the things to investigate are:

1. PARENTAL ATTENTION

Is parental attention in short supply? If it is, *or if the children think it is,* then they will compete with each other for parental attention. Most of the time, this is a competition for approval, but sometimes, a child who feels unnoticed will resort to misbehavior to get parental attention.

If there are five hundred students in a school, and they know that there are only 499 lunch portions in the cafeteria, there will be pushing on the way down to the dining hall. The odds are only

500 to one that any given student will lose his portion, but there will be pushing anyway. How much more so in the home, where parental love and approval are so urgently needed and the odds seem far greater that one will lose one's share of that positive attention. Then the "pushing" can get really serious, as the children jockey for position in the household hierarchy.

2. Selective Parental Approval

If parental approval is tied to some specific talent, achievement or trait, this sets the stage for many grave problems, and sibling rivalry may not be the worst of them. Parents court disaster if their approval is bestowed only upon certain types of behavior and achievement, or if approval isn't related to who the children are, but rather to the parents' own value system, or to their desire for social approval.

For some time each child will try to excel in the "approved" areas, but if one or more of them feels unsuccessful in this competition, he or she may "drop out of the race." Then there may be untold anguish in store for the family.

3. Differences: A Double-Edged Sword

As with many areas of life, differences between people can be a source of either love or hatred. Rav Tzadok says that Yehudah and Yosef had a centuries-long enmity because they were so different.[1]

---

1. This enmity began when Yehudah confronted Yosef over Binyamin (*Bereishis* 44:18) and culminated, centuries later, with the split in the Jewish kingdom whereby ten tribes followed Ephraim, Yosef's chief son, out of the kingdom headed by King David's descendants. See Rav Tzadok, *Ohr Zarua LaTzaddik*, pp. 28–9, where he shows that as a descendant of Leah, Yehudah's greatness lay in speech, while as a child of Rachel, Yosef's greatness lay in silence (see *Bereishis Rabbah* 71:5). In addition, Yosef's greatest moment was when he passed a test involving a woman, and both Yehudah and his descendant King David faltered when tested with women.

On the other hand, differences can be a source of love, for people who are different from each other can complement each other.[2]

Children need to be shown nonverbally that they are treasured, and that what they say means a lot to us. This is a crucial source of self-esteem and pleasure to the child. There is probably no greater source of anguish for a child than the realization that his parent is deeply disappointed in him.[3] This feeling, often unjustified, must never take root in the child's soul. If it does, then the child who feels unappreciated will try, among other things, to "bring down" his more-appreciated sibling. The stage is then set for arguments and bitterness between them.

4. Negative Attention-Getting

As stated, sometimes children will act out in order to gain parental attention. Sometimes a child is consciously bitter about what he perceives as his parents' lack of respect for him, and the tension caused by his interactions with his siblings is — to put it bluntly — revenge. In addition, dislike for a brother or sister may be rooted in his feeling that this sibling has stolen away parental love that was rightly his.

---

2. See *Sefas Emes*, in which it is stated that Yitzchak's wife needed to excel in *chessed*, kindness (as manifested by Rivkah's giving drinks to Eliezer and his camels), because Yitzchak himself embodied *din*, justice, which is the opposite ideal. Similarly, Sarah stood for *din*, while her husband Avraham was the personification of *chessed*. In a similar vein, Rav Aharon Kotler, zt"l, said that the reason Yaakov realized that Rachel was his intended was because she excelled in the trait of silence (as was later evinced when she remained quiet as her sister Leah stood under the marriage canopy with Yaakov), while he, Yaakov, was the pillar of Torah, which is the finest use of speech. They indeed complemented each other.
3. Mild disappointment, however, can sometimes be used as a means of conveying parental displeasure to a child.

5. Having a Child with Special Needs at Home

Sometimes the extra attention showered upon a particular child is not due to parental approval, but because the child has special needs. These may be a result of physical illness, a learning disability, or an emotional problem. While it is understandable that parents must devote disproportionately greater time to the needy child, there are things that can be done to alleviate the resulting problems with the other children. For instance, express sincere gratitude to your children for the help they extend in caring for their special-needs sibling. This should be done, when possible, individually. Consult them in the decisions you make regarding a younger sibling, remarking that their mature behavior encourages you to ask for their input. Do this, however, only when the situation allows for their input to be seriously considered. In addition, teachers should be informed of the child's help in the home and should be asked to praise him or her for it.[4]

It must be noted, however, that having a special-needs child at home can help siblings achieve remarkably good character and maturity, for they learn early on what it means to lovingly attend to the needs of another. As in many areas of life, problematic situations can create wonderful human beings.

Briefly stated, parents need to utilize the children and make them part of the caregiving effort. Their help should be:

- Of real value — not "busy work."
- Sincerely appreciated.
- Not desperately needed. If the parent is at a loss and cannot cope, household help or professional caregivers should be hired. *Children cannot feel pressed into work, for it will surely, sooner or later, backfire.*

---

[4]. What we have said here is also applicable when a new baby arrives in the home. The potential for jealousy is enormous: Here is a brand-new, completely needy, highly successful competitor for parental — especially maternal — attention.

Talking It Through

Again, just as in many other areas of life, there is inestimable value in talking things out openly and honestly. Children need to air their grievances without fear. (I refer the reader to the chapter on listening.)

Listening with an open ear and heart can be difficult, but it must be done.

Parents must arrive at a sure knowledge of their own worth, that they are good people even if they've made mistakes, and this self-confidence permits them to be clear-sighted about what is causing the sibling rivalry. Young as they are, children can be carrying around some extremely heavy baggage. Abnormally intense sibling rivalry is not created overnight and children may not have been able to articulate their feelings.

In a family with a special-needs child, speaking things out can, in a certain sense, be easier. Problems can be couched in technical terms, not emotional ones, and it's more straightforward that the child in question is in fact in greater need of attention, practically speaking. It is more self-evident that this does not mean that the other children are valued or loved less.

Yaakov and His Children

Yaakov, our paradigm of a successful parent,[5] understood that each child was different, and gave each of them a unique blessing.[6] When he was on his deathbed, his children exclaimed, "Hear, O

---

5. See Part 7, chapter 31.
6. *Bereishis* 49:28. See also verses 3–27. Even Reuven, Shimon and Levi received a blessing. It was important for Reuven to realize that he couldn't be the leader (see *Sefas Emes, Bereishis*, p. 171, paragraph beginning *"BaPasuk ha-yeled,"* in which he sees that Yosef is no longer in the pit, and exclaims, "What will become of me?" for he realizes that his success in life is tied up in Yosef's leadership). The tribes of

Israel, Hashem our God is One!" What united these different personalities was One God.[7]

This, at the end of the day, is the only real resolution for sibling rivalry. Children often quarrel, sometimes fiercely, but when each one is treasured for who he is, and open communication keeps that awareness uppermost in everyone's minds, then sibling rivalry, at least in its pathological form, will not make your home an unhappy place. Again, a happy home is the best defense against destructive influences from the outside.

Shimon and Levi were not given their share in the Land of Israel, and were therefore scattered among the other tribes; for a person who has a temper is healed when he is exiled, and therefore compelled to become the guest of others (Rav Avigdor Miller, zt"l). See *Tzidkas HaTzaddik*, section 80.

7. This was one of the functions of the thrice-yearly pilgrimage to Jerusalem, which was to serve as a reminder to the Tribes that even though they were different, they were still united by One God. Differences can be a source of anger and hatred, or they can be a source of love and unity.

❧ EXERCISES

1. With your spouse, make a list of the positive, valuable character traits that each of your children have, taking care to find at least one trait which is uniquely that child's.

2. See how that trait can find expression and recognition in the home.

3. Plan individual time with each child, at least once every two weeks. The child's preference for inside the home or outside should be respected, whenever possible. This time should be pleasant bonding time, not a "working vacation."

4. Plan a project in which two or more of the siblings can work together, each one being able to contribute something that reflects his or her specific strengths.

❧ Points to Remember

Some level of sibling rivalry is normal.

If parental attention is in short supply, or if the children think it is, then they will compete with each other for it.

Listening with an open ear and heart can be difficult, but it must be done.

A happy home is the best defense against destructive influences from the outside.

CHAPTER TWENTY-TWO

Criticalness

We often encounter people who are critical of themselves. This tendency is often at the root of an inability to accept oneself. Though we are discussing child-rearing, it is an inescapable fact that people who are overly self-critical will be overly critical of their children, often with disastrous results. A few thoughts on how parents can deal with their own self-criticalness is vital for the creation of a happy home environment for children.

If I'm self-critical, then what I notice about myself is what I'm doing wrong, or incompletely, or too slowly, or any number of other negative ways of viewing behavior. It is hard to accept myself when I'm constantly noticing my inadequacies.

There is no question that the ability to criticize oneself is also at the root of many wonderful accomplishments, just as the ability to accept criticism from others is a crucial factor in character growth, and in the honing and perfecting of one's accomplishments. What I'm referring to here, then, is the kind of self-criticalness which causes unhappiness with oneself and effectively prevents a person from accomplishing.

An understanding of the roots of criticalness and self-criticalness is important. We will now be examining some of them.

Noticing Details

At the root of negative criticalness is the ability to notice the imperfections in a person or situation. The critically inclined individual then attaches so much importance to these imperfections that they cloud the happiness or satisfaction to be had from what may be, overall, a generally positive picture.[1]

Noticing What's Right As Well As What's Wrong

It is extremely difficult to change a character trait. Rav Yisroel Salanter is said to have declared that it is easier to complete the study of the entire Talmud than to change one character trait. When seeking to change, even to a modest degree, some tendency rooted in a person's essential character or habitual behavior, one basic rule must be heeded: *It is far better to rechannel a well-*

---

1. The word for criticism in modern Hebrew is *bikoret*. This seems to be derived from the same word in the Torah (*Vayikra* 19:20) meaning "investigation," the attention paid to small details. The Ramban (*Bereishis* 1:5) says that the word for "morning" in Hebrew, *boker,* is related to the ability to pick out details which were unperceived during the night. The Ramban says that *erev*, evening, refers to the mixing (in Hebrew, *eeruv*) of objects, and their becoming progressively more of one mixed mass, due to lack of light. See the Ramban, ibid., and the *mishnah* in tractate *Berachos* (1:2) in which daytime is measured by the ability to distinguish between various colors. Rav Yitzchok Hutner, *zt"l*, tells us (*Igros Pachad Yitzchok*, Letter #33) that to visit the sick, *bikur cholim*, really means to investigate the sick, i.e., to see what they lack.
2. Based on the verse in *Tehillim* 34:15 and 37:27, *sur me-ra ve'asei tov,* turn away from evil and do good. This interpretation tells us that the best way to turn away from evil is to be involved in doing good. This concept can be found in many Torah sources. An expression of this idea can be found in *Mishnas Rav Aharon*, vol. 1, the chapter entitled *Banim Atem LaShem Elokeichem*, in which he writes, "And every person is obligated to introspect and to recognize the greatness within himself …and this (recognition) is the greatest of all causative factors in enabling a person to correct himself."

ingrained negative trait or habit into some positive action, than to try to repress it. I sum up this rule for my students with the phrase, "The best *sur me-ra* ('turning from evil') is an *asei tov* ('doing good')."[2]

What this means is that *if a person has already habituated himself to noticing negative details,*[3] *he should now habituate himself to noticing positive details also.*

I am reminded of a story that puts this idea into proper focus:

> *A parent consulted me concerning his young child who came home every day with complaints about his rebbe. I advised the parent that he should continue to hear his child out, provided that for each complaint the child had against his rebbe, he would also find something good the rebbe had done that day. After several days, the complaining stopped, as the child realized that his rebbe, like everyone else, had good points as well as bad ones.*

Similarly, whenever a person finds something negative about himself, he should immediately think of something about himself in which he can take pride. It is important that this become a habit, for when a person feels emotionally low, it is difficult to see the positive, especially in oneself. A habit enables us to "go on automatic pilot," and do something even when we lack the psychic energy for it.

---

3. This is basic human nature. The Vilna Gaon, commenting on the Gemara in *Berachos* 8a, stresses this. He notes that there are two verses in the Written Law referring to wives, one describing the good wife and the other the evil wife. In the verse mentioning the good wife, the past tense is used מצא — "He who has found a (good) wife found good" (*Mishlei* 18:22). On the other hand, the evil wife is described in the present tense — מוצא, "I find the woman more bitter than death" (*Koheles* 7:26). According to the Vilna Gaon, this is because a person takes good fortune for granted, not realizing how much it is a part of his present, yet never ceases to complain about his present ill fortune. See *Beis HaLevi, Shemos* 3:7, the section beginning *"Ra'ah raisi,"* where the same concept is expressed.
4. *Duties of the Heart,* the immortal medieval work delineating the duties that a Jew has in his service of Hashem. Written by Rabbeinu Bachya ibn Pekuda (ca. 1080).

The *Chovos HaLevovos*[4] expresses this beautifully:

> *A tzaddik was once walking with Eliyahu HaNavi when they passed a carcass. The tzaddik held his nose, commenting on the stench. Eliyahu commented, "But look at how white its teeth are!"*[5]

To sum up, a critical person who has the tendency to notice details shouldn't attempt to repress the habit. Instead, he can develop a habit of noticing what is right in addition to what is wrong.

There is another factor that may cause a person to be too self-critical. When a person bases his self-worth on a specific accomplishment or array of accomplishments, he sets himself up for a situation where, should he not accomplish as much as he would like to in this area or areas, he will begin to put himself down. This is especially true if the society in which he lives also attaches worth to these particular accomplishments. This is a common phenomenon, and must be addressed as follows:

Who I Am Is Distinct from What I Accomplish

As stated, we live in a world in which people measure themselves and others in terms of their "accomplishments," whether this has to do with career success or material attainments. Precious little recognition is granted to the person who, by dint of years of labor, has perfected his or her inner world, and who has polished and refined his or her own personality. This labor may have consisted of building upon the positive character traits endowed upon him by way of genetic inheritance, or parental training, or early environmental influences. It may have involved the gradual erasure and rechanneling of the negative energy generated by negative character traits.

---

5. Gate Six, *Sha'ar HaKeniah* (The Gate of Submission), chapter 6.

In any case, I think the reason for humanity's lack of appreciation for such labor is twofold. The first is that this person's exertions are unseen; Hashem is the only One Who perceives this person's toil, his fellowman being unaware and incapable of evaluating the years and decades of effort that went into refining his character.[6] The second is that we live in an era of superficiality. What is easily seen is given credence, while the more meaningful, less visible, achievements go undervalued.

The Torah, however, gives enormous credit to these private "victories of the soul." As we will soon explain, several aspects of Torah become clearer when we know that there exist these two realms of accomplishment: the external and visible, and the internal and invisible. The latter bears fruit of the soul, even when there are no "worldly" accomplishments one can point to.

Your Greatest Weakness Is the Area of Your Greatest Success

Using this concept, that our toil in perfecting ourselves is the highest measure of success, we can understand the words of Rav Tzadok HaKohen:[7] Where your greatest weaknesses lie, therein lies, as well, your greatest opportunity for perfection. This concept can be understood in several ways, and one of them is certainly this: For each "small" victory brought about with much spiritual toil in the area of a person's greatest weakness, the reward for success is proportionately greater.

---

6. As it is written (*I Shemuel* 16:7), "For man sees with his eyes [i.e., superficially] and Hashem sees the heart."
7. Rav Tzadok writes that in the place where a person has fallen, and in the area where the *yetzer ha-ra* strikes him the hardest, in that very area does the potential for his greatest success lie. See *Tzidkas HaTzaddik*, section 70, where he writes that when something is hard for a person, whether on account of his nature or because he has sinned in that area, the reward for his struggles is the greatest.

The Two Reasons for Reward

These two forms of spiritual victory, accomplishment and toil, are reflected in the two reasons that Hashem rewards someone:

1. **Spiritual accomplishment.** The *Sifri*[8] tells us that if a person loses money and a poor man finds it, then the loser is rewarded. A person is rewarded (and punished) for the results of his actions.

2. **Spiritual labor.** "According to the pain, so is the reward."[9] Hashem rewards us for our labor, for it is this labor that demonstrates our love for and loyalty toward Him. The reward is closeness to Hashem, measure for measure: To the extent that we want to be close to Hashem and serve Him, He rewards us by bringing us closer.[10]

Rewarding Children

It seems to me that rewards for children should be based more on their efforts than on their accomplishments. Children have dif-

---

8. Mentioned in Rashi, *Devarim* 24:19. The *Chovos HaLevovos* tells us, in the sixth chapter of *Sha'ar Avodas Hashem* (The Gate of Love of God), that when someone works for the community by instructing others in the proper service of Hashem, his reward is greater than what he could have accomplished by himself. In this case, we see the results of his outward actions, teaching others, being given greater weight than his internal struggles.
9. *Pirkei Avos* 5:23.
10. See Rav Dessler, *Michtav Me'Eliyahu*, vol. 3, pp. 13–21, in which he states that the ability of a person to understand and derive pleasure from the Divine Presence and wisdom in the World to Come is commensurate with the amount of his toil. A genius who never had to toil hard with his mind in this world may well be a dunce in the Next World, while someone of weak intelligence, who toiled hard in this world with the intellect he was granted, may be a genius in the next. For this reason, in the *berachah* upon Torah study, we ask *la'asok*, to become engrossed, in the words of Torah. The legendary Chazon Ish (1878–1953) also writes in his Letters (#2) that all the benefits of Torah study are related to the degree of toil. In this vein, Rav Dessler explains (*Michtav Me'Eliyahu*, vol. 2, p. 205), that the greatness of Yitzchak was that he laboriously created a new approach to serving Hashem, rather than taking the easier path of following in his illustrious father Avraham's footsteps.

ferent capabilities, and it is common for one child to succeed more easily in a particular area than does his sibling or peer. Recognition based on too narrow a definition of accomplishment will eventually lead a child to feel less loved and appreciated by his parents. Such circumstances have set the stage for countless tragic situations. Sometimes parents have lost their children altogether.

WHO YOU ARE — THE TWO FACTORS

The Telsher Rosh Yeshiva, Rav Yosef Leib Bloch, *zt"l*,[11] explains a famous story in the Gemara:

> *Rabbi Chanina ben Dosa, one of the pious giants of the Tannaic period [10–200 CE], came to learn Torah from Rabbi Yochanan ben Zakkai, the recognized Torah giant and leader of his generation. Rabbi Yochanan's child took deathly ill, and Rabbi Yochanan requested from Rabbi Chanina that he pray for his son's recovery.*
>
> *Rabbi Chanina's prayers were answered. Rabbi Yochanan commented that his own prayers would have proved ineffective. To his wife's wondering response, he replied: "Chanina is like a servant before the King, while I am as a minister before the King."*[12]

There are two forms of greatness, said Rav Bloch: One is that of the "minister," and the other, of the "servant."

The minister facilitates the king's rulership, by helping to execute those laws that the king promulgates. The servant, on the other hand, serves the king on a more personal level. He washes the

---

11. 1860–1929, the author of the monumental work *Shiurei Da'as*, and one of the twentieth century's great thinkers and educators. See *Shiurei Da'as*, "Chayim."
12. *Berachos* 34b.

king's feet, brings him his tea the way he likes it, hands him his royal garments each morning, and so forth.

In the above analogy, Rabbi Yochanan ben Zakkai referred to himself as the "minister." He was a great scholar, teacher, and disseminator of Torah, whose command of Torah was such that it was he who was responsible for the Oral Law's safe transmission to the next generation. He was not close enough to the King, however, to submit personal requests.

The "servant" is Rabbi Chanina ben Dosa, who put all his spiritual energy into *transforming himself into a person dedicated to doing the King's will,* in all areas of his life. His knowledge did not equal that of his teacher, Rabbi Yochanan ben Zakkai, yet he was lovingly referred to by Hashem as "My son."[13]

---

13. Ibid. Rabbi Yochanan ben Zakkai was "a minister before the King," the greatest disseminator of Torah in his generation, while Rabbi Chanina ben Dosa, although a student of Rabbi Yochanan ben Zakkai in Torah learning, had purified his inner world so perfectly that he was close to Hashem, and could ask for Hashem's grace on a more intimate level. He was close to Hashem ("a servant before the king") by dint of the degree of his personal toil and true service of Hashem, service whose magnitude and depth was not seen, and certainly not appreciated, by anyone other than the Creator Himself.
The Ozhrover, Rav Moshe Epstein, *zt"l* (1890–1971), one of the great Chassidic *Geonim* and *tzaddikim* of our times, writes in *Be'er Moshe, Bemidbar,* pp. 205–6, that this is what is meant when it says: "against My servant Moshe" (*Bemidbar* 12:8). Moshe was great, both as a minister of Hashem ("Moshe"), and as His servant ("My servant"). Moshe had both forms of greatness, that of the servant to Hashem, like Rabbi Chanina ben Dosa, and that of the minister, like Rabbi Yochanan ben Zakkai.
This difference between a servant and a minister, as far as approaching a king is concerned, is related eloquently by Rav Yaakov Lifshitz in his classic history of Eastern European Jewry, *Zichron Yaakov.* The Rabbis, seeing they were unable to nullify an anti-Semitic decree of the Czar, bribed the Czarina's hairdresser to convince the Czarina to speak to her husband about nullifying the proposed legislation. A hairdresser can often speak to the queen about matters that an official member of the government cannot.

Rav Yitzchok Hutner, *zt"l,* said[14] that "prince" and "servant" are two factors which determine a person's level in Hashem's eyes:

1. **The level of a person's knowledge, understanding, and accomplishments,** regardless of whether these things result from his inherited native intelligence, his own intellectual and spiritual labor, or his upbringing ("prince").

2. **The tests that a person undergoes,** and his or her internal struggle to achieve closeness to Hashem ("servant").

We may conclude from all of the above that more than knowledge or external achievement, it is the internal struggle to perfect oneself, and to transform oneself into a servant of Hashem, that creates closeness to Him.

How We View Ourselves

We can now learn to appreciate ourselves in a new light.

The degree of honest effort we invest in something, *regardless of the fruitfulness of our efforts,* is in itself an accurate measure of our genuine success in Hashem's eyes. Just as a person can take justifiable pride in all the measurable accomplishments that Hashem has helped him or her achieve, so, too, should a person derive pleasure simply from the *effort* he has invested in any worthwhile undertaking — whether it be trying to perfect his internal world or trying to constructively help those around him.

While it is true that we should not be blind to our shortcomings, we likewise should not fail to recognize, *and derive pleasure from,* either our inborn traits and capabilities, or our acquired ones. The more prone we are to notice every small defect from which we

---

14. When talking about the greatness of Rav Aharon Kotler, *zt"l,* who possessed both forms of greatness.

may suffer, the more must we balance this criticalness with recognition of each and every small gem in our crown. To quote the immortal Rav Yeruchem Levovitz, *zt"l*:

> *Woe to him who does not recognize his faults, but a double woe to him who does not recognize his good qualities, for he then has failed to recognize his tools.*[15]

Self-acceptance is the foundation of good self-esteem, and a healthy self-esteem is the foundation of our ability to care, cope and communicate. These three elements are the building blocks of a happy and successful life, whether in a relationship between man and man, man and God, or man and himself.

It is in this spirit of valuing our own efforts and accomplishments that we can now consider how we view our children, why we are critical of them, and how to develop a happy atmosphere at home.

---

15. *Alei Shur*, p.169.

❧ POINTS TO REMEMBER

WHERE your greatest weaknesses lie, therein lie your greatest opportunities for perfection.

PEOPLE who are overly self-critical will be overly critical of their children, often with disastrous results.

IT IS FAR better to rechannel a well-ingrained trait or habit into some positive action, than to try to repress it.

A CRITICAL person can develop a habit of noticing what is right in addition to what is wrong.

THE TORAH gives enormous credit to private "victories of the soul."

REWARDS for children should be based more on their efforts than on their accomplishments.

TO THE EXTENT that we want to be close to Hashem and serve Him, He rewards us by bringing us closer.

CHAPTER TWENTY-THREE

Successful, and Unsuccessful, Criticism

An ongoing atmosphere of criticalness creates an unhappy home. Many parents, for various reasons, deem it right to find fault with their children. This faultfinding can be expressed over the child's academic record, his mannerisms, his friends, and the untidiness of his room, etc. The list can be endless.

There is no question that parents need to carefully examine their children's actions and correct them. In this chapter, *b'ezras Hashem*, we will distinguish, however, between destructive criticism and criticism that can build a person.

First, however, we must take a careful look at why parents criticize, even when their own personal experience has amply proven that it almost never works. There seems to be something within people that almost compels them to criticize their children. This phenomenon calls for careful examination, since a flawed mindset must be corrected before any suggestions can be implemented.

WHY PARENTS CRITICIZE

There are several reasons why parents criticize their children.

1. To Help Their Children Succeed in Life. Parents often consider it an obligation to criticize their children. The feeling is, "How else will they grow up to be *menschen*?" Parents feel that their role and purpose is to make sure their kids do things the right way so that their lives will turn out well. It is criticism dealt out for the child's sake.

It is usually young parents, who have less perspective (and more energy), who make this mistake. What for more experienced parents seems to be a minor matter, or a "stage," looms large for the less experienced. To them, their five-year old looks so old compared with his two younger siblings, and they thus hold him to inappropriately high standards of behavior and performance. As stated earlier, it is often the firstborn who get this kind of criticism.

2. The Two Dangerous Assumptions. Let's examine the two assumptions behind this mind-set:

"If I tell them what they're doing wrong, then they'll do it right and things will get better."

"They won't grow up to be menschen otherwise."

Both assumptions are patently false. There's much more to successful criticism than just "telling it like it is." And the idea that a child won't grow up to be a *mensch* without ongoing criticism implies that he won't make it without having it constantly pointed out to him where he's going wrong.

The truth is, these assumptions are not only false, they're downright dangerous.

"Telling it like it is" is more likely to turn a person off than to help him. Properly directed criticism is indeed one facet of education, but it must be done in such a way that it produces positive changes. If the child is showing resentment or sulking, that's an indication that the criticism is hurtful, not helpful.

The assumption that my child is intrinsically incapable of succeeding unless I carefully and constantly monitor and correct him sends a dangerous message. Children (especially younger ones, but it's true for all ages) respect and take on many of their parents' attitudes, including the parents' view of who they, the children, are. If there is a sense, even unspoken, that the child is essentially *not good*, the child will pick up on this. This will lead, eventually, to either poor self-image or rebellion. *Parents must see their child in a positive, good light — always.*

3. Parents See Their Child's Failures as a Reflection of Their Own. Parents often fail to differentiate between their children's successes and failures and their own. It's the old "my son the doctor" syndrome again. The idea is that if my son is a success, then so am I. Similarly, many parents who view themselves as less than successful want to make sure that their children, at least, will live "better" lives.

This mind-set makes parents overanxious about every success or failure their child experiences, and criticism and correction are sure to become his regular fare.

4. Perfectionist Parents. Sometimes parents are perfectionists, and feel that it is their children's job to deliver the perfection. When a child comes home with a 90 on a test, the question is asked, "Why did you get that one wrong?"

Such parents usually expect perfection of themselves (whether or not they satisfy their own expectations), and this attitude is either verbally or nonverbally projected, and passed on, to the child.

I define a perfectionist as someone who can't separate *how well am I doing?* from *how good am I?* The feeling is: *I'm only as good as my performance. My accomplishments, or lack thereof, define my value as a person.*

Although Torah Judaism teaches that we should strive for perfection, it also recognizes that we'll never get there. As the *Sefas Emes* says,[1] quoting the verse, *"Ein tzaddik ba'aretz asher ya'aseh tov velo yecheta,"*[2] "There is no righteous person who can only **do** good without any error." In this world, the world of action, it is impossible to be perfect. Perfection exists only in the World of the Mind *(Olam HaMachashavah)*. It is what we strive for. We should indeed desire perfection, but according to Judaism, perfection is only a point of reference, a yardstick by which to measure our progress.

A perfectionist, one who is unable to separate his attitude toward himself from how well he does, never considers himself as being essentially good. There are always those imperfections to focus on and make him feel unworthy.

> *I was once in a car with Rav Zelig Pliskin, shlita, and I remarked that, except for snowflakes, nothing is perfect in this world. His response was, "Snowflakes aren't perfect, either. They melt quickly."*
>
> *(That is, I would add, except for at the North Pole, where there are many other things to be unhappy about.)*

Rav Pliskin was teaching me that *nothing* in the world is perfect — even perfectly formed, exquisite snowflakes.

REBUKE — EVEN A HUNDRED TIMES

The Torah does enjoin us to criticize others when we see them doing something wrong. In fact, our Sages teach us that the verse, *"Hoche'ach tochi'ach es amisecha,"*[3] "You shall surely rebuke your companion," carries with it the implication that we must reiterate

---

1. *Shemos*, p. 26, paragraph beginning *"Vayedabber Elokim."*
2. *Koheles* 7:20.
3. *Vayikra* 19:17.

our criticism even a hundred times.[4] This, however, is contingent upon its being done in such a way that no embarrassment occurs as a result, and that it is not done for the sake of "telling him off."[5]

At the same time, rebuke must be expressed only when there is a chance it will be accepted. If there is a good chance of its being scorned, the rebuke should be withheld.[6]

It is essential that parents recognize, *and internalize,* the principles of successful criticism and rebuke. Otherwise, their criticism will be counterproductive, and certainly won't constitute a mitzvah.

SUCCESSFUL CRITICISM

A parent must always remember the elements of successful criticism. They are:

1. Building — *beforehand* — the right relationship with the person being criticized.
2. Finding the right time.
3. Using the right nonverbal messages.
4. Giving useful advice about correction.
5. Never criticizing in public.
6. No labeling.
7. Ending up positively.

Each of these points deserves a brief explanation.

---

4. *Bava Metzia* 31a.
5. See Rashi, *Vayikra* 19:17.
6. *Yevamos* 65b. This is not necessarily a contradiction to saying it even a hundred times (which would indicate that the person isn't willing to hear), since as long as the rebuke is accepted, even if it needs repeating a hundred times, it is not falling on deaf ears. See *Chochmah U'Mussar,* vol. 1, *ma'amar* 87.

1. **Building the Right Relationship Beforehand.** Rabbeinu Yonah[7] points out that one of the functions of a true friend is to give criticism. *This means that in order to criticize someone you must first establish yourself as a friend.*

This idea is an example of the principle that *we must invest in a relationship beforehand in order to weather problems that may develop in that relationship later on.* This is true in regard to husband and wife, student and teacher, employer and employee, and parent and child. Most children are not mature enough to understand that criticism and rebuke can be a sign of caring, love, and a sincere desire for the person being rebuked to have a good life. Love must be securely in place if the rebuke is to have the desired effect, without straining the relationship. As stated, we must take the time and make the effort to develop the kind of relationship with our children that fosters effective communication, even when that communication is less than pleasant.

People often fail to look ahead. They don't take the time and trouble to establish the kind of relationship we are speaking of, one that can not only weather criticism, but will, indeed, prosper from it. In such a relationship, criticism is an additional sign of love and caring.

2. **Finding the Right Time.** When a child has just had a disappointing day, or is troubled by some mistake he has made, be careful to avoid criticism. At such moments, he's too vulnerable. Even if your words strike home, they are bound to leave a scar. It is much more important to be there for your child when he's down, and to empathize, than to seize this propitious moment to make a point. This is so even though the time may seem to you so tantalizingly opportune.

---

7. d. 1263. Rav Mattisyahu Solomon, *shlita*, *mashgiach* of Beis Medrash Govoha in Lakewood, NJ, commenting upon the law that when a person hits you as a result of your rebuke, you are absolved from further criticism, says that Rav Yaakov Kamenetsky, *zt"l*, interprets the violence as a sign that the person you are rebuking does not consider you to be a friend. Only a friend can give rebuke.

Does he view you as being with him? In the long run, the way he experiences you in relation to him is far more important than your being right. As the saying goes, you can be right — dead right. You can play an irreplaceable role in your child's life by giving him or her a secure, loving relationship. This is what will help him identify with you and your ideals. As my brother Michael said when our father, of blessed memory, passed away, "Fathers are one to a customer."

When, indeed, is the right time to make a point? The right moment will come along naturally when the relationship is close and accepting. Then, using empathy (see below), we'll make far better headway than by being "right" a million times over. Remember, a child's emotional component is far greater than his intellectual one. A message of love will have greater impact than his message about what's right and who's wrong.

3. **Using the Right Nonverbal Messages.** We have noted that since they are dominated by their emotions, children react more deeply and totally than adults to the nonverbal components of speech. These are tone of voice, facial expression, and how sincere we are about what we're saying. Touch is also a powerful nonverbal message that can sometimes be used together with words, provided the parent–child connection allows for it.

4. **Giving Corrective Advice.** The Vilna Gaon[8] tells us that when advice is given along with rebuke, it's a sign that it is being given with love. Advice, when suited well to the recipient, conveys the message that the rebuker wishes to help his friend improve and achieve greater success in life, and that the rebuke is not just a way to tear the person down.

Try to find some positive, practical ways of helping your child improve and to avoid repeating his mistakes. This is the nonverbal message: your intention is not to rebuke, but to correct.

---

8. *Mishlei* 1:25, 24:26.

5. Not in Public. The Gemara[9] points out that Yeravam ben Nevat merited royalty because he rebuked Shlomo HaMelech (King Solomon), but that he lost his share in the World to Come because he did so in public.

Children, like all of us, are sensitive to being rebuked in public. If they are emotionally healthy, they will feel stung by such assaults to their dignity and self-image. Simply in order to save face, they will refuse to acknowledge the correctness of the rebuke, and will often become defiant. This is a corollary of our saying that a child "would rather die than lose."

6. Don't Label. Similarly, in order to preserve the child's dignity, don't label him. He isn't a liar, a thief, a failure. Such words can be self-fulfilling prophecies. When we label a child, we convey to him that *this is who you are; you're not going to change.* If only our children would take our praise as seriously as they take our labeling![10]

Labels are catch-alls, and in this way they affect the child's emotional side. It is the nature of emotion to perceive totalities — things are either black or white. The intellect, on the other hand, can distinguish between the person and his many different deeds.

Misconduct must be considered a technical matter, not as something that reflects upon the person as a whole. The essence of the person is

---

9. *Sanhedrin* 101b.
10. See the introduction to *Chovos HaTalmidim*, the master work of Rav Klonimus Kalman Shapiro, *hy"d* (d. 1943), in which he quotes the holy Shlah's (1560–1630) explanation of the verse, "Do not reprove the mocker, lest he hate you; reprove the wise man, and he will love you" (*Mishlei* 9:8): "When you are about to reprove someone, do not denigrate him by calling him a mocker, for then he will hate you and not heed you. Rather, 'Reprove the wise man,' saying to him, 'aren't you wise? Why should you behave this way?' Then 'he will love you' and heed you." See also *HaBayis HaYehudi*, p. 449: "When you reprimand a child for some misbehavior, do not label him negatively. Do not say to him, for example, 'You are a thief' or 'you are lazy,' etc."

immutably good. "The soul that You have placed in me is pure,"[11] is one of the basic tenets of Judaism, and should never be forgotten.

7. Ending Positively. The way something ends up is usually the way it is remembered most distinctly, so finish up any rebuke on a positive note. This can be a sincere statement that you're sure there will be now be improvement, or an affirmation of the many good things the child does and the wonderful traits he possesses. It can mean, after delivering your rebuke, that you'll be turning your shared attention to something positive. For example, the child can be brought into the decision-making process in regard to something important or happy (such as an upcoming birthday party for himself or a sibling, or plans for a family trip). This is a nonverbal message that life goes on, and that he is always regarded with love and respect.

To sum up, while it is necessary sometimes to give rebuke or to criticize, much preparation is necessary to ensure that it will not harm the relationship. This can only be accomplished if parents have the foresight to build that relationship beforehand. *It is also vital to give the rebuke in a manner that preserves the essential self-worth of the child.* Remember that the action is being criticized — not the person.[12]

USE REBUKE SPARINGLY

It goes without saying that rebuke, like punishment, should be used sparingly. As we have stated elsewhere, rebuke and punishment are like antibiotics: The more you use them the more their

---

11. From the morning prayers.
12. It is interesting to note that Moshe is not rebuked for telling his people, "You have been rebellious with Hashem (*Devarim* 9:24)," for it was a description of what they had done. On the other hand, when he *labeled* them, "Hear, please, you rebellious ones" (*Bemidbar* 20:10), he lost his right, according to some opinions, to enter the Land of Israel. See *Midrashei HaTorah, parashas Chukas* (*Bemidbar* 20:10).

effectiveness wanes, and the higher the required dosage. *Catch children doing things right, and praise them for it sincerely and often.* Do not forget to consistently notice, as well, their good traits as well as their good actions. When your children realize how much you see the good, then they will be better able to hear you whenever you find the need to rebuke them.

❧ Exercises

1. Ask your spouse or a good friend if they consider you a critical person.

2. Find a pattern. What are you critical about?

3. Is there a time of day or the week when you tend to be more critical?

4. Practice, with your spouse or friend, ways of saying things that don't sound as if you're upset with the person, but rather, that you only seek a change in the behavior.

5. If you must point out something negative, mention something positive as well. In other words, make sure to find something to praise before and after expressing criticism. (Bear in mind, however, that if you only give praise when it's accompanied by rebukes, others will start getting wary of your praises.)

🌹Points to Remember

PARENTS must see their child in a positive light — always.

A PERFECTIONIST is unable to separate his attitude toward himself from how well he does, and thus never considers himself as being essentially good.

MISCONDUCT must be considered a technical matter, not as something that reflects upon the person as a whole.

IN ORDER to criticize someone, you must first establish yourself as a friend.

FINISH up any rebuke on a positive note.

CATCH children doing things right, and praise them for it, sincerely and often.

CHAPTER TWENTY-FOUR

Confrontations: Where There Are No Winners

A Child Would Rather Die than Lose

Parents often complain that their children have "chutzpah," that they don't obey, that they have no respect for their parents' instructions and are all too vocal about their opposition to following orders.

The complaint is also heard: "I've got to scream at them before they do what I say!" Of course, the reason for this is that the parent is willing to scream in order to ensure compliance with his orders. The child in such a home learns that "all's well" until a certain decibel is reached. Then, and only then, need he (reluctantly) comply.

The same goes for parents who repeat instructions many times, then complain, "I've got to say it ten times before he listens!" Their child has learned that up until the tenth time, he doesn't have to take the order seriously.

Too many parents feel forced into yelling, and other forms of intimidation, to get their children to obey. Yelling, constant repetition, chutzpah — these are some of the characteristics of a confrontational home atmosphere.

What role should confrontation have as a way of getting things done in the home?

Before addressing the above question, I would like to give an earthy, but accurate, definition of a child. *A child is someone who would rather die than lose.* What does this mean, and why is it so? And how does it relate to our discussion about confrontations?

WHO ARE WE, ANYWAY?

It's necessary for the understanding of this subject to mention the following life principle: *Only an internal definition of self, unrelated to our surroundings, can be a true barometer of who we really are.*

The Maharal[1] teaches that we cannot measure a person by comparing him to anything external. Wealth, strength, and wisdom are not measured by how much money a person has, how big his muscles are, or how much he knows, for all of this is relative to his surroundings. A middle-income American tourist in Uganda may be perceived as being fabulously wealthy. In a kindergarten, any adult appears big and strong. Amongst the ignorant, anyone with a little learning is considered a scholar.

It is for this reason, the Maharal tells us, that the *mishnah* in *Pirkei Avos* uses self-based definitions of strength, wealth and wisdom. Strength is measured by our ability to conquer ourselves, that is, to control those negative traits and attitudes that wreak havoc with our lives. Wealth is relative to how happy we are with our lot. Wisdom is personified by the individual who loves wisdom so much that he seeks to learn from everyone, even those who are supposedly his juniors in knowledge and in the understanding of life.

---

1. See his commentary on *Pirkei Avos* 4:1.

Self-Worth and a Sense of Security

The same idea, that who I am is based entirely on what my inner world is, applies as well to self-worth.

The Mishnah teaches, "Who is honored? He who honors others."[2] Those who possess a secure inner feeling of self-worth can freely honor others without fearing that their own honor will thereby be diminished. The Telsher Rosh Yeshiva, Rav Yosef Leib Bloch, *zt"l*, teaches this principle with the following beautiful example:

> *When someone arrives late for a meeting and all the available chairs are taken, who is most likely to give up his chair for the newcomer? Certainly the most distinguished one, for he feels secure and at ease. The others worry that they might seem less important or distinguished than the newcomer if they give up their seats for him.*[3]

This concept is taken to its ultimate conclusion with this statement of our Sages: "Whenever we see (i.e., in the Scriptures) the greatness of *HaKadosh Baruch Hu*, we find also (verses that refer to) His humility."[4]

What this means is that the essential sign of Hashem's *innate* greatness is the fact the He is humble. Not only does this not detract from His greatness, it *reveals* His greatness.[5]

"Winning" and "Losing"

Now we can return to our discussion about children and confrontations.

---

2. *Pirkei Avos* 4:1.
3. *Shiurei Da'as*, "Meluchah."
4. *Megillah* 31a.
5. See Maharal, *Nesivos Olam, Nesiv HaAnavah*, chapter 1; and *Ma'archei Lev*, by the Gateshead *mashgiach*, Rav Moshe Schwab, *zt"l* (1917–1979), vol. 3, p. 212.

An internal sense of identity and self-worth is something children generally have not yet had time to acquire. They therefore take their cues as to who they are from their surroundings. *Children often measure themselves by what goes on around them.*[6] It is the external world that tells them how good or how capable they are.

In contrast, a mature adult can reach into his inner world of values, which he has come over time to treasure, and thereby maintain his self-respect no matter what goes on in the external world.

One area in which we can observe this characteristic most easily is in game-playing. Children love all sorts of games, but especially competitive ones, and they often get distraught and angry when it seems that they or their side are losing. Children don't want to lose in the worst way. I think they associate losing with the idea that this somehow indicates that they're less worthy, or intrinsically less capable.[7]

CONFRONTATIONS BEGET MORE CONFRONTATIONS

What often occurs when a parent sets up a confrontation is that he or she is taken very much by surprise when he gets an excessively

---

6. Several important ideas flow from this concept:
   (1) The effect of the environment: Children, rightly or wrongly, look outside of themselves to learn how to behave. As we have stated before, *Mori VeRabi, zt"l*, said, a child is like a new immigrant who learns how the citizens of his newly adopted country behave and then copies them. It is therefore of paramount importance to choose a proper environment for children.
   (2) I was taught by *Mori VeRabi HaGaon* Rav Chaim Pinchas Scheinberg, *shlita*, that when the Mishnah teaches us (*Pirkei Avos* 4:15) that it is "better to be the tail of a lion rather than the head of a weasel" (that is, a person grows more as a junior member in a strong group of scholars than as the leader of a weaker group), this does not refer to children. A more mature person can see the larger picture and deal with the fact that in his surroundings he is considered small and weak, but to a child, *his surroundings are his world*. He will simply consider himself a tail, without appreciating that he's part of a lion.
7. This is similar to the perfectionist, who defines his or her self-worth by how well they do. See chapter twenty-two in this part.

mindless, stubborn, "*chutzpahdik*" reaction on the child's part. Perhaps it's about taking a bath, or coming on time to dinner, or doing homework — in any case, the parent deems this issue important enough to merit a confrontational ultimatum ("Do it... RIGHT NOW!" "Get into that... OR ELSE!") *But the child has much more invested emotionally in not obeying the command than the parent does in having it obeyed.*

Unless the child has been emotionally broken, God forbid, he'll hear the confrontational language just the way a bull sees the red cloth waving in the hands of the toreador. Obeying the order is seen as "losing." The order is equivalent to a challenge, *and obedience is equated with defeat.* The child either ignores the order totally or reacts negatively with more energy and emotion than the parent ever anticipated. After all, maybe baths are important, but they're not *that* important.

So what happens now? The parent, caught off guard by the level of resistance, more often than not backs down.

This backing down will have monumental consequences. The child has learned two things. One, *I can win a confrontation.* Two, *the taste of victory is sweet.* These lessons will not be lost on him. The next time Mother or Father uses confrontational language, the child will probably be looking forward to a repeat performance by all concerned.

Confrontations — Usually a "No-Win" Situation

It is for this reason that we must avoid, as much as possible, confrontational situations. When children hear an order being barked out at them, they either stubbornly refuse or comply out of fear, and *neither option is healthy, especially when it becomes a common occurrence.* Certainly, we need to let children know when a request or order is urgent and calls for immediate compliance. But something has gone very wrong when stern orders, meant to be obeyed immediately, become a way of life.

Parents may think that they can browbeat children into doing what they want, but they're unaware of the effect this has upon their children's development, and the price they'll pay for their children's total, fearful compliance. If the child, as can often be expected, refuses, then the stage is set for a long and protracted battle of wills, and this battle has no victors. If the child succeeds in defying parental authority (that is, if the parent, having issued a stern command, backs down in the face of the child's intransigence), then the parent can be assured, as already mentioned, that more stubborn refusals are on the way. Even if the child is "successfully" forced on subsequent occasions to comply, the very pleasant memory of that single "victory" will remain in the child's mind, and he or she will continue to defy the parents, in the hope of winning the next round. It's sort of like winning big in Las Vegas. The sweet memory of all those coins rushing out of the slot machine will bring a person back to Las Vegas time and time again.

If, on the other hand, it's always the parent who "wins," forcing compliance by brute force or by bullying, then the child will eventually end up broken, one way or another. He or she could develop a poor self-image, or be lacking in personal initiative. I have seen this many times in the last twenty-five years, and it is not a pretty thing to behold.

Therefore, it follows that this rule should ring true: *Confront as infrequently as possible. But when a confrontation is inevitable, then the parent must emerge, **for the child's sake**, as the "victor."*

WHY CONFRONTATIONS OCCUR

Confrontations are usually preventable, but in many homes they become a way of life. To mention some of the main reasons that confrontations occur:

1. Poor Planning. When a parent doesn't plan things out properly, emergencies arise. This could be because too little time has been allotted for everything that needs doing, or too little thought was invested in all that a given activity entails. Under circumstances such as these, departure time for a trip arrives, for example, and preparations are still incomplete. Or bedtime arrives and many little tasks still need attending to.

So the parent goes into "take charge" mode and starts issuing brisk commands, and upon not being immediately obeyed, shifts into confrontation mode. Perhaps the most common example of this is *erev Shabbos* (Friday afternoon), with all the myriad tasks that need attending to and the pressure felt by all, especially by the mother.

Erev Shabbos is often a time of tension and strife.[8] There's often more work than can be handled, and children are frequently pressed into service, sometimes against their will. This leads to tension, arguments, and recriminations.

It would be far better for the parent to either begin preparations on Wednesday or Thursday night or cut back on the level of Shabbos preparation, and explain, truthfully, that he or she could not manage everything alone, and therefore didn't make the usual dessert, etc. Better to have a simpler Shabbos meal than an *erev Shabbos* battle.[9]

It must be stressed, however, that this approach is not meant as a punishment, but rather, as a natural outcome of the reality of the situation.

---

8. This is explicitly mentioned in *Gittin* 7a and 52a.
9. It says (*Mishlei* 17:1), "Dry bread with peace is better than a home full of strife." In addition, our Sages teach us (*Shabbos* 118a), "Make your Shabbos as a weekday, and do not become dependent on people." While the Sages are speaking of financial issues, I believe that "people" can refer to your children, as well. It is better to have fewer special dishes on Shabbos than to fight over them before Shabbos.

There's no doubt that children should help prepare the home for Shabbos, just as there is no doubt that they need to participate, as responsible family members, in many other aspects of life in the home. What we're referring to here is an example of what happens when things have been allowed to go much farther than they should have. At that point we need to cut back somewhere. *This cutback is done without rancor, bitterness or anger, but it must be done.*

2. Poor Preparation for New Situations. Children, being dominated by their emotions, react poorly to surprises. One example is when the parent fails to prepare the child about what to expect — or what is expected of him. For instance, before taking a child to a supermarket, clearly prepare him for what he will see there. Map out your visit: First we'll select the vegetables, then the cold cuts, then the cereals. After that, if you have behaved well — *and be specific about what good behavior entails* (no whining, rushing ahead, etc.) — then we can buy some specific treat for you.

Make sure the child understands that if he misbehaves, then you will put everything back on the shelves that had been selected and leave the supermarket. The child will forfeit the next trip to the supermarket and will stay at a neighbor's or with a babysitter, and no amount of howling will help.

For the third trip to the supermarket, the rules should be spelled out again and the child given another chance to accompany his mother. There is an excellent possibility that the child, now prepared for what to expect, will behave well.

3. Parental Self-Esteem. Sometimes the parent, too, feels that he must "win," lest his status in the home be undermined. The parent feels insecure, so he digs in his heels and feels that for "the good of the home" he must show who's boss.[10] It becomes an emotional issue, with each side intent on victory. Often, as stated, the parent

---

10. In fact, to me, this is a sign that he is definitely *not* the boss.

loses, and his status in the home is indeed diminished. If this was supposed to be a test of who's the boss, it's clear that whoever it is, it's not the parent.

This is but one of the many reasons mothers and fathers must build up their own sense of authentic self-worth. Although we have discussed in many places how parents can build their own self-esteem, a complete treatment of this crucially important subject is beyond the scope of this work.

4. **Poor Sleep and Diet.** When a person doesn't sleep or eat properly, his patience wears thin. This quickly increases the chances that the home climate will become confrontational.

5. **Generally Disrespectful Language.** When family members don't talk to each other respectfully, confrontational language becomes the norm and people dig in to defend their positions. *Parents must especially take extra care to speak to each other lovingly and respectfully.* The children will follow suit, at least in the context of the home, and then they can be taught to speak that way outside of the house as well. An insecure individual may fear that speaking respectfully somehow suggests that he is in an inferior position, but on the contrary, speaking respectfully to others is a sign of one's own dignity.

Let the children see that respectful speech pays off.

6. **Lifestyle.** If a parent is overburdened with various responsibilities or worries, in or out of the home, this creates added stress. At such times, the parent may feel more insistent upon everything "working out smoothly," and the glitch-free running of the family becomes for that parent a pressing emotional requirement. The reality is that in all families — especially those with an infant, or several younger children, or a few teenagers, or all of the above — it's normal for things *not* to go smoothly. But this does not have to result in the anger, shouting and confrontations that can too easily become commonplace.

If you feel that stress is an unavoidable part of your normal daily life, then thought needs to be given to which of your outside commitments can be eliminated or toned down. Priorities must be set. Even some important matters might need, for the time being (perhaps throughout the years your children are growing up!), to be put on hold. Consider the fact that rebellious, sullen children, or children with no self-motivation, or children with a negative self-image, will eventually be a far greater burden on your soul, not to mention your time and probably your pocketbook, than the lost income resulting from a lighter schedule. It is far better to cut back and allow yourself more time so as to be even-tempered with your child today, than to endure the deep pain of shattered relationships at a later stage in life.

That Basic Principle Again

Each and every confrontation strains a relationship. Sometimes these stresses are unavoidable, although, as stated, they should never be part of a child's daily fare.

But there's one rule that we've mentioned a number of times, and it bears repeating: *Before putting strain on a relationship, first it is necessary to build, nurture and develop the relationship's positive side.*[11]

Therefore, first and foremost, a parent must build a relationship with the child in such a way that if a tight moment comes along, the parent will be able to give a curt command and the child won't feel put down, or demeaned, or like a "loser," but will understand that this is a difficult moment for Mommy or Daddy. He or she

---

11. From this idea, I believe, flows the principle of *shanah rishonah*, the special laws governing the first year of a marital relationship (see *Devarim* 24:5). The Torah knows that there are bound to be stresses in a marriage, and the first year of marriage is intended as a time of investment, during which the love between husband and wife can blossom and mature.

will comply with the request, mindful of the unusual urgency that the parent is displaying.

More Reason to Avoid Confrontations

Confrontations contribute significantly to an unhappy home atmosphere. This is a vital point, for if we want our children off the street, then we want them to be happy at home.

In addition, when we confront or bully our children, we are in effect teaching them that this is the way to solve problems and to "get your way." Sometimes the bullying is subtle.

> *I remember several instances in which parents told their children that if the parent wasn't obeyed, the father would have a heart attack. Certainly a parent's health is a top priority, but matters should never deteriorate to such a point that only a threat such as this will convince a child to do what the parents want.*

Such expressions of emotion, besides the terribly negative effect they have on the atmosphere of a family, are in themselves confrontational. They constitute an attempt to bully the other person into compliance, either through emotional force or through guilt. But bullying is still bullying; it never works in the long run and it has bitter side effects.

"Catching Them Red-Handed"

Confrontations arise when we show a child that we've "caught him red-handed." While sometimes this is necessary, in the long run it's usually counterproductive. Perhaps you'll prove your point with incontrovertible evidence, but there will be long-term damage to the relationship, *for the child will now assume that you have a low opinion of him.*

This has many negative repercussions, not least of which is that the child will no longer seek to maintain a modicum of good behavior in order to maintain his reputation.[12] This is especially true of teenagers, to whom self-image is so important. The decision regarding whether or not to share with the child that you have clear evidence of misbehavior is a difficult one. Much of the decision will be predicated, I think, on two things:

1. What the past relationship between parent and child has been like.

2. How vital it is that the behavior be stopped as quickly as possible.

WHEN AND WHERE DO WE CONFRONT OUR CHILDREN?

On some occasions, there must be a confrontation. Some of the most important guidelines are as follows:

1. Does It Affect the "Inner Person?" If the child's behavior is touching upon something that will affect his inner world, that is, his character or basic ideals, a clear and firm stand is in order. These matters include honesty, bullying others, or a tendency to erupt in fits of temper. These behavior patterns will affect a person's chance at a successful life, and must be dealt with as soon as they become apparent.

The best way to react to a temper tantrum is to make sure that whatever it is the child wants, he doesn't get it. If temper tantrums don't pay off, they'll stop. However, there may be underlying frustrations at the root of the anger, and these must be addressed.

---

12. See *Zichron Yehoshua*, by Rav Hillel Brisk, *shlita*, p. 51, where this concept is dealt with at length.

Otherwise, the anger will be expressed in other, more subtle, or perhaps more violent, ways.

2. Is It Common Knowledge? If a particular form of gross misbehavior has become public household knowledge, a parent may need to react. This is particularly true if you are dealing with an older child, whose actions are often copied by younger siblings. Enormous care must be taken here, for the older child will be especially sensitive to a public confrontation, and will go to great lengths to "win." A delicate balance must be struck between letting the younger children know you don't approve, and making sure they see you exercising firm control over behavior you consider bad. At the same time, everyone should see that you preserve the dignity of the child in question.

One way of doing this is to offer explanations for the child's misbehavior that cast him or her in a better light. Statements such as, "You probably thought…" "It must have been a very difficult day for you to have spoken this way to me," "You probably didn't know where this could lead," "This probably wasn't your idea," can all help preserve a child's self-image while simultaneously demonstrating your disapproval.

3. Can You — and Your Spouse — Weather the Confrontation? Remember that adults often underestimate the lengths to which children will go to avoid losing a battle of wills, so you must be firm in your resolve and convinced that the situation does call for confrontation. Otherwise you may end up giving in, and find yourself, as a result, in a far worse position than if you hadn't started out on this course in the first place.

This also refers to your spouse's resolve. If your husband or wife is not convinced of the correctness of your cause, or lacks the emotional fortitude to weather the difficult moments every confrontation brings in its wake, then don't start. Children are experts at "divide and conquer," and will sense your spouse's weakness and exploit it to the hilt. This is especially true if they've won confrontations in the past, because they believe in their ability to pull it off again.

It is truly amazing just how much effort a child is willing to invest in scoring a victory.

4. Is It a Precedent? If the behavior is the kind that is likely to repeat itself, that is all the more reason to put a quick stop to it. Often, however, problematic behavior is an expression of some "stage" the child is going through, or is the natural consequence of certain environmental causes. These could be the boredom of a long summer, or emotional and physical exhaustion the day after a wedding, or countless other events and circumstances that can upset the equilibrium of a child and cause him or her to act out. The proper approach to such forms of misbehavior is to address, on a practical level, the underlying causes. Then the behavior will disappear of its own accord.

Under this category is behavior that the child will eventually grow out of.[13]

5. Do You Have Clarity? Sometimes the reason for a certain pattern of misbehavior is unknown to the parents, but the confrontation seems to eliminate the misbehavior anyway.

Usually, however, if the cause is not taken into consideration, then the misbehavior will repeat itself one way or another, which in turn will invite more confrontations. I would therefore hesitate before confronting a child over any misbehavior if I am unsure what is causing it.

This is analogous to defeating a pneumonia with a powerful drug, but not making sure that the home is properly heated and free of cold, windy, drafts.

---

13. See *Reb Yaakov*, by Rav Yonasan Rosenblum (New York: Mesorah Publications, 1993), p. 328, where several examples of this concept are given, such as the young child who sat in Reb Yaakov's seat in shul. Reb Yaakov said there was no need to rebuke him, for when he grew older he certainly would refrain from sitting in the Rav's seat.

Gifts, War and, Especially, Prayer

I think that this chapter will come to a fitting close if we apply the principle set forth by the *Sefas Emes* in describing how Yaakov dealt with Esav.[14]

A confrontation between Yaakov and Esav was brewing, and Yaakov wanted to avoid it if possible.[15] The *Sefas Emes* discusses here the related issue of how to deal with the *yetzer ha-ra*, with whom every person has countless confrontations in the course of a lifetime. What he says, I believe, holds true equally when dealing with children, for as *Mori VeRabi, zt"l,* said, children are dominated by their *yetzer ha-ra*.[16]

The *Sefas Emes* notes that Yaakov employed three stratagems.

The first was *doron*, sending gifts. We deal with the *yetzer ha-ra* by remembering the vast kindnesses that Hashem bestows upon us. This cultivates a love for Hashem, and is the first line of defense against the *yetzer ha-ra*.

The second strategy, should this be insufficient, is *milchamah*, direct confrontation.

The third — *and the Sefas Emes calls this the main weapon in our possession* — is *tefillah*, prayer. For without Hashem's help, we stand no chance at all against the *yetzer ha-ra*.

The same, I think, is true in regard to our children.

---

14. *Bereishis*, p. 148, paragraph beginning "*Ve-hiskin.*"
15. See *Lev Aharon*, by the Suvalker Rav and great *maggid*, Rav Aharon Bakst, *hy"d* ("Reb Archik," 1869–1941), pp. 92–4, for an ingenious treatment of how to deal with anger. He says that to confront Esav with brute force and defeat his 400 men, would have caused Esav to return with 800, and then 1600. It would never end. Esav, the epitome of the *yetzer ha-ra*, would — like a child — never give up. Interestingly enough, Rav Yonasan Eibshitz (d. 1762) points out that Yaakov was as afraid of killing Esav as he was of being killed, for his mother had prophesied that both would die on the same day. Indeed, Esav died on the day of Yaakov's burial.
16. See the Ari, *z"l* (*Sefer HaLikkutim, Shemos*, paragraph beginning "*Vayomar*").

First we must draw them close, developing a positive relationship with them. This is *doron*. Only then can we contemplate *milchamah* — confrontation. But above all, we cannot succeed at anything with our children without Hashem's blessing — for which we must offer earnest, deeply felt *tefillah*, which expresses our joyous recognition that we are totally dependent on Him for everything.

❧ EXERCISES

1. Keep a record of how many confrontations you've had recently with your child.

2. Find a pattern. Were the confrontations over a particular activity, such as cleaning his room or doing homework, or was it at a particular time of the day or week, such as Fridays or bedtime?

3. Together with your spouse, plan out a better way of handling things.

❦ Points to Remember

PARENTS must take special care to speak to each other lovingly and respectfully.

ONLY an internal definition of self, unrelated to our surroundings, can be a true barometer of who we really are.

CHILDREN often measure themselves by what goes on around them.

CHILDREN associate "losing" with the idea that this somehow indicates that they're less worthy, or intrinsically less capable.

A CHILD has much more invested emotionally in not obeying a parental command than the parent does in having it obeyed.

CONFRONT as infrequently as possible. When a confrontation is inevitable, the parent must emerge, *for the child's sake,* as the "victor."

BULLYING never works in the long run.

"CATCHING them red-handed" is usually counterproductive.

THE BEST way to react to a temper tantrum is to make sure that whatever it is the child wants, he doesn't get it.

IT IS FAR better to cut back and allow yourself more time so as to be even-tempered with your child today, than to endure the deep pain of shattered relationships at a later stage in life.

CHAPTER TWENTY-FIVE

Children and Domestic Strife

CHILDREN ARE SENSITIVE TO THE HOME'S "EMOTIONAL TEMPERATURE"

In the same way that children are so sensitive to nonverbal messages, they are also sensitive to the "emotional temperature" in the home. Children can sense when their parents are worried, angry, or frustrated with themselves, each other, or other family members, and the reverse is also true: when parents are feeling secure, content, and happy, this is conveyed to the children.

Children are affected by negative emotional temperature in several ways:

1. Children Feel Insecure and Frightened. It has been said that even nursing infants can sense when the mother is tense, worried, angry, or affected by other negative emotions. This is especially true for younger children, from birth until puberty. When parents are fearful — even when the fear is justified, such as fear of an earthquake (as in Los Angeles) or of a carjacking (Johannesburg) — there is an enormous difference between fear that is primarily emotional (when the parents are communicating emotional terror) and fear that is primarily intellectual (which is focused more on problem-solving.) Although fear of dangerous situations is justified, our approach has to be that of first doing whatever we can to alleviate or avoid the problem, then of exercising *bitachon* in Hashem regarding events over which we have little control.[1]

2. Children Blame Themselves. Sometimes children blame themselves for the parents' negative frame of mind. This is true even when the source of the negativity is marital discord. Children need and want to respect and admire their parents and therefore they instinctively blame themselves, rather than their mother or father, for problems in the home.[2] This can be likened to a child adopting his parents' accent or mannerisms. As the child grows older, of course, he'll increasingly adopt customs and habits of the society in which he was raised, but children's first models, and heroes, are their parents.

3. Diminished Respect. Children can feel diminished respect for a parent who doesn't seem to be in control of himself. Children can be extremely judgmental, and without perceiving what may be an understandable reason for tenseness and impatience, they may feel that since their parents are incapable of handling their own emotions, they're not worthy of handling their children, either. From such an attitude, brazen disrespect and disobedience are but a short step away.

WE WANT OUR CHILDREN TO WANT TO BE HOME

One of the best ways to prevent the street from influencing your children is to have them at home (when they're not in school) as much of the time as possible. A number of factors can help you

---

1. The truth is that everything we do is anchored in *bitachon*, even when we take the steps that are within our control. See Part 1, chapter 5.
2. I think this is because of the feeling, *If my parent is a nobody, then so am I.* Healthy people don't want to be nobodies. My friend, Dr. Meir Wikler, offers this idea: Children are very self-centered, and assume that what goes on around them must be because of them.

succeed at this, but the first requirement is that the home atmosphere be a happy one. *And the greatest single factor in how it feels to be home is how parents get along with each other.*

Children, especially younger ones, are terrified when parents quarrel.[3] Their entire world is shaking. An analogy I once heard comes to mind:

> *Two people are sitting on an airplane that is preparing for takeoff. One understands English, the other doesn't. An announcement comes over the PA system: "In about forty-five minutes we will be encountering turbulence. The plane will shake a lot, but we won't be in any danger. The turbulence is normal for this route at this time of year." When the plane begins to shake forty-five minutes later, the one who understood the announcement remains calm. His fellow passenger, though, is petrified. He doesn't understand what is happening to the plane, which is the only thing standing between him and the deep blue sea.*[4]

A child in a home with marital discord can be compared to that baffled, terrified passenger. All he knows is that his whole world is shaking.

---

3. Someone showed me a quote from the book, *The Optimistic Child*, by Dr. Martin Seligman (Boston: Houghton Mifflin, 1995), p. 272, and I feel I must share it with others:
"Research has shown that even very young children are strongly hurt by conflict between their parents. Preschoolers show adverse *physiological* [emphasis mine], behavioral, and emotional responses to anger between parents. Even videotapes of two adults disagreeing nonverbally upset young children."
How much more will deep conflict between parents affect children. Children can be quite judgmental, and will often perceive — as in fairy tales — one parent as the "good one" and the other as the "bad one," or hero and villain, or victim and persecutor. In the real world this is rarely true, but children's perceptions are dominated by their emotions.

4. Dr. Binyomin Surovsky, of Jerusalem, uses this analogy to help us understand the broad strokes of Jewish history. One who has the perspective, and has heard the "announcement" of the Torah in regard to the true causes of Jewish success and tragedy, is not overwhelmed or broken by our national travails. To him, it's expected that such things should occur along the route destined for the Jewish People.

Although domestic tranquility is not the subject of this book, we must nevertheless point out that if the home atmosphere is frightening or unhappy, the children will take every opportunity to leave it as soon as possible. Their emotional welfare depends to a large extent on their parents' getting to the source of the marital discord and doing something about it.[5]

Just as with any other factor that can make a home unpleasant, much can be done to alleviate marital discord. Competent help can be sought, small initial changes in the marital relationship can come about, and the dynamics behind the problem can truly be worked through. With Hashem's help, enormous progress can eventually be made. People who might once have thought their relationship was hopeless, and who might undertake to work on it just for the sake of their children, may be greatly surprised and delighted at how radically their relationship can change for the better.

> *Rav Shach, zt"l, once told someone who had questioned him about education, "Der beste chinuch iz tzufreedena elteren." "The best education is happy parents."*[6]

We must, as parents, do everything we can to make all aspects of our home contribute to a happy home atmosphere. Then the effects of the outside culture can be better combated.

---

5. It has been said that this is why when parents disagree over how to handle a child, the child cannot be legally considered a "wayward son" (a *ben sorer umoreh*; see *Sanhedrin* 71a). His poor character and behavior are a direct result of parents who could not agree on how to raise him. (Heard from Rav Yeruchem Praga, *shlita*, of Jerusalem.)
6. Heard from Rav Avrohom Fishman, principal of the Beis Yehudah school in Detroit, Michigan.

🌸 Points to Remember

Children are sensitive to the "emotional temperature" in the home.

Children's first models and heroes are their parents.

Children can feel diminished respect for a parent who doesn't seem to be in control of himself.

The greatest single factor in how it feels to be home is how parents get along with each other.

We must do everything we can to make all aspects of our home contribute to a happy home atmosphere.

PART SIX

COPING WITH A HOSTILE ENVIRONMENT

CHAPTER TWENTY-SIX

Compete Where You're Strongest

How Do We Compete?

A number of years ago, an interesting incident occurred in one of Jerusalem's *yeshivos* for young men seeking to learn more about their Jewish heritage — and it sheds light on the subject of this chapter.

> *A delegation from the Israeli government was touring Yeshivas Ohr Somayach, and when they heard that there was a successful public relations expert among the students, they asked to be introduced. After the initial pleasantries, one of the government officials asked how the student would recommend that they "sell" Israel.*
>
> *The young man replied that they'd never find a product whose advertising theme was, "Our product is as good as anything else you can buy." Marketers seek to extol that which is unique to their product. Similarly, Israel shouldn't market itself on the basis of its scenic beaches and nightlife, etc., because for that, a person can find it bigger and better elsewhere. What Israel should do is market the thing that makes it so special — its spirituality.*

This principle, that we should compete in the areas in which we excel, is one of the most useful tools I know of when trying to protect our children from negative influences. We need to realize that what our children need most — our love and our caring — are things that the street cannot give them, and we must see to it that they get these things at home in abundance. True Torah Judaism and a warm, loving family are a combination that can, with Hashem's help, withstand superbly the influences of the street.

Satirize, But Polish Your Own Apples

Over thirty years ago, I heard the following story:

> Rav Sholom Schwadron, zt"l,[1] who was a master of satire and who had an ingenious knack for poking fun at secular, materialistic values, was once accused of being merely a *"leitz,"* a clown. He went to the Chazon Ish,[2] who asked for a demonstration performance. Upon hearing Rav Sholom's witty, piercing, scholarly presentation, he responded, *"A zoi darf men redden,"* "That's how you have to speak."

There is no question that we must poke fun at the materialistic, pleasure-seeking world around us, but as Rav Sholom, *zt"l*, himself stressed, nothing is better than emphasizing what *we* have to offer, our own strengths. It isn't enough to throw mud on the apples of others; you have to polish your own. And you have to present an excellent product.

---

1. (1912–1997). A great scholar and orator, he was one of the greatest maggidim of our time, speaking, literally, around the globe, and inspiring countless thousands with his wit, his storytelling, and, above all, his deeply rooted awe and love of Hashem.
2. Rav Avrohom Yeshaya Karelitz (1878–1953), one of the great Torah leaders of the twentieth century.

HOME AND THE FAMILY — AN INVINCIBLE PAIR

Parents must know that they have no competition out there. What they give cannot be duplicated. When you give your child time, understanding and acceptance, then the connection will never be permanently broken. As in all relationships, especially close ones, there can be stormy moments, but after all is said and done, the security of a happy, loving home has nothing to rival it. There may be times when a child will, out of frustration and anger, do things that infuriate you, but the bond will never be severed. *They will never totally repudiate what you stand for.*

> *Rav Yechiel Yaakovson, shlita, one of Israel's foremost experts on troubled teenagers, often asks children from Orthodox homes, who have chosen to stray from their Torah heritage, how he, as a father, can prevent such a thing from happening to his own children. The answer he received one time startled him: "Oh, you have nothing to worry about, your children won't leave you. They won't leave what you believe in. They know that you love them."*

A great educator once shared with me the following remark that his son had come out with. The boy, a teenager, wasn't interested at that time in the intensive Torah study which is the hallmark of many children in today's Orthodox homes.

> *"Abba, don't worry. Torah study doesn't 'pull' me, but I'm never going to 'go off' (abandon a Torah-observant lifestyle). I know you love me."*

This is not to say that families with children who have left traditional Judaism do not, or did not, love their children. But too often, *the message didn't get through clearly enough.*

There are a number of possibilities as to why the love isn't felt. Sometimes, children perceive that their parents' love is conditional, that it's predicated upon their *doing* or *being* something. This kind of love is often eventually rejected, and hatred takes its place. Sometimes, the love, acceptance and respect of the parents toward the child is contingent upon some secular accomplishment, such as a professional or academic distinction, or depends on how helpful the child is to them. *And sometimes, it depends upon how successful the child is in his Torah studies.*[3]

Parents tread on thin ice when they too closely tie their love, respect and acceptance to any particular condition — and this includes success in Torah study. The following letter, received by Rav Yaakovson, *shlita*, from a child who had run away from home, speaks for itself. It is worthy of our close attention.

> *"I don't care about him (my father) because he doesn't really care about me. Only when I brought him recognition, or good grades, or I would help him a lot — only then would he smile at me, and once, maybe twice, he even hugged and kissed me.... He'd get enraged and he'd hit me when I went to my aunt, since they're not so religious. But I went, because my aunt always smiled at me. I'd just open the door and she was already smiling, she was just glad I'd come. She hugged me as if I were her own son. Even when I hadn't done anything good to deserve it."*[4]

The boy who wrote this letter had definite opinions regarding whether his father really loved him. It is very likely that the son was totally wrong. His father almost certainly did (and hopefully still does) love his child. Parents naturally love their children — gener-

---

3. *Mori VeRabi, zt"l,* said that the "generation gap" of decades ago had its roots in, "My son, the doctor." Parents often tied their respect for their children on their becoming doctors, lawyers, or some other esteemed professional, and the children sensed that their benefit was not always uppermost in their parents' minds. Today, in some places it has become, "My son, the Rosh Yeshiva." While Torah greatness is arguably the highest ideal for which a Jew can strive, *parental love cannot be contingent upon it.*
4. *Al Techetu BaYeled,* vol. 2, p. 7. All three volumes are powerful, practical reading. The first two volumes have been translated into English, and are available from Yeshivas Sha'arei Yosher, Jerusalem.

ally speaking, it's a fact of life.[5] Why, then, the total misconception on the part of the child?

Different People — Different Languages

The aforementioned child, in his letter, emphasized what being hugged and kissed meant to him. This brings to mind one situation which left an indelible impression on me as to how far these misunderstandings can go.

> *A child felt his mother didn't love him. In fact, this woman loved her child so intensely that she wrote him loving notes and put them in his lunch box. But that was totally lost on the child, because what this particular child needed, more than anything else, was to be hugged.*[6]

For various reasons, many adults don't express love by way of touch. They rarely kiss or hug. That's fine, for there are other ways to express affection. The problem arises when they live with someone (either a spouse or a child) who does need to be frequently hugged and kissed. Words of affection, or actions which manifest their affection, are not "heard," and as far as the child or spouse is concerned, there is only a deafening silence, an atmosphere and relationship devoid of love. Again, this may not reflect the reality at all — the spouse, or father or mother, may actually love this family member deeply — *but it is not coming across.*

---

5. There's a saying from the Kotzker Rebbe (Rav Menachem Mendel Morgenstern, zt"l, 1787–1859), that parents love children more than children love parents because Adam, the first man, had children but not parents. Therefore, the love for children is more a part of the natural way of the world. This powerful potential to feel a loved one's emotion can sometimes render a parent incapable of making proper decisions on emotionally charged issues. Then the parent must have the good sense to realize that it is time to consult with others.
6. Children are often more affected by touch than by words.

What then, can be done when the child needs touch, hugging, and kissing, and the parent simply doesn't speak that language? I think there are several possibilities:

In the world of electricity, whenever you have an appliance that runs on, say, 110 volts, and you're plugging it into a wall outlet that sends 220 volts, you need a transformer. Otherwise a level of current that it can't handle will destroy the appliance in seconds. In effect, the transformer acts as a translator, changing the language that the electricity source "speaks" into one that the appliance can "hear."

What this means is that when two people speak two different emotional languages, each needs to recognize, learn, and respect the other's language. When they recognize each other's language and understand that what the other person is expressing is love, then they can use their "transformer," and feel the love that's coming their way.

The problem arises when children are not mature enough emotionally to do this "translating." In such a situation, the parent has to be more creative. He has to search for ways to show love, from more conventional ways such as reading stories aloud, to the more unconventional, such as taking the child out of school from time to time for ice cream.

It may even be possible, in such a situation, for the parent to *learn how to hug*. Not cold, forced ones, but real ones, the kind the child so desperately wants. How?

WHAT'S IMPORTANT TO YOU IS IMPORTANT TO ME

When a male student marries, I often give the following advice:

Let's say your wife wants you to accompany her when she goes to buy drapes and you aren't one bit interested. You couldn't care less which color or kind of drapes she buys. You have three choices of action:

A. Don't go. That would be a mistake.

B. Go and make believe you're interested. That would be an even bigger mistake. Women generally have good instincts, and pretended feelings on the part of a husband can be very painful to them.

C. Go and be interested. How can you be interested in something you aren't interested in? By feeling, "If it's important to you, it's important to me."

I emphasize *feeling*. When you care for someone, their feelings can be transmitted to you, if you let it happen. You can share their emotional reality. This applies not only to a spouse, but to a child as well. You can be interested in something you aren't interested in by feeling, "If it's important to you, it's important to me."

WINNING — AGAINST ALL ODDS

That a truly warm and loving home can compete — and succeed — against the powerful, seemingly irresistible lure of the street is well-illustrated by the following true story:

A father, recently divorced, who had custody of his nine-year-old son and had placed him in a Torah school, consulted me. The mother had custody for one weekend a month, and would usually take the child with her to Las Vegas. How could the father compete with Las Vegas, and the terrible moral lessons it would teach his son?

The answer was clear. He needed to compete by using his strengths. It was impossible to give the child more "fun" than Las Vegas. But he could give the child a warm, loving, and interested father, and in this respect, Las Vegas didn't have a chance. Nothing could rival what the father had at his disposal.

Several years have passed since this question arose. The father triumphed. His son, recognizing where his home truly was, has espoused his father's values.

This father recognized that he needed to give his son an even higher level of love and attention than most children normally receive. This is similar to a person who is working in a typhus ward: He has to be more careful than normal about his diet, sleep patterns, etc., in order to maintain a higher level of resistance than would usually be necessary. *So, too, with our children in today's world.* Parents may need to invest more time and love than was necessary in past generations, for the "germs" of the street demand that we fortify our children even more than was previously thought necessary. Our homes must be places of happiness, encouragement, and nurturing. Then there is much cause for optimism that children will choose the home over the street.

❧ EXERCISE

Find something about your household that can make your child proud to be a member of the family. If you can't think of anything… get to work.

❧ POINTS TO REMEMBER

COMPETE in the areas in which you excel.

WHEN you give your child time, understanding and acceptance, then the connection will never be permanently broken.

CONDITIONAL love is often eventually rejected, and hatred takes its place.

WHEN two people speak two different emotional languages, each needs to recognize, learn, and respect the other's language.

WHEN you care for someone, their feelings can be transmitted to you. You can share their emotional reality.

CHAPTER TWENTY-SEVEN

The Big Question

The world of the twenty-first century is one which virtually all parents and educators, including the secular, consider inimical to a child's spiritual and character development. It follows that one of the most serious decisions facing parents today is how far to go in protecting their children from the surrounding culture. A corollary question is how best to prepare a child for the inevitable occasions on which he or she will come into contact with that society, and be affected by it.

THE PARENT IS THE CHILD'S YETZER HA-TOV

Mori VeRabi, zt"l, said that a child has no *yetzer ha-tov* (Good Inclination), and that therefore it is the parent who must serve the child in that capacity.

Children live in the here and now, because it is the nature of the *yetzer ha-ra* to consider only the present gain or pleasure, not the long-term effects, of any particular action. This is how blind emotion operates, unguided by the vision of the intellect. It is the parents who can correctly foresee the outcome of any given course of action, and then either prevent it or encourage it. They are the child's *yetzer ha-tov*.

It is therefore a parental obligation to weigh the pluses and minuses inherent in both answers to this monumental question: *To shield or not to shield?* The answer to this question is highly individualized, with the situation varying greatly from family to family and city to city. Parents must search for the response that is in keeping with their own unique family history, the community in which they live, and the personalities of their children. Competent, experienced Torah authorities must be consulted. To look away, to ignore the question, to abdicate responsibility for arriving at a decision in regard to this dilemma, can have fateful implications for our children.

In my opinion, the longer we can shield a child from a negative environment, the better. A young person often lacks the maturity to resist the seductiveness of today's hedonistic, pleasure-seeking society, even if intellectually he recognizes how demeaning it is to human dignity. Numerous Torah sources point to the fact that even when a person has witnessed the bankruptcy of a culture he can still be drawn to it.[1]

There comes a time, however, when parents do have to face the fact that we live in exile. Our children will be exposed to negative, destructive influences.

---

1. See *Michtav Me'Eliyahu*, vol. 2, pp. 188–9, who brings the verse in *Devarim* 12:30 warning us not to be swayed by the Canaanite culture. We had to be warned even though we had witnessed its downfall. The point is made in *Devarim* 29:15, that even after the Jewish People had seen with their own eyes that the idols were "as disgusting as dung," a warning not to be tempted by them was still necessary. Such is the power of the environment! Today we see the tragic consequences of Western hedonism, yet some people living in Israel still enthusiastically seek to import its culture.

BUILDING OUR CHILDREN'S RESISTANCE

When discussing whether to expose a child (or ourselves, for that matter) to an inimical environment or to remain apart from it, a fundamental point needs to be considered.

Everyone understands that when a person begins work in a typhus ward he must maintain a high standard of precautionary measures, both in sleep and diet. His resistance needs to be gradually built up, both before and during exposure.

In the same way, anyone whose fate it is to have to function successfully in a world that's rampant with innumerable spiritual "viruses" must take precautions beforehand to build up the "resistance" in our souls to ward off the spiritual menaces that may come our way.

How to build up this resistance is the purpose of this entire book. Let us name the most powerful ones:

1. **Love of Hashem.** A child must have at least the beginnings of a love for God, along with a deep, abiding belief that God loves him, at all times and under all circumstances. These two aspects of his relationship to the Almighty are inextricably intertwined. An outgrowth of this love is the knowledge that misdeeds can be rectified, and that indeed, God wants this and helps us accomplish it.

2. **A Model of a Warm, Caring, and Positive Relationship.** A child, in order to succeed in his relationships with others and, indeed, in his relationship with Hashem, needs a model of a deep, warm and caring relationship, preferably one within the home, and preferably one that has been presented at an early age. If for any reason his own family cannot serve as a model of a good Jewish home, he should be given opportunities to spend time with families that can fill this gap.

3. **A Love of Learning.** A love of learning and spiritual growth, and a commitment to these as a lifelong process, are indis-

pensable to a person's continued development. Such growth is the only reliable safeguard against spiritual deterioration.

4. A Place to Renew Oneself. People need a place to "recharge," that is, to renew and reaffirm commitments to those spiritual ideals that are the basis of a Torah life. Often this is a quiet and tranquil spot which is conducive to allowing us to once again access and appreciate the importance and value of our life goals.

This renewal is necessary in order to develop the resistance which anyone growing up in the twenty-first century desperately needs. We live in a very uninsulated world, and young people will be exposed, probably sooner than later, to spiritual "viruses." These viruses are not only anti-Jewish and anti-religious, but give rise to hedonistic ideas and produce unethical, pleasure-seeking individuals.

WHEN EXPOSURE IS INEVITABLE

Yaakov, upon hearing that he would have to spend time in Lavan's home, first prepared himself by staying fourteen years in the yeshiva of Shem and Ever. What this means is that when we know it is inevitable that our child is going to be exposed to a dangerous environment, we must give him preparation, and if it is to mirror the Shem and Ever experience, it must have two vital elements:

1. It Must Be Pure. In order to experience, and then to reject, the bad taste of impurity, one must first have experienced the good taste of purity. Sometimes, it is true, we can appreciate things that are good and pure after having been exposed to the impure. But that's a dangerous way of doing things and sometimes doesn't work, as we will soon see. If *first* we can experience the taste of holiness, there's a better chance we will recognize its overwhelming superiority to impurity, because we ourselves are still unsullied, and can experience the purity totally and take it in.

What this means is that for as long as possible, we must shield our young children's hearts and minds from exposure to the immorality and violence that they will eventually be witness to, one way or another. As long as possible, their soft, pure hearts and minds must be shielded. They have not yet tasted enough of the pure happiness of kedushah, holiness, and have not yet developed the antibodies to withstand all that they may one day have to weather. We the parents still serve as their *yetzer ha-tov*, their Good Inclination, and just as we wouldn't let them cross the street by themselves, we wouldn't willingly expose them to other grave dangers, either.

The Jewish People, in their first years as a nation, were given forty years of purity. Indeed, as they prepared to enter one of the most decadent lands of antiquity, they were, and were destined to remain, "a nation that dwells alone."[2]

It does constitute greatness to live within, yet stand apart from, a decadent environment,[3] but we dare not attempt this unless it is preceded by a period of purity. There is, in addition, another condition:

2. It Must Be Positive. Yaakov gave Yosef invaluable lessons on coping in exile, by which he himself had been sustained during

---

2. Bemidbar 23:24. See *Toras Kohanim, Vayikra* 131; Rashi, *Vayikra* 18:3. This was part of the divine plan, that the Jewish people should be exposed to the worst environments in the world. See *Da'as Torah*, by Rav Yeruchem Levovitz, *Kedoshim*, pp. 137–9.
3. We ask Hashem never to bring us to the test, for we fear failure. *Growth from a negative environment can come only when Hashem has decided to thrust the person into the situation.* There are many examples of this, such as Moshe's having been raised in Pharaoh's household and Ruth in Moab. In fact, this pattern has been present throughout the history of the Jewish People. It says (*Shir HaShirim Rabbah* 4:6) that there were more righteous people raised in the time of Destruction than when the Temple stood (*Yeshayahu* 54:1). Indeed, the crucible for our nation's greatness was the Egyptian Exile. In addition, our Sages tell us (*Sanhedrin* 97a) *Mashiach* can arise from a completely degenerate generation. *How is it that a degenerate generation is more likely to merit the Redemption than one that is "average"? There must be a quality of greatness that is brought out by dwelling in — and resisting — a terrible environment.* See *Michtav Me'Eliyahu*, vol. 1, pp. 157–9.

the difficult period in Lavan's home. All the Torah that Yosef learned during those precious years spent with his father were regarded by him as a treasure, and the joyous memories sustained him throughout the almost impossibly difficult years in Egypt.

Something of great importance emerges here: *One's memories of the time spent in a pure environment must be happy ones.*[4] If we are to keep our children safe from the seductiveness of the outside world, we must be the first to "seduce" them with sweet associations from home, school and peer groups.

GETTING THERE FIRST

There is a principle in Torah jurisprudence that a judge cannot listen to the argument of a litigant before the latter's opponent arrives. This is so because what a person hears first, should it go unopposed, takes root in the heart and mind and is difficult to dislodge.[5]

The same holds true for what will have first taken root in our children's minds and hearts.

When we know that our children will be exposed to ideas we consider alien to their well-being, we have to be sure to get there first.

Parents need to make children aware of the tests they will face and give them the wherewithal to cope. Most often, the major asset a child has is his love for home and school and, by extension, what they stand for.

---

4. When Yosef sent a message to his father that he was still alive, he referred to where they had been studying when he left. Those were indeed joyous times for him. See Rashi, *Bereishis* 45:27. Rav Moshe Rabanowitz, *shlita*, of Jerusalem, says that perhaps this is what the Torah is hinting at with: "And Yisrael loved Yosef more than his brothers" (*Bereishis* 37:3). Perhaps the ability of Yosef to survive in such a terrible environment arose from the love that Yaakov had showered upon him.
5. *Sanhedrin* 7b; *Shulchan Aruch, Choshen Mishpat* 17:5,8.

How NOT to Expose Them

Exposure to the dominant, materialistic culture is not an ideal, but it is sometimes a necessary part of living in a world that is completely at odds with our belief system. However, when a child has already shown a tendency to forsake his Jewish heritage, it can be a momentous error to expose him even further to a irreligious and immoral environment.

> *An unhappy, misbehaving teenage boy had already developed negative peer relationships outside the school and was now a candidate for expulsion. His parents consulted a counselor, whose advice was to send him to public school. There, the counselor predicted, the boy would see how wonderful his old school was, and would mend his ways.*
>
> *When consulted about this, my response was that this advice was so dangerous, another twenty-two people would have to rule on it.*[6]
>
> *I recommended that the child be sent to an out-of-town school, where I knew that there was a staff and environment that would care for him with warmth and understanding, for it was clear that his home was no place to be.*
>
> *In the end it was too late. The boy had already gone to the high school orientation and was "sold" on his newfound "freedom." Today this person is a lost soul, far from his heritage.*

We can't expect young people who have already become enamored with the secular, materialistic, freewheeling environment to foresee the tragedy that such a society brings in its wake.

---

6. In capital cases, a court of twenty-three judges is needed.

Hashem has placed us in exile, and sometimes we must be exposed to alien ideals. Eventually this exposure may make us stronger, but while our children's minds are young and their powers of discrimination not fully developed, such an encounter would be better avoided. If it cannot be avoided — which is often the case — then our children must be prepared beforehand with an educational and family experience that will see them through the test. And that experience must be thoroughly laced with Judaism and love, and must be as pure and as happy as possible.

Then, with Hashem's help, we will have withstood the terrible test of exile, and merit redemption. For there is a good chance that once we pass a test, it will get taken away. May this come to pass speedily, in our days.

❧ Points to Remember

THE LONGER we can shield a child from a negative environment, the better.

WHAT a person hears first takes root in the heart and mind and is difficult to dislodge.

IT CONSTITUTES greatness to live within, yet stand apart from, a decadent environment, but we dare not attempt this unless it is preceded by a period of purity.

ONE'S memories of the time spent in a pure environment must be happy ones.

A LOVE of learning and spiritual growth are indispensable to a person's continued development.

A CHILD needs a model of a deep, warm and caring relationship in order to succeed in his relationship with Hashem.

MISDEEDS can be rectified.

CHAPTER TWENTY-EIGHT

TV, Videos, and Who Knows What Else: Not Only a Torah Issue

Television, videos, movies, and other modern forms of visual entertainment occupy a prominent position in the world today, so no effort to protect children from a spiritually hostile environment can be complete without mentioning these influences. In this chapter I will limit myself to a brief presentation of the effects of the media on our children. It is patently clear, from a Torah perspective, that a person who exposes his child to television, videos, and movies (not to mention questionable magazines and books, etc.) is not merely playing with the child's soul, he is actively destroying it. No person hoping to raise a child imbued with Torah values can allow exposure to this immoral and sadistic "education." My hope, in the few words that I will devote to the subject, is to present the reality that this is not solely an issue of whether our children will grow up as Torah Jews. *Exposure to modern media "entertainment" will destroy them as human beings, from the standpoint of both morals and character. This is not a "religious" issue, it is an issue of life or, God forbid, death.*

> *Someone once mentioned to Mori VeRabi, zt"l, that television is idolatry. His response was that TV isn't idolatry, it's brain death.*

Television makes it exceedingly difficult to produce your own thoughts. It is so comfortable to have someone else take over. Thinking becomes a chore, a burden.

> *I remember that once, on a flight from New York to Los Angeles, the PA system announced that because of the harsh winter caused by the phenomenon known as El Niño, we would be battling high winds and the flight would take an additional half hour. But there was no need to worry — there would be an extra movie.*

Rav Tzvi Zobin of Jerusalem, an expert on learning disabilities, pointed out to me an interesting fact:

> *Television, because of the rapidly changing screen, trains you not to pay attention to details. If you focus too much on any one detail in the picture, you lose the flow of the script. If, after several years of exposure to TV, a child then begins school, where he is asked to differentiate between a B and a P, or an E and an F, the search for detail is a burden to him. He has long since learned that details are unimportant. School becomes "hard" and "unpleasant," and the stage is set for a negative experience. Even "educational" programs such as "Sesame Street" make it difficult to sustain the child's interest in class, for the teacher can never match the excitement generated by the TV program.*

Speaking of "Sesame Street," it is generally not a good idea to teach preschoolers what they'll be learning in first grade, since once they reach the classroom, they'll be bored and will learn what it means not to pay attention in class, Furthermore, the teacher, for her part, will, simply because of the pressures to teach an entire group of children, tend to pay less attention to a child who already knows how to read or do arithmetic.

That paragon of Jewish educators, Rav Samson Raphael Hirsch, *zt"l*, writes in this regard:

Should the mother attempt to anticipate the work of the school? Should she see to it that her child is already able to read and recite the multiplication tables and so forth by the time he enters school? The answer is No! She should not concern herself with anything that will be the specific function of the school, for such haphazard anticipation of the work that should be done by the school is often more damaging than helpful.[1]

I'm certainly not opposed to teaching young children, but this should be in matters that stir the child's imagination, such as telling inspiring stories. In addition, personal bonding time with the mother at preschool age develops the child far more than any specific information the mother might impart.

TV "Withdrawal" and Misbehavior

Nothing seems so tantalizing to the parent as a cheap, constant "babysitter," one that keeps the children mesmerized and "out of trouble." Even the knowledge that TV is harmful doesn't seem to deter the most caring and responsible of parents. For the parent needs relief *now*, and a little television, the reasoning goes, couldn't be that terrible. Indeed, it has been said that an overwhelming majority of American parents polled agreed that TV isn't good for children, but almost 100 percent of their homes have at least one TV set.

But there is a big downside to TV as babysitter. Without it, you feel lost. Children, unable to occupy themselves, spin out of control.

In a parenting seminar, one mother asked me why her children act up so much in the car. My response was that this was the only place where they were not being "entertained" by the TV. After the seminar, another woman came up to me to

---

1. See *The Collected Writings of Rabbi Samson Raphael Hirsch* (Jerusalem: Feldheim Publishers, 1997), vol. 7, pp.111–12.

say that they had just had a TV installed in their minivan. They simply had no other way of keeping things under control.

THE MOVING PARTS OF AN ADDICTION

The basic dynamic of an addiction is that it offers immediate, total gratification, without too much effort. TV fits this description. Turn on the set and your troubles are over. Fights over which program to see are also easy to solve. Each person can have his or her own TV set. Then the destruction of the family unit is complete.

The degree to which TV has power over our children is illustrated by the following. I posed a question to two of the finest principals I know, Rav Kalman Baumann of Toras Emes Academy of Miami, and Rav Shlomo Goldberg of Ohr Eliyahu Academy of Los Angeles: "If parents choose something 'wholesome' for their children to see on TV, with the stipulation that it will then be discussed by the family afterwards, do you think that maybe then it would be okay? That way, the children wouldn't feel deprived vis-à-vis their classmates." The immediate response of both principals was amazing: It wouldn't work. Within a short period of time, the set would be on indiscriminately again and the children would be watching their usual programs.

Mr. Avi Shulman of Monsey, New York, an authority on children and television viewing, also decries the myth that parents can exercise meaningful control over their children's television viewing. It usually can't be done, he says, not in their own homes, and certainly not in their neighbors'.

There is no way around it: TV is addictive, and the only way to deal with it is to get rid of it. I would recommend consulting *To Kindle a Soul,* by Rabbi Lawrence Kelemen, for useful and frightening statistics about what television can do to your child.[2] Information documenting the damage inflicted by television should be shown to anyone who does not appreciate the harm to which they are exposing their child.

What You Can Do

There is a secular organization in the United States that helps people who want to get their families off TV. It is called TV-Free America, and it can be contacted by mail, telephone, fax or e-mail.

TV-Free America
1611 Connecticut Avenue NW — Suite 3A
Washington, DC 20009

Tel. (202) 887–0436
Fax (202) 518–5560
tvfa@essential.org
http://www.essentialorg/orgs/tvfa

Rav Ephraim Applebaum, a teacher at Eitz Chaim of Toronto, has put out an excellent collection of articles, tips and valuable information on how to get kids off TV. He can be reached by telephone at (905) 881–8438 or by fax at (905) 886–6525. Or write to Parents Concerned With Media Influence, 8950 Bathurst Street, Thornhill, Ontario L4J 8A7, Canada.

When It's Everywhere

Parents often ask me, "Even if I get rid of my TV, my kids can still see it at their friends' houses." True enough, it is difficult turn-

---

2. Jerusalem: Targum Press, 2001. See pp. 153-190 for an excellent overview of the damage inflicted upon children by television.

ing your child into the only pariah on the block, especially when in many elementary schools across the United States, one of the recurring topics of conversation is the programs the children saw the night before.

A parent should attempt to mitigate, as much as possible, the effects and quantity of TV and video viewing. Sometimes it may be necessary, for limited periods, to have nature videos, documentaries, etc. at home. Friends can be invited over, and good food made available. Be creative. This approach is better accomplished in consultation with a local educator, one who is familiar with the reality in your child's school but who still subscribes to the idea that television is inimical to your child's welfare.

It is a good idea also to have a well-stocked recreation room. There should be interesting games that can compete with the television, and parental participation can serve as an incentive to play rather than watch a program. As we have said many times, create a good connection with your children and they'll love being with you. In addition, the best way to avoid the negative is to be involved in something positive. Even if the game isn't exactly educational, it's still better than "brain death."

❧ Exercises

1. Together with your children, plan a TV-free week, starting on Saturday night. If your children have no school on Sunday morning and/or afternoon, have some games ready and be prepared to play along with them. When the week is finished, go for a special family outing. Manipulate things so that the second Saturday night as well as that Sunday are free of TV as well, and by Monday morning, when it's time to go back to school, it will have been more than a week.

2. Plan a long-term, big family prize if the family can stay off TV for a month.

3. If the above seems too hard, then reduce TV viewing-time per evening and spend that time with the children doing something you all enjoy. It is best, however, to go "cold turkey." Endure the initial difficulty and win big in the end.

4. Get the families of one or two of your children's friends involved as well. This will make it much easier. "Freedom from Television" can even become a status symbol in school, especially if the school administration actively encourages and rewards abstinence from TV. If this sounds too haughty or snobby to you, don't worry; just get them off of TV and deal with the arrogance (I call it kosher pride) later.

❧ Points to Remember

A PERSON who exposes his child to television, videos, and movies is not merely playing with his child's soul, he is actively destroying it.

PERSONAL bonding time with the mother at preschool age develops the child far more than any specific information the mother might impart.

AN ADDICTION offers immediate, total gratification, without too much effort.

TELEVISION is addictive, and the only way to deal with it is to get rid of it.

PART SEVEN

Using the Lessons of History to Build a Better Future

CHAPTER TWENTY-NINE

Bridging the Generation Gap

When the guns of World War I fell silent, the war within the world of European Jewry had only just begun.[1] Family life was shattered, and the very fiber of Jewish community life lay smashed economically, socially and religiously. In Poland and Lithuania, anti-Semitism was a national creed, and in the Soviet Union, Torah Jewry faced its most implacable enemies since Roman times, the Communists, who were aided and abetted by the *Yevseksia*, the Jewish section of the Communist party.

World War II would be a shattering six-million-fold blow, and when by 1946 the destruction of European Jewry was complete, the battle for the spiritual and physical survival of the Jews was picked up and carried on by the community's remnants. The War of Independence in the fledgling State of Israel occurred shortly thereafter, thrusting the new country into a state of war which persists to this day.

The Sephardic community, although not as hard-hit during World War II as the Ashkenazic (European) one, was to experience its own spiritual Holocaust in Israel. The older generation looked

---

1. The author remembers when Rav Elozor Menachem Man Shach, *zt"l*, made this statement several years ago.

on helplessly as their children succumbed to the secular values of the leaders of the newly established state. Our people's struggle was and continues to be not only for physical survival among external enemies but for spiritual survival: We are engaged in an ongoing ideological battle about Jewish identity that is being waged internally between the various sectors of Israel's own population.

All these cataclysms have brought in their wake a series of generation gaps, whereby the older generation was Torah-oriented in world outlook and religious in practice, while the younger generation, seeking to create what they felt would be a better world, often espoused various secular causes — whether it was Communism in Eastern Europe or assimilation and Americanization in the United States. As stated, Sephardic Jewry followed this pattern as well, after the establishment of the Jewish State.

Today, an amazing thing is happening. Many members of the younger generation, disillusioned with the false promises of happiness which materialism offers, are adopting a more religious outlook, thereby giving rise to a new sort of generation gap. Now it is the younger generation that is espousing the ancient values rejected by their parents and grandparents.[2]

Indeed, it was, and continues to be, a War of the Worlds.

---

2. This widespread phenomenon has given rise, in turn, to an entirely new set of generational conflicts and challenges. There is one particular manifestation of this phenomenon, the interrelationships between the children of *ba'alei teshuvah* (the newly religious) and their less observant grandparents. I think one of the reasons for these generation gaps is that most parents want to make sure that their children don't experience the suffering they themselves had to endure. The generations following World War I underwent the ordeal of poverty and material deprivation, and parents who experienced these tribulations wanted to protect their children from this fate. They saw (in the United States) secularization, primarily though education, as the vehicle that would ensure their children a more secure life, and (in Eastern Europe) they saw communism as the harbinger of a more fair distribution of wealth and as the espouser of equal opportunity.

BRIDGING THE GENERATION GAP

For many reasons, both national and personal, all generation gaps must be bridged. In this chapter, we will be concentrating on the problems that arise for children whose parents and grandparents differ regarding how they should be brought up. It will not be for us to discuss here who's right and who's wrong, but rather, how this generational rift can affect the children.

Rifts within a family reflect those of the society of which it is part. Since the conflict of which we speak is so close to home — in fact, within the home — dealing constructively with it is even more crucial than dealing with the larger issue of the conflict between Judaism and the "outside world." In other words, before teaching a child how to live a successful and full Jewish religious life in a secular or Christian society, he must often learn how to live successfully with his own extended family.

GRANDPARENTS

Everything that God created has a function, or many functions. Indeed, this is one of the hallmarks of Creation.[3]

There are many amazing twists in the modern *ba'al teshuvah* phenomenon. *And the Angels Laughed* (Brooklyn: Artscroll, 1997), a book about Rav Levi Yitzchok Horowitz, the Bostoner Rebbe, tells the story of a young woman who discovered the road back to Judaism as a *result* of inter-generational differences and her father's determined anti-religiosity. The woman's grandfather had once told her: "I want you to remember three things: Remember that you are Jewish. Remember Shabbos. And remember me." These words made a profound impression on her, but since her family was not observant, she decided to start out simply by lighting Shabbos candles every Friday night. Her father would then proceed, week by week, to snuff out the flames. It was her father's diligence and persistence at undoing the candle lighting that gave her the strength, she said, to be equally diligent and persistent. "I [realized] that I could just as stubbornly keep them burning," she said. "So I became religious because of both of them, my father and my grandfather."

3. See *Chovos HaLevovos*, Second Gate, *Sha'ar HaBechinah* (The Gate of Reflection), for a beautiful treatment of this subject.

Grandparents, like parents, have manifold purposes, and naturally these will vary according to their unique circumstances and personalities. But one purpose can be fulfilled by virtually all grandparents across the board, and it is particularly relevant for us here. It is a service that cannot be performed by anyone else: *The existence of grandparents makes it possible for parents to role-model the honoring of parents.* Since parental example is by far the most powerful form of education,[4] the greatest possible education regarding this mitzvah is provided when children see their own parents fulfilling it.

Parents should therefore not only get along with the grandparents, but also honor them, if only for the sake of their children.

Shielding our children from exposure to generational strife is so crucial that when the relationship between parents and grandparents is strained, and the parties find no way to ameliorate the situation, then living at a distance is one option. But it is not the ideal solution.[5]

Trying to Understand Each Other

Mori VeRabi, *zt"l*, was once asked by a group of students at Yeshivas Ohr Somayach how they could get their parents (who gen-

---

4. For it utilizes the sense of sight, which powerfully impacts on the emotion. See *My Child, My Disciple*, by this author (Jerusalem: Feldheim Publishers, 1993), chapter 11, p. 53.
5. Immigrant parents, when they leave behind their own parents in the "Old Country," are in effect depriving their children of this nutrient. Although frequent phone calls, and sending family videos and cassettes are an important way we can show our children how much we love our parents, it is not the same as when the parents interact, in person, with their own parents, in a loving and respectful manner. They need to find "spiritual supplements" to ensure that their children learn what proper honor, love and respect consists of. But like all supplements, substitutes are never as good as the real thing. Immigrants often have good and altruistic reasons for immigrating, and history has shown immigrants to be a hardy and creative breed, but this is one of the risks they run when changing countries.

uinely believed that their children were in a cult) to understand them.[6] His answer is classic:

> *You cannot get anyone to understand you. What you can do is to try to understand them, and hope they will reciprocate.*[7]

Mori VeRabi, zt"l, was really expressing what King Solomon said long ago: "As water reflects a face, so, too, does the heart of a man reflect [the heart of] his fellowman."[8] We tend to treat others as we are treated, and to feel toward others as they feel toward us. It is this honest effort to value and understand the other that will enable us to honor and be patient with those with whom we disagree.[9]

Sometimes grandparents find it truly difficult to comprehend what their *ba'al teshuvah* children are so concerned about, and can unwittingly, from love and enthusiastic goodwill, introduce their grandchildren to a highly entertaining secular world, offering them videos, non-kosher food, television, and so forth. In such a case, it is the responsibility of the parents to lovingly provide enough clear information to the grandparents so as to avoid inadvertent mistakes.[10]

It is true that there are the rare cases of grandparents who do knowingly try to influence their observant grandchildren into adopting a secular lifestyle, in which case the child does indeed need to

---

6. I recall a case in which a student at Aish HaTorah, another school for returnees to their Jewish heritage, was actually lured back to the States by his parents and put into the hands of "cult busters." After several days, the three men told the parents that their child was not in a cult, for his ability to think and question had been enhanced, while a cult robs its members of these abilities.
7. *Mori VeRabi, zt"l*, gave the same advice to people who felt they lacked friends. You cannot make anyone be your friend, he said, but you can befriend them and hope they will reciprocate.
8. *Mishlei* 27:19.
9. See *HaIsh al HaChomah*, vol. 3, p. 350, where Rav Yosef Chaim Sonnenfeld, *zt"l*, eloquently espoused this as a prime way to heal the rift between religious and secular elements in the Holy Land.
10. Rabbi Lawrence (Leib) Kelemen, *shlita*, author of *To Kindle a Soul*, says, "Whenever anyone questions my hesitance to expose my kids to TV, I just quote two or three statistics from the book (pp. 153-190), and my nonreligious relatives are left speechless.... Even by secular standards, the 'idiot box' is only for idiots."

be distanced from them. But this is unlikely to occur if there is love and peace in the family, regardless of religious differences.

Dear parents, if your *chinuch* is good and your home is as warm and loving as you can make it, and if you send your children to the proper schools, then the danger that grandparents will serve as undesirable role models is far less significant than the emotional and spiritual dangers brought about by strife and bickering.

Communicating Nonverbally

People communicate in two ways, verbally and nonverbally. This has been discussed many times in this book, but one difference between the two is important to mention here.

In verbal communication, the speaker uses words to try to gain acceptance for some idea that he himself already believes, or to convey an emotion that he wants the other person to understand. The message then passes through the listener's brain, which may be predisposed to resisting and invalidating it.

In nonverbal communication, an idea or emotion is communicated by means of some physical action or gesture, which is then interpreted involuntarily by the other person — whereupon he reaches his own conclusion. A conclusion reached on his own will carry more weight with him. This, I think, is what is meant by the saying, "actions speak louder than words."

Verbal communication is more important than the nonverbal mode when, for example, the goal is to give some sort of directive, or to teach a skill.[11] Verbal detail then becomes a valuable tool for avoiding misunderstanding. However, when it comes to human

---

11. The truth is that even when teaching a new skill to an adult, nonverbal encouragement and a good relationship will have a direct bearing on how well and how quickly the subject or skill is mastered.

relationships and the communication of emotion, the nonverbal route is by far the more potent.

The desire to understand another person, and to convey the importance you place on whatever he or she is expressing, is best communicated nonverbally. Here are a few examples that apply specifically to parents and grandparents:

1. **Ask Advice.** When a person's counsel is honestly sought, a clear message is being sent: *I value you and I value your opinions.* There is a virtually endless list of topics upon which one can solicit grandparents for extremely valuable advice, both on technical issues (medical questions, for example) and on a general level (discipline, sibling relationships, etc.).[12] Such interchange not only fosters close, warm relationships, but accords recognition to the wisdom that life bestows as people grow older. (May we all, God willing, have the merit to be in their shoes one day.) If your attitude toward the older generation is that they have little of value to offer, then you should prepare yourself for being similarly viewed by your own grown children.

Being treated respectfully is a basic necessity for any human being, and plays no small role in emotional and physical health. All the more so is this the case for the elderly, who may by this time have suffered many losses in life.

> *I remember the case of a student at yeshiva whose grandfather was critically ill in a Paris hospital. The boy was unable to fly immediately to France, and came to discuss the situation. I advised him to send a video to his grandfather, telling him how much he looked forward to seeing him soon and that he had so many questions, about life and about the family, that he wanted to ask.*

---

12. Wise parents hesitate before offering advice to a son- or daughter-in-law, and must be made to feel that their input is sincerely sought and welcomed. The Yiddish word for mother-in-law is *shviger*, which, it is said, is related to the word *shveig*, to be silent, for a mother-in-law must learn the art of silence.

2. Remember What They Once Taught You. When grown children remind their parents of the lessons that they have learned from them, they're sending a life-giving message: *What you taught me has remained with me and is part of my world outlook. I treasure what you say and keep it uppermost in my consciousness.* It is also a message that this son or daughter, though now grown, still regards him- or herself as their child.

3. "And He Will Bring Back the Heart of the Fathers..." When people feel appreciated and valued, then differences in religious outlook are rarely an emotional sore point. These differences can be addressed technically and solved in an amicable atmosphere. There are many things children can do with grandparents that don't threaten their religious training. They have only to gain from knowing the caring and loving people who most grandparents are.

The prophet Malachi teaches us, "And he [the prophet Eliyahu] will bring back the hearts of the fathers [through] the children, and the hearts of the children [through] the fathers."[13] I think that the key word here is "heart." It is the heart, the emotional component, which will in the final analysis bring families closer together again. It will not be done by way of intellectual debate, whereby each party defends his own position, lest someone be proven wrong and lose the respect of his loved ones.

Any kind of hostile battle between parents and grandparents is a bitter one with high stakes, and children are the suffering pawns in such conflict.

> *Rav Mendel Kaplan, zt"l,[14] once told a recent ba'al teshuvah (who, it seems, was likely to be at odds with his parents) that he had only one mitzvah to perform when returning home — to honor his parents. He was to constantly look for physical things, such as cleaning or errand-running, to do for them.*

---

13. *Malachi* 3:24. Here, the word "fathers" refers to parents.
14. See *Reb Mendel*, by Rav Yisroel Greenwald (New York: Mesorah Publications, 1994), p. 169.

Teaching Children History

I recommend that parents give their children a lesson in Jewish history. It is for this reason that we devoted several opening paragraphs to the reasons for the secularization of the Jewish People. The history lesson should be as detailed, graphic, and interesting as possible. Children need to know the world in which their grandparents and great-grandparents grew up. This is especially important for children of *ba'alei teshuvah*, who might not understand why their grandparents are not observant.

For example, if a Jew, until World War II, observed Shabbos in the United States, then he would usually need to look for a new job every week. In addition, there was an almost total unavailability of Jewish education. Furthermore, many parents feared that Jewish education was deficient compared with secular education, and that it would render their children inferior in the eyes of the Americans — thus further hindering their absorption into the society that was so good to them.[15]

The lure of this free society, that offered equal opportunity, was mind-boggling to the European immigrant. In his country of origin, being Jewish had meant that for him that all doors to earning a decent and dignified livelihood had been closed, while in America, it seemed that Jews were being treated better than they ever had been in history. Rav Shlomo Brevda, *shlita*, tells the following story, which brings to life the trials that these people faced when con-

---

15. Rav Berel Wein, *shlita*, has pointed out that this may be the reason so many American Jews were afraid to vigorously protest the destruction of European Jewry and support any and all efforts to send them financial support, or to encourage the endangerment of United States military personnel in efforts to hinder the Nazi's Final Solution. They were terrified of American society turning on them and saying, in effect, "Oh, we thought you were Americans first and Jews second. Now we see it's the other way around. Your loyalty to the United States is only secondary." We today cannot imagine the overwhelming gratitude of Jewish immigrants toward the United States, for giving them a haven from European oppression, and how strongly they felt that such a response on the part of the American public was to be avoided at all costs.

fronted by unexpected fairness and decency on the part of the American culture:

> *It was 1946. The parents of a refugee student studying at an American yeshiva were stranded in Europe, refused an entry visa to the United States because one was suffering from tuberculosis. The Rosh Yeshiva went with the student to the State Department in Washington, DC, where he knew high-ranking officials from the days when he had gone to Washington to try to save Jews trapped in Nazi-occupied Europe.*
>
> *In 1946, the entire world was in ashes. The United States wasn't just a superpower, it was the only power. American prestige and power were unchallenged and feared. So entering the State Department meant entering into the very pinnacle of world power.*
>
> *Upon entering the reception room of some important official, the secretary asked the Rosh Yeshiva who he was and what he wanted. He replied, "Tell your boss that Rabbi ____ is here."*
>
> *The secretary did so, and the official immediately emerged from his office. "Rabbi ____," he exclaimed, "what can I do for you? I'm in a meeting now, but I'll be out as soon as possible." The Rosh Yeshiva and the student were then ushered into another room and most cordially served drinks and made to feel extremely honored and comfortable while they waited.*
>
> *So bewitching to this student was American hospitality and decency, he later said, "If they had asked me to take off my yarmulka and throw it to the floor, I would have done it in a second."*[16]

---

16. Rav Shlomo Brevda, *shlita*, used this story in the context of speaking about the greatness of Esther, who was not only *not influenced* by the luxury and friendliness of Achashveirosh's palace, but indeed, despised it and became physically ill by it. See the commentary of the Vilna Gaon to *Esther* 2:15.

The Two Lies

The Vilna Gaon[17] says that the *yetzer ha-ra* (Evil Inclination) has two ways of working:

1. He Claims that the Torah Is Too Difficult to Keep. When the Serpent sought to entice Chavah into partaking from the Tree of Knowledge, he said that God wouldn't let them eat from any of the fruits in the Garden. It's so hard to not eat *any* of the fruits in the Garden.

The implication of this was: This prohibition is too difficult to keep.

2. He Distorts the Truth. When you eat from the Tree, the Serpent was saying, you won't die. God was able to be a creator because He, too, ate from the Tree, and now He wants to make sure you don't do the same.

This was, of course, a ludicrous fabrication.

These two methods have been used and repeated down through the centuries, right up until our own time. In America, there were those who claimed that though keeping Shabbos would of course be preferable, it was far too difficult to do so in the United States. This was also the case, they maintained, when it came to sending a child to yeshiva or to establishing a *cheder*.

Then there were those who maintained that the right and good thing to do was to let go of Shabbos. Orthodoxy was outmoded, this was a new world, and the best thing for the children would be to help them adapt.

Both groups of people were saying that it was a new world and that Jews should conform to it. Those in the first group, who said

---

17. *Aderes Eliyahu, Bereishis* 3:1,4.

that Torah was too difficult to keep, admitted that the observant way of life was a better one, but that the old ways were impossible to maintain under the circumstances. The second group, who distorted the truth, said that the new world was superior, and that it was therefore correct to cast off the old ways.

I have a poignant memory of a victim of the first school of thought.

> One Friday evening over twenty years ago, when we were living in the Sanhedriah HaMurchevet neighborhood of Jerusalem, a student from Yeshivas Aish HaTorah brought his mother to Rav Moshe Lazerus's house for Shabbos. When she saw Mrs. Lazerus lighting the Shabbos candles, she suddenly broke down. It was the first time she had seen candle lighting in over forty years. She recalled the first Shabbos that she had gone to work, feeling that she would be struck dead because of her desecration of Shabbos. Later, of course, it became easier.

USING PICTURES

No matter what problems may exist between the generations, children should not be made to feel ashamed of their grandparents. This is so for a multitude of reasons, not the least of which is that such feelings engender low self-image in the children themselves.

On the contrary, parents should do their utmost to instill love and respect in children toward their grandparents, regardless of their religious beliefs. One way of accomplishing this with younger children is with pictures.

A picture is worth at least ten thousand words. There are many pictorial histories of American and pre-war European Jewry which can impress upon children a greater understanding of their great-grandparents. If it was the great-grandparents' misfortune to lose their *Yiddishkeit*, parents can expound upon all the tests that they faced. If their great-grandparents continued being observant in spite of the enormous societal pressures that they encountered in the so-called "New World," the children can be taught to respect their great-grandparents' spiritual heroism and nobility.

In any case, it is generally characteristic of the particular generations of Jews about whom we are speaking that whatever else was lost, they resisted intermarriage in spite of all the temptations around them to totally assimilate. Parents can speak of the remarkable strength of spirit behind this retention of Jewish identity.

Children love stories, and the more details the better. Parents can research the history of the times and places where their parents and grandparents grew up, making several enjoyable storytelling occasions out of this with the children.

Difficult Grandparents

Even when grandparents or in-laws have difficult natures, the restraint, patience and loving respect accorded to them will not be lost on the maturing child. The parents themselves will eventually reap a rich harvest of respect from their children as reward for their endurance and perseverance in the fulfillment of this mitzvah.

To sum up, children need grandparents. Differences in religious outlook need not be a reason to deny children this natural and vital nutrient. Almost as much as children need to see their own parents living together in peace, they must also witness, for their own healthy development as nurturing, loving human beings, love and peace between the previous generations.

❧ Points to Remember

EVERYTHING that God created has a function.

PARENTAL example is by far the most powerful form of education.

BEFORE teaching a child how to live a successful and full Jewish religious life in a secular or Christian society, he must often learn how to live successfully with his own extended family.

HONEST effort to value and understand others will enable us to honor and be patient with those with whom we disagree.

BEING treated respectfully is a basic necessity for any human being.

WHEN people feel appreciated and valued, then differences in religious outlook are rarely an emotional sore point.

PARENTS should do their utmost to instill love and respect in children toward their grandparents, regardless of their religious beliefs.

CHAPTER THIRTY

The Ba'al Teshuvah Family in a Torah Society

THE MIRACLE IN CONTEMPORARY JEWISH HISTORY

It was the oft-expressed opinion of *Mori VeRabi, zt"l,* that we are witnessing a miracle in our time. In the past, Jews embraced Torah as a result of persecution or political hardship, or on account of some physical threat to their security from their country of residence. Today, for the first time in our history, secular Jews are doing *teshuvah* (returning to Hashem and His Torah) in spite of having been raised in an environment that is comfortable both economically and socially.

Mori VeRabi said that this switch is a sign that we are in the Generation of *Mashiach*.[1] When discussing this subject, he would sometimes cite the following story to show how close people are today to *teshuvah*.

---

1. Dr. Alan Weiss, a prominent cardiologist from St. Louis, who enjoyed a close relationship with Rav Elozor Shach, *zt"l*, quoted Rav Shach as having told him that although the *yeshivos* are the heart of the Jewish People, it is the *ba'alei teshuvah* who will be the ones to bring *Mashiach*.

Someone from Los Angeles was in Rochester, NY, when his mother passed away. Before her passing he had promised her that he would recite the mourner's Kaddish for one month.

Upon his return to Los Angeles, he rushed to a Reform temple on Wilshire Boulevard to catch the Afternoon Service, but found that during the week the Temple was closed. He then rushed over to the Orthodox Beth Jacob Congregation on Olympic Boulevard, but arrived too late, and had to await the commencement of the Evening Service.

As he sat there waiting, he noticed a Jew sitting and learning Torah with a sweet melody. Captivated by the purity of the melody and by the enthusiasm of the learner, the man resolved to "check out" what this brand of Judaism was.

From that one small spark, he eventually found his way to a Torah life.

This return to Judaism is a blessing for us all. Every *ba'al teshuvah* injects the Jewish People with fresh spiritual energy and a renewed appreciation for Judaism. These can sometimes be lacking in those who have grown up with it and take it for granted as a natural part of life.

However, *ba'alei teshuvah* often run into grave disappointments, particularly as parents.

Disenchantment

We've all heard the saying that the grass is always greener on the other side of the fence. I think that this refers to the human tendency to believe that life should proceed in a certain prescribed way. Since grass is supposed to be green, and it doesn't look all that green in our own yard, then somewhere "out there" people are surely enjoying grass that's as green as it should be.

Once our emotions create these generalized idealizations, we carry the images around with us and project them onto everything in our lives: from other people (especially our marriage partners) and the careers we choose to follow, to the institutions in which we participate and the ideas we believe in — all the way down to how this summer vacation is going to turn out.

We imagine that if only these idealizations would become the reality, then everything that bothers us about the present would disappear.

Then, sure enough, we find ourselves feeling disappointed in our lives.

The *ba'al teshuvah* often views the Torah world as a place where perfection can be expected and realized. However, in many places around the globe today, the Torah community is under siege, because of the secular, hedonistic society's inroads into the observant society and observant home. Since the Torah world consists of human beings, it has imperfections. Some flaws are easier to explain than others, but to the *ba'al teshuvah*, any one of them can be disenchanting.

STRENGTHS AND WEAKNESSES

Sometimes a person comes in from the outside world having been highly appreciated and highly trained in a field in which the Torah world is weak, or uninvolved with for halachic reasons. For example, let's say a landscape designer, or dietician, or violinist, enters Orthodox society and sees that world as not living correctly or not being appreciative of certain facets of life. Sometimes the low quality of secular studies in some Torah schools is worrisome to the *ba'al teshuvah* parent.

Sometimes parents can be critical of a school they see as being under par in certain areas, and their criticism is expressed loudly enough for the children to hear. The truth is, however, that even unspoken disrespect will be picked up on, and manifested alarmingly in the children. As Rav Tzadok says, children express openly what parents feel secretly in their hearts.[2]

> *A man once brought his daughter to the local rav to have him dissuade her from intermarriage. The rav, however, failed at this assignment, and said to the father, "All these years, I've been undermined too much in your home to have any effect now." This is analogous to the thief who holds up a doctor on the road and tosses the doctor's medical bag into the river. The next day the thief's daughter falls ill. He comes running to the doctor for help, but the doctor has nothing to treat her with.*

Just as we may overly idealize people and institutions, we sometimes also overly discredit them.

Children need to feel that their parents support the school they attend, and the environment in which they're being raised. Certainly a parent has the right, and the obligation, to point out to their children's educators the defects in the child's education and environment, but this should be done unemotionally, and against the backdrop of a general respect for their children's activities at school and in the Torah world at large.

How People View Themselves

Sometimes a *ba'al teshuvah* begins a life centered around Torah Judaism, quickly changes his or her name, manner of dress and language, and even some of his or her mannerisms. All these constitute rejections of the person's previous lifestyle. If the rejection is total and sudden, it may be more indicative of a rejection of self.

---

2. *Tzidkas HaTzaddik*, section 63.

Ba'alei teshuvah need to find ways of retaining the positive facets of their pre-*ba'al teshuvah* days. There is no question that the strength of character behind the courageous changes they've made in their lives comes from somewhere — and it's often from their morally sensitive, principle-centered parents.

The problems that *ba'alei teshuvah* encounter in their adaptation to the Torah world, especially in regard to their children's upbringing, must be addressed, like all problems, with an understanding of the unique strengths and abilities germane to *ba'alei teshuvah*. Then problems turn into challenges, and can be addressed in that spirit.

Ba'alei teshuvah, having seen the falsehoods of materialism, and having successfully rejected the dominant culture, now face a new challenge. The Torah-oriented society that they've chosen, the culture that is molding their children, is in many ways foreign territory. While they find this society far superior to the one they themselves grew up in, they still find themselves in situations in which they have no experience. In addition, *ba'alei teshuvah* very often are at an added disadvantage, as they have no *frum* family to steer them through the waters of child-rearing in the Torah world.

FAMILY SIZE

The average American family has two children. The average Torah home has at least double that, and five to seven children per family is not unusual. What this means is that most *ba'al teshuvah* parents have no personal model on which to manage a family considerably larger than the one in which they were raised. In addition, the *ba'al teshuvah* usually encounters opposition from his or her parents and/or siblings, who are critical of the "burden" being imposed on their family member by this big-family lifestyle. Furthermore, having chosen a stronger Torah community in which to live, the *ba'al teshuvah* often lives far away from his or her family of origin, and the help — with child-raising, household maintenance, and finances, that in the Torah world is often gladly given by grandparents and siblings — is lacking.

This experience is not limited to *ba'al teshuvah* couples, however. On a personal level, my wife and I were one of those young American couples who were establishing families in Israel in the 1960's and early 1970's. The families of people like ourselves were in the United States, and there was a dearth of help for young mothers who were blessed with a good "head start" in raising beautiful families. We felt the lack of parental help keenly. We would have welcomed our parents' physical presence, as well as their parenting expertise.

My wife and I were new immigrants, and there is a great similarity between raising children in a new country and raising children in an unfamiliar society. But just as the new immigrant has deemed it worthwhile to make the move across the world, a move which my wife and I have never regretted, so, too, does the *ba'al teshuvah* deem it worthwhile to become part of what is, after all is said and done, the finest society of all — the people who are loyal to Hashem and His Torah, even in the twenty-first century.

Lack of Familial Support

For those immigrants to Israel in the 1960's and 1970's, what happened during those years was that young families facing similar challenges grew close to each other, and forged friendships that would last a lifetime. Both material and moral support were there for young parents facing the challenge of raising a family without the normal parental help.

In just the same way, it is important that young *ba'al teshuvah* families join together and give to each other. Parenting advice should be forthcoming, and is indeed invaluable when offered by experienced, sensitive, sensible mothers. Both younger mothers and mothers who are five to ten years (or more) past their own child-rearing experiences, should join to share their expertise and encouragement. In addition, I believe it to be an important responsibility of those families who are veterans of the Torah world to reach out and respectfully, and tactfully, offer their advice and encouragement to those wonderful families who are now choosing this life direction.

Extended Family

Ba'al teshuvah families should, if possible, maintain good relations with their extended family, siblings, cousins, aunts and uncles, and, of course, grandparents. There are often difficulties that need to be addressed, for while the *ba'al teshuvah* wants to have his children benefit from knowing their relatives, some of the influences of the dominant society creep in. What to an average secular family is quite acceptable is, in a Torah family, a profound threat to the children's healthy spiritual development. It is vital to build on what binds you together, not what separates you. This is especially the case with extended family living close by.

There are many recreational activities, such as rowing or a trip to an aquarium, which can be enjoyable for all. When visiting secular relatives, remember to bring an interesting game that will occupy the children and distract them from viewing the "idiot box." Television, even when "educational," can open a whole panorama of difficulties. It should stay off, and, in my opinion, out of sight.

School

There is no question that one of the great advantages of living in the Torah world is that for children, the environment is much healthier than "modern" society, in which children are exposed at early ages to extremely damaging influences. His or her teachers will, in the grand majority of cases, be better personal role models, and the social setting will be on a far higher level morally and personally, than one would find in today's general school system.

However, the yeshiva or day school is a very different place from the public or private secular school in which the *ba'al teshuvah* parent himself was educated. The day is likely to be substantially longer, and the curriculum vastly different. Parents may have difficulty communicating with teachers who lack an understanding of their background, and may feel that they themselves are inadequately equipped to help their children with their Torah studies, since the material is unfamiliar to them. Indeed, not only can the material be unfamiliar, and very different from what they themselves learned as children, but also it can be taught in Hebrew or Yiddish, rather than the parents' native tongue. Similarities can be drawn between these *ba'al teshuvah* parents and the new immigrants to the United States at the turn of the twentieth century.

While it's absolutely necessary for their children to learn in a Torah school, parents can take steps to mitigate all these normal problems. I recommend the following:

Choosing the School

It is important to choose, if possible, a school that is open to meaningful parent-teacher dialogue. That is, if the parent starts early in the year to get acquainted with the teacher, the curriculum, and the school's goals, then the school should gladly help the parents keep abreast of their child's progress and be open to parental input as to who their child is and what kind of interaction with the teacher would work best for him or her.

It is vital that the school respect the fact that the *ba'al teshuvah* parent is indeed a unique individual, and that he or she will be its best source of information about such a family's special needs.

Principals have found that *ba'al teshuvah* parents, who do not take for granted the benefits of a Torah education, make the best allies in arousing a greater parental awareness of the school's needs in the general parent body. They realize that the so-called *"frum-*

from-birth" have a lot to learn from the excitement of people who understand full well what a gift it is to have a Torah education from a young age. If the principal himself is a *ba'al teshuvah*, then this augers well for your child's "career" at that school.

STUDYING WHAT YOUR CHILD IS LEARNING

Some schools provide either classes or resources that keep parents apprised of what their child is learning. This enables the parent to master all, or some of, the material that the child is studying. While this isn't absolutely necessary, it is a good way for a parent to keep in touch with his or her child's world, and to be of some assistance academically — certainly on the elementary school level.

BUILDING ON YOUR STRENGTHS

As stated earlier, the *ba'al teshuvah* parent needs to build on his personal strengths and create a relationship with his child which transcends the academic arena. Children can be helped to respect the fact that their parent never had the same opportunity to study Torah as a child. When the parent shares his life wisdom, life experience and skills (either academic or manual) with his child, the bond between them will be deep. The parent's ability to have changed his course in life for the right reasons, and his dedication to truth, will not be lost on the child.

UNREALISTIC EXPECTATIONS

All parents can have unrealistic expectations of their children. As has been pointed out, parents coming from Europe were particularly enchanted with the idea of their child having an opportunity to become a doctor. (*Mori VeRabi, zt"l,* once said that in Eastern Europe, the doctor had an almost divine aura.) But the children, sensing that their parents wanted *"nachas"* in ways that weren't always right for the children themselves, started to pull away.

There's still another variation on this theme. Rabbi Shlomo Goldberg, *shlita*, an expert educator in Los Angeles, was the first to bring this problem to my attention.

It is normal for parents to want for their children what they themselves never had, whether it be education, financial security, or certain life experiences. The parent lives vicariously through the child. This pattern is normal, generally speaking, but Rabbi Goldberg points out that it can be patently dangerous if the *ba'al teshuvah* parent wants his child to become a "super-FFB" (*frum-from-birth*). Children need to be loved, respected, and helped in every way. But they cannot carry their parents' unrealized life expectations on their shoulders.

For Us All

This need to build mutually loving and respectful relationships with our children obviously applies to all parents, not only to *ba'alei teshuvah*, for as we've said before, we live in such a fast-changing world that it is common for children to get the feeling that their parents are hopelessly "out of it." When that happens, the parents' power to protect and influence their children wanes.

Even parents who are sending their children to the same school they themselves attended, and whose children patronize the same corner pizza shop, are probably completely out of touch with their children's world if they rely on their own knowledge of the school and the pizza shop that dates back one or two decades, from the era of their own formative years. Today, even the passage of three or four years can signal massive change. In a pizza shop that was an innocent meeting place a few years ago, our children can learn things today and be exposed to things that are literally life-threatening, not just to their spiritual well-being, but physically as well.

In this respect, the *ba'al teshuvah* family is at an advantage. They realize that they need to understand their children's world, for it is clearly different from the one in which they grew up. They're not lulled into a false sense of security that they know what their children's day is like, whom they might meet up with, and what they're likely to see and hear.

The *nachas* they will have is indeed enormous. For they are the "Avrahams," the ones who began a new life for themselves and for their children.

❧ Points to Remember

CHILDREN express openly what parents feel secretly in their hearts.

WE IMAGINE that if only our idealizations would become the reality, then everything that bothers us about the present would disappear.

BA'ALEI TESHUVAH need to find ways of retaining the positive facets of their pre-*ba'al teshuvah* days.

VETERANS of the Torah world have a responsibility to reach out and offer advice and encouragement to those wonderful families who are now choosing a Torah-true lifestyle.

THE BA'AL TESHUVAH parent needs to build on his personal strengths and create a relationship with his child which transcends the academic arena.

CHILDREN cannot carry their parents' unrealized expectations on their shoulders.

CHAPTER THIRTY-ONE

Being a Parent: The Example of Yaakov

YAAKOV IN JEWISH HISTORY

Yaakov Avinu is the paradigm of a parent who successfully raised great Jewish children in exile (in Lavan's house), and Yaakov's son Yosef carried on his work in Egypt, where he raised two exemplary sons.[1] When today we bless our children, "God should make you as Ephraim and as Menashe,"[2] the *Ksav Sofer*[3] explains the blessing as follows: Just as Ephraim and Menashe grew into upright Jews, and even achieved greatness in decadent Egypt, so, too, can the Jewish children of later generations, destined similarly to grow up in a negative environment, be upright and great.

If we look at how Yaakov raised his children, we can glean some important insights into how to successfully raise our children in exile.

---

1. If we look through the eyes of our Sages and the commentaries on *Bereishis*, even the "sins" of Yaakov's children are seen as mistakes and not transgressions.
2. *Bereishis* 48:20.
3. The illustrious Avrohom Shmuel Binyomin Sofer (1815–1872). See *Yalkut Yehudah*, *Bereishis* 48, section 15.

Allow Them to Grow Up

When Yaakov parted ways with Lavan, we are told that he instructed his "brothers" to gather stones.[4] Yaakov, however, had only one brother, and not only was he far away in Canaan at the time, but he was full of hatred for Yaakov.

Who, then, were these "brothers"?

Rashi[5] explains that Yaakov's "brothers" were his children, who were at his side to help in time of need, including when a war had to be waged.

This reveals an important detail in Yaakov's parenting.

If Yaakov had been treating his sons as if they were still immature children, they never would have come forward to help him in time of danger. They would have felt too weak and incompetent. We see from this that the goal of every parent, like every good teacher, is to imbue his children with a realistic sense of their own competence. No one is ever rid of the need to seek wise counsel, but as people mature, the areas in which they feel capable and confident should always be expanding.

I have often said, tongue-in-cheek, that it's every parent's job to make him or herself obsolete as quickly as possible. While the relationship between parent and child is meant to be an unending one — growing deeper throughout life — there is some truth to the saying. It is the goal of a good parent to guide his children toward independence, and it is the ultimate purpose of the parent–child relationship to serve as a paradigm for the child's relationship with Hashem.

---

4. *Bereishis* 31:46.
5. Commentary on *Bereishis*, ibid.

Show Them that You Know Them

The Alter of Kelm[6] says that the reason children don't love parents as much as parents love children is that they don't think the parent knows what's best for them. Today, especially, we are at constant risk of losing our parental influence. In our fast-changing society, our children often have valid reason to doubt that we understand them or their world.

Yaakov spoke with each child separately, showing great understanding of the deepest recesses of each child's soul. Parents must never stop observing their children, keeping in step with all the changes they undergo. If parents take it upon themselves to seriously consider what is going on inside their children, then the children will, in most cases, respond in kind, with more sensitivity to the parents' concerns.

This is a giant step toward the child's choosing the ideology of his home over that of the street.

---

6. *Chochmah U'Mussar*, vol. 2, *ma'amar* 225.

❧Points to Remember

THE GOAL of every parent, like every good teacher, is to imbue his children with a realistic sense of their own competence.

IF PARENTS take it upon themselves to seriously consider what is going on inside their children, then the children will, in most cases, respond with more sensitivity to the parents' concerns.

CHAPTER THIRTY-TWO

A Rose among the Thorns

The Jewish People, destined to spend the greater portion of their national history in exile, survived against all odds. In the face of powerful forces bent on destroying them either by persecution or by assimilation, the Jews' survival is the world's greatest demonstration of loyalty to Hashem at all costs. This loyalty is movingly and eloquently expressed in the following *midrash*:

> *A king once betrothed a noblewoman and wrote her a long marriage contract. He said to her, "Such and such a number of canopies will I make for you, and such and such a number of fine, royal purple garments will I give to you." He left her and went abroad, and was delayed there. The woman's neighbors ridiculed her, saying, "The king has left you. He will never return." She would cry and groan bitterly, then enter her home and read the marriage contract which the king had written for her, promising her such and such a number of canopies and such and such a number of fine, royal purple garments, and she would be instantly consoled.*
>
> *Some time later the king returned, and said to her in amazement, "My daughter, how were you able to wait for me so many years?" She replied, "My master the king, if not for*

the contract that you wrote and presented me with, my neighbors would have long ago surely destroyed me."

So, too, do the nations of the world ridicule the Jewish People, and say to them, "Your God has hidden His face from you and removed His Divine Presence from you. He will never return to you." And the Jews cry and groan. But when they enter their halls of prayer and study and read in the Torah (Vayikra 26:9), "And I will turn to you, cause you to multiply and place My Sanctuary among you, and I will go among you," they are consoled.

Later, when the Redemption comes, Hashem will say to them, "My dear children, I wonder how were you able to wait for me all those years," and they shall reply, "Master of the World, if not for Your Torah that you gave us, the nations would have long ago destroyed us."[1]

---

1. *Eichah Rabbah* 3:7. Indeed, this was the claim of the Church — that Hashem had deserted the Jewish People. See *Chagigah* 5b, in which we see this claim being made in a debate during Roman times. The prophet foretold this when he said (*Yeshayahu* 49:1) that the day would come when Zion would say Hashem has forsaken her. The Gemara (*Berachos* 32b) describes the detailed refutation with which Hashem responded to this claim.
Rav Shlomo Brevda, *shlita*, once quoted a Rabbinic source as saying that the reason Rabbeinu Gershom (1050–1130) was called the "Light of the Exile" was because he addressed the feeling of being forsaken which was enveloping the Jewish People at that time in history, when it seemed as if the Church would be victorious throughout the world. Rabbeinu Gershom first instituted an edict which said that no one could divorce his wife against her will, which was analogous to decreeing that Hashem could not send the Jewish People away. (As we know, there is a principle, whose exploration is beyond the scope of this work, that the law in Heaven follows the law as laid down on earth by the great scholars of the Jewish People.) If, in the hypothetical case that Hashem, while not sending away the Jewish People, would "take" the Christians as a "second wife," to this Rabbeinu Gershom responded with a second decree that from then on, no man could take two wives.
In this manner, Rabbeinu Gershom lifted the spirits of his people. Never, he was telling them, never would Hashem desert them, never would He "marry" another nation. Rabbeinu Gershom was truly "the Light of the Exile," for he gave his people renewed hope.

The Torah has not only been our comfort throughout history, but also our guide to a successful life, nationally and individually. Indeed, Rav Samson Raphael Hirsch, *zt"l*, wrote that the reason the poles remained in the rings of the Ark[2] (where the Tablets of the Law were kept) is to tell us "that the Law and its function are not confined to the soil on which the Temple and its Sanctuary stand at any given time. Rather, the Law is ready to accompany the People of Israel wherever their God may lead them."[3]

We would do well to listen to the Torah's guidelines for successfully coping with our exile, especially in regard to raising our children in a society which opposes and ridicules Judaism's ideals.

Roses and Thorns

One of the most poignant metaphors describing the Jewish People in exile was written by King Solomon in *Shir HaShirim*, the Song of Songs, which is the expression of Hashem's eternal love for His Chosen People.

When King Solomon, the wisest of men, described the Jewish People, he likened them to a rose among the thorns.[4] This analogy bears much contemplation, for in it are contained some of the greatest insights into how the Jewish People have been able to survive their long and bitter exile among the nations of the world.

The Vilna Gaon[5] points out two salient characteristics of a rose among the thorns.

First, a rose's beauty and uniqueness are heightened by its contrast to its surroundings. It is a single fragrant blossom surrounded by thorns possessing neither odor nor color. Were that flower on a

---

2. *Shemos* 25:5.
3. *Collected Writings* (Jerusalem: Feldheim Publishers, 1988), vol. 3, pp. 197–8.
4. *Shir HaShirim* 2:2.
5. Commentary on *Shir HaShirim*, ibid.

fruit tree, its precious scent would be overwhelmed by the much stronger scent of the fruit. Its color, too, would go unappreciated.

Second, the rose's soft texture allows it to be unaffected by the penetrations of the thorns. Even should a thorn prick the blossom, the flower will revert to its previous soft completeness once the thorn is removed. It is never permanently marred by the thorn.

These two traits are keys to understanding how we can help our children — and ourselves — cope with the fact that we live in a "thorny" society.

1. Appreciation by Contrast. People often appreciate good fortune when seen in the light of misfortune. Health is appreciated when we see sickness. The happiness of daylight is all the more evident to us because we have night.[6] Winter makes springtime all the more beloved.

The same holds true in a spiritual sense. Moshe was raised in Pharaoh's household, and thereby gained a truer understanding of the beauty of what his people stood for. Yaakov grew spiritually in Lavan's household more than in all the years spent in the Yeshiva of Shem and Ever.[7] Indeed, the development of great Jews, true "sons" of Hashem, has always been even more noteworthy in exile than within Eretz Yisrael's own borders. As it is written,[8] "For more numerous are the children of the desolate [woman, the Jewish

---

6. Rav Avigdor Miller, *zt"l*.
7. When fleeing from his brother Esav's wrath, Yaakov spent fourteen years in intense study, never even lying down to sleep, after which he merited to see angels in his sleep (*Bereishis* 28:12; see Rashi, verse 11). When he had finished twenty years in the negative environment of Padan Aram and Lavan's house, he merited seeing angels when he was awake (*Bereishis* 32:3; said by Rav Avigdor Miller, *zt"l*). There is no question, of course, that Yaakov could not have attained the heights he did reach while living with Lavan, had he not first spent such quality time in yeshiva.
8. *Yeshayahu* 54:1.

People in exile] than [are the children] of the wedded one [the Jewish People in their own land.]" The Midrash[9] comments:

> *She [Zion] raised up for me more righteous people when she was destroyed [i.e., when the Temple was destroyed] than when she was built [when the Temple stood].*

What this means is that in exile, where there is an overwhelming negative influence from the host culture, the potential for spiritual growth is greater than when the Jew lives in his own land, where he needn't guard himself from alien influences. That need to be constantly warding off alien influences, and the effort expended in self-protection, strengthens the Jew in a way that does not occur when he lives in peaceful isolation.

Sometimes, as stated, this growth comes from an increased appreciation of the chasm separating the lives of the righteous from the lives of those who have chosen to follow the directives and ideologies of the dominant host culture.[10]

Let us now focus on the other aspect of the rose, cited by the Vilna Gaon, in which it symbolizes our resistance to the negative influences that can invade our homes. While it is relevant for any Jew, I believe it is especially so for parents.

2. **The Softness of the Rose.** The Gemara[11] states that a person should be soft as a reed, not unyielding as a cedar tree. When the wind blows with intense force, the reed bends. Yet when the fierce winds eventually stop, it regains its former upright position.

---

9. *Shir HaShirim Rabbah* 4:6. See *Pachad Yitzchok,* Chanukah, *ma'amar* 8, for a beautiful explanation of this *midrash.*
10. However, the reverse is also true. The influence of an environment is palpable even when it is obvious to all that it is negative and disgusting. See *Michtav Me'Eliyahu,* vol. 2, pp. 188–9, who brings the verse warning us not to be swayed by the Canaanite culture after we had witnessed its downfall.
11. *Ta'anis* 20a.

The cedar tree, on the other hand, refuses to yield and eventually breaks.

Let us study this gemara through the eyes of the Ben Ish Chai:[12]

> *So, too (like the reed), a person would do well to be of a pleasant nature, understanding all sorts of people, so that he can interact with everyone according to their nature. In the end, such a person will remain in his place [secure], with everyone pleased with him and without enemies. The cedar, being tough and unyielding to any wind, will eventually encounter a powerful southerly wind[13] that will totally uproot it. So, too, will the unyielding person eventually meet an even stronger person, who will then entirely destroy him.*

A HOME IS WHERE A PERSON CAN SPEAK — AND STILL BE LOVED

We must learn to be soft and flexible, with a friendly countenance and a genuine desire to understand where each person is coming from and where his or her needs lie. We cannot constantly be confronting our children, forcefully overwhelming them over every issue on which there is disagreement. When we seek to assert our will with the blatant force of our personalities, the strength of our economic control over them, or with our physical advantage by way of corporal punishment, we will find ourselves caught in a highly undesirable position.

When it comes to truly important issues, extreme stands are sometimes necessary. There are red lines in life. But their use must be governed by the same rules that apply to strong antibiotics: The

---

12. Rav Yosef Chaim (1832–1909), the legendary Chief Rabbi of Baghdad, whose Aggadic commentaries throughout the Talmud are of enormous beauty and insight.
13. See *Gittin* 31b, where the power of the South Wind is described.

more you resort to them, the less effective they become, and the more powerful the next strain of medicine must be in order to combat future illness.

A child's home must be a place where he can speak his mind. Where there is sufficient love and mutual respect, just knowing that certain activities would cause his parent(s) distress would to some extent serve to deter him from engaging in such activities.

Admittedly, this dynamic is not in itself sufficient to protect our children from some of the more alluring aspects of a modern hedonistic society. *Nonetheless, if this dynamic of love and openness is lacking, I'd be hard pressed to think of a substitute for it.* If a child is toying with the idea of deserting Torah ideals and morality, what pedagogical technique could we come up with that would convince him not to take the primrose path to self-destruction? Nothing can take the place of love.

As *Mori VeRabi* said, *the single greatest ingredient in successful chinuch is love.*

Coming Back

The Vilna Gaon, as we have said, wrote of the ability of the rose to restore itself after the thorn is withdrawn. This alludes to the ability to come back, to restore oneself, even if the dominant culture has had a temporarily negative impact on one of the family members.

This means that even when there is a temporary victory of the *yetzer ha-ra* and our children are pulled into its net, there is always hope. As long as love and openness endure in the family, there is an excellent chance that the child will eventually come home. This may take time, and some children may never walk exactly in the footsteps of their parents, but return they will, *for today there is no substitute for the love and warmth of a family, one in which the child is really cared for, and effort is made to understand him.*

An amazing story unfolded not long ago to reaffirm the ability of a Jew to always return:

> *The phone rang one evening in the home of Rav Nachman Bulman, shlita, menahel ruchani of Yeshivas Ohr Somayach. On the other end of the line came the voice of a woman, a voice that Rav Bulman had not heard in decades. Thirty years before, this woman had intermarried. Rav Bulman, in disbelief, said, "Judy [not her real name], is it really you?" The answer came quickly. "Rabbi Bulman, I want to come home."*

WE NEED TO BE SOFT AS A REED — ESPECIALLY IN EXILE

The Gemara in *Ta'anis* 20a, which contrasts the cedar tree with the reed, uses these words to describe the Jewish People: "This reed which stands in the water." The nations of the world are likened to powerful mighty waters.[14] What the Gemara is telling us, says the *Iyun Yaakov*, is that when the Jewish People finds itself in exile, this trait of being soft as a reed will enable us, as a people, to endure.

WE NEED RED LINES, BUT NOT TOO MANY

The softness of the rose is applicable in another way, as well. For all people, but especially for teenagers, it is very difficult living in a home where "everything's a big deal." While parents need to inculcate values into their children, and though there are ideals in

---

14. See *Shir HaShirim*, 8:7. See also the commentary of the Vilna Gaon on the Gemara in *Tamid* 32a, and the *Maharsha* at the beginning of the fifth chapter of *Bava Basra*, and the Gemara in *Yevamos* 121a. A full treatment of this subject is worthy of a book in its own right.

life about which there can be no compromise, these things should be as few in number as possible. "Laying down the law" to them is not something that should happen too often. If we as parents are too quick to make a big issue of things, then the power of our opposition will lose its effect. Either we lose our credibility that way (as well as the issue at hand) or we'll need to exercise more and more firmness in the future in order to continually "get our way." As stated, both punishment and extreme opposition need to be used with caution, lest they lose their potency. If not, we have to resort to higher and higher doses of "medicine," or end up switching to more powerful brands, just to keep our children "in line."

What this means is that we need to inculcate in our children those ideals of life that we consider most important in a soft, nonconfrontational manner.[15] This is generally achieved best by way of our example. Children want naturally to emulate their parents, and the younger the child, the more that emulation takes place.

If we establish a warm, loving relationship with our children early on, then there's great reason to hope that the dominant culture will not sway them.

---

15. See *Chofetz Chaim*, Part 1, 8:14, where the author discusses the obligation of a parent to exhort his family members to guard their tongues. He says, "and *only* with soft speech."

🌸 Points to Remember

THE SINGLE greatest ingredient in successful *chinuch* is love.

PEOPLE often appreciate good fortune when seen in the light of misfortune.

WHERE there is an overwhelming influence from the host culture, the potential for spiritual growth is greater.

THE MORE you resort to extreme stands, the less effective they become.

ALTHOUGH there are ideals in life about which there can be no compromise, these things should be as few in number as possible.

EPILOGUE

Exile as an Opportunity

Rav Tzadok HaKohen writes[1] that the reason the Jewish People have had to travel the world during their long exile is to demonstrate that they can withstand any sort of negative environment.[2] No nation can claim that if only the Jews had lived in that specific nation's midst, then they, too, would have succumbed to the same influences which held such a strong sway over the local populace.

This means that we are capable, with God's help, of giving our children an education that will protect them from the dominant culture's insidious influences.

---

1. *Resisei Lailah*, #37: "Every nation has its own unique power of evil. This is the function of the exile among the nations, to demonstrate that the Jewish People are not ensnared in the same evil power that engulfs other nations, for the nations claim that the Jewish People, even though they accepted the Torah, did not fulfill it."
2. The truth is that the Jewish People were exiled to the worst places. See the *Toras Kohanim* on *Acharei Mos*, and the sixth chapter of the Maharal's *Gevuros Hashem*. See also *Da'as Torah*, by Rav Yeruchem Levovitz, pp. 137–9.

I think we can take it a step further. Rav Dessler writes[3] that the happiness of life consists of this realization: *My contribution to glorifying Hashem's Name is unique. It cannot be duplicated by anyone else.*[4]

Those of us who are bringing up children in countries steeped in Western culture — a culture rife with hedonism, materialism and immorality — can take courage in the fact that when they do cope with the challenges that this culture poses, our children achieve an unprecedented, unequaled level of perfection, one that even surpasses the loyalty shown by our ancestors in extreme circumstances, in so many lands. Our children occupy a unique place in Jewish history.

THE ROSE OF JERICHO

The Malbim[5] explains that in the verse, "I will be like the dew to Yisrael, he will blossom like *the* rose,"[6] the word used is *KaShoshanah*, like *the* rose, as opposed to *KeShoshanah*, like *a* rose. For the word refers to a specific flower, the Rose of Jericho, which shares with the Jewish People a characteristic that has stayed with them throughout their exile. This flower, the Malbim says, even when driven by the wind through a desert area, can come to rest and derive its nourishment from the dew. So, too, will Hashem be like the dew for His people. The Jew will not only survive, but thrive, in all the circumstances into which Hashem sends him.

The Jew can thrive as a Jew no matter where he is.

---

3. *Michtav Me'Eliyahu*, vol. 1, pp. 22–3.
4. This idea, that each person's contribution to history is unique, is expressed in *Sefas Emes, Vayikra*, p. 203. The idea that each generation has its unique place in Jewish history is discussed in *Sefas Emes, Devarim*, p. 2. It can also be found in *The Bridge of Life (Gesher HaChayim)*, vol. 3, by Rav Y.M. Tukatchinsky, zt"l.
5. Rav Meir Leibush Malbim (1809–1879), whose commentary on the Written Law is a work of genius and is held in high regard by scholars and laymen alike.
6. *Hoshea* 14:6.

Our Uniqueness

At the end of our exile, when all the generations line up to present themselves before Hashem, each with its unique luster, I can imagine the Chofetz Chaim — to whom no one in our generation can even approach in piety, studiousness and Torah greatness — leaning forward to look upon the parents of our poor generation and saying: "You raised Torah-true children even though you lived in the most decadent world since the Generation of the Flood. How did you *do* that?"[7]

It is in such a spirit that we must approach the challenges that face us in the latest and, *b'ezras Hashem*, last great Exile before the coming of *Mashiach*. May the dedicated parents of today be encouraged in all their efforts to raise children who will be wonderful people and loyal Jews, no matter where they are.

---

7. See *Shemiras HaLoshon*, at the end of the tenth chapter of *Sha'ar HaTorah*, where the Chofetz Chaim clearly expresses the unique reward the generation preceding the *Mashiach* will receive because of their efforts at rearing Torah-true Jews against all odds.

❧ Points to Remember

Happiness in life consists of the following realization: "My contribution to glorifying Hashem's Name is unique."

The Jew can thrive as a Jew no matter where he is.

Glossary

AVINU – our father.
BA'AL TESHUVAH – lit., penitent; a formerly non-observant Jew who returns to the Torah.
BEIS HAMIKDASH – the Temple in Jerusalem.
B'EZRAS HASHEM – with God's help.
CHEDER – Torah-oriented elementary school.
CHINUCH – education.
DAVENING – praying.
EREV SHABBOS – Friday.
FRUM – religious.
FRUM-FROM-BIRTH – colloquialism referring to a person/family that grew up religious; i.e., not a BA'AL TESHUVAH.
GEMARA – commentary on the MISHNAH (together they comprise the Talmud); a volume of the Talmud.
HALACHAH – Jewish law.
HY"D – Hebrew acronym for "may Hashem avenge his blood"; referring to someone who was murdered.
KORBAN PESACH – Paschal Lamb, the sacrifice brought by the Jewish People immediately prior to their leaving Egypt.
MA'AMAR – essay.

MASHGIACH – dean of students.
MASHIACH – the Messiah.
MECHANECH – educator.
MECHUTAN – the parent of one's son- or daughter-in-law.
MIDRASH – a collection of Tannaic teaching, based on the verses of the Written Law.
MISHNAH – the codified Oral Law redacted by Rabbi Yehudah HaNasi; a specific paragraph of the Oral Law.
RAV – competent, trained Rabbi.
SHLITA – Hebrew acronym for "may he live long."
SHEMONEH ESREH – lit., eighteen; the eighteen blessings of the *Amidah* prayer.
TOSAFISTS – medieval French and German commentators on the Babylonian Talmud.
YIRAS SHAMAYIM – fear of Heaven.
ZT"L – Hebrew acronym for "may the memory of a righteous one be for a blessing."

בזכות זה

יהי רצון שיחזק אבינו שבשמים אנחנו
וצאצאינו וצאצאי צאצאינו לשמור מצוותיו
ולדבוק בדרכיו ולאהוב בריותיו.

₪

אברהם הערץ ותמר וורגה
משה יחזקאל. רבקה לאה. חנה פרימה. מיכל דבורה.
קלמן יצחק. טוביה. אלעזר שמחה

In Memoriam
לעילוי נשמת

YAAKOV BEN REUVEN
LEAH BAS PINCHOS MOSHE

In Memoriam
לעילוי נשמת

יהודה לב בן יוסף הלוי
YEHUDA LEV BEN YOSEF HALEVI
עלקא בת ישראל מאיר
ELKA BAS YISROEL MEIR
יצחק דב בן עזרא
YITZCHOK DOV BEN EZRA
שפרה בת יהושע מרדכי
SHIFRA BAS YEHOSHUA MORDECHAI

In לעילוי *Memoriam* נשמת

Dr. Asenath Petrie
Asenath bas Avigdor
20 Teves 5761

In לעילוי *Memoriam* נשמת

Mr. Gerald Gundle   Mr. Kurt Bendheim
Mrs. Phyllis Gundle   Mrs. Lizzie Bendheim

Dedicated by their children
Clifford and Sooozee Gundle
and their grandchildren
Kimberley and David Gundle-Mark
Kevin and Deborah Gundle
Bryan and Gail Gundle
Brigitte and Daniel Glinert